IN THE
GODFATHER GARDEN

Rivergate Regionals

Rivergate Regionals is a collection of books published by Rutgers University Press focusing on New Jersey and the surrounding area. Since its founding in 1936, Rutgers University Press has been devoted to serving the people of New Jersey and this collection solidifies that tradition. The books in the Rivergate Regionals Collection explore history, politics, nature and the environment, recreation, sports, health and medicine, and the arts. By incorporating the collection within the larger Rutgers University Press editorial program, the Rivergate Regionals Collection enhances our commitment to publishing the best books about our great state and the surrounding region.

IN THE
GODFATHER GARDEN

The Long Life and Times of
Richie "the Boot" Boiardo

RICHARD LINNETT

RUTGERS UNIVERSITY PRESS
NEW BRUNSWICK, NEW JERSEY, AND LONDON

Library of Congress Cataloging-in-Publication Data

Linnett, Richard, 1957–

   In the Godfather garden : the long life and times of Richie "the Boot" Boiardo /
Richard Linnett.

     p. cm.

   Includes bibliographical references and index.

   ISBN 978–0–8135–6061–8 (hbk. : alk. paper) — ISBN 978–0–8135–6062–5
(e-book)

   1. Boiardo, Richie (Richard), 1890–1984. 2. Criminals—New Jersey—Case studies. 3. Mafia—New Jersey—Case studies. 4. Organized crime—New Jersey—Case
studies. I. Title.

   HV6452.N5L56 2013

   364.1092—dc23

                                  2012023500

A British Cataloging-in-Publication record for this book is available from the British
Library.

Visit our website: http://rutgerspress.rutgers.edu

Manufactured in the United States of America

Dedicated to
Rosina Boiardo Hanos and Arlene Moretti Linnett

CONTENTS

THE GARDEN

The garden was terraced, with the first tier on top of a three-foot-high brownstone wall and with a stone stairway leading to the second level above that. The Boot raked and turned the soil in the spring; he painted tomato poles and planted the best seeds and seedlings from the previous year's harvest. He experimented with fertilizers. His favorite was rabbit manure; he believed it was best for his *pomodori*, or tomatoes, which grew round and heavy like red bocce balls. He also grew bright yellow sunflowers, or *girasole*, and *cetrioli* (cucumbers), *melanzana* (eggplant), *gagoots* (zucchini), *basilico* (basil), and his favorite—*rose rosse*, or red roses. The vegetation was so dense one had to look very carefully to see him puttering around inside.

When certain people came to visit him, like John "Big Pussy" Russo and his brother Anthony "Little Pussy" Russo or the Boot's son, Anthony "Tony Boy" Boiardo, the Boot would guide them up the stone steps to the second tier, deep into the thick of the garden, and they would talk in whispers, as if in a confessional.

Beyond the garden, in the endless, gloomy woods, there was another sanctuary. The Boot was known to quietly take certain people there too. These were special people who never went willingly. Little Pussy once had to drag one of them back there at the end of a chain tied around his throat. "Stay away from there," Little Pussy warned an associate in a conversation taped by the FBI. "So many guys have been hit there. There's this furnace way up in the back. That's where they burned them."

ACKNOWLEDGMENTS

The research, writing, and production of this book took five long years, and many individuals helped make it happen. I would like to thank, first and foremost, Roger Hanos. Without his dedication, hard work, patience, inspiration, guidance, stellar connections, killer research, writing skills, and profound rememberings, through many years of fits and starts and the overcoming of obstacles real and imagined, this book never would have made it to press. Although he modestly refused to put his name on the cover, he is as much an author of this book as I am.

I would also like to express my sincere appreciation to Marlie Wasserman and the entire staff at Rutgers University Press for their expert guidance, administration, tolerance, and cajoling. She and her team know better than most publishers that real books about subject matter that is challenging and engaging—not just entertaining—are rare and delicate things that need to be encouraged, nourished, and finally published. Thank you for all that.

Special gratitude to Chris Allegaert, Kevin MacMillan, and David Berger at the law firm Allegaert Berger & Vogel for their expert counsel, enthusiasm, and support. Sincere thanks to the Newark Library staff under the supervision of George Hawley, Ph.D., who assisted in retrieving incredible photos and newspaper articles. The staff at Alexander Library at Rutgers University was also supportive, generously making available their newspaper archives. The FBI's local and central Freedom of Information and Privacy Act offices, in particular David Hardy of the Records Information and Dissemination Section and his staff and David Sobonya of the FBI's Public Information Office, provided invaluable services. Approximately thirty thousand pages of FBI documents were retrieved and researched for this project. A special thank you to Roger Sr.'s late mother, Rosina, and his wife, Janet, his son Roger Jr., and his daughter Mia Hanos Zimmermann, for their support and assistance; Roger Sr.'s brother, Darrel, for assisting in the research and for verification of certain aspects of this story; and his sister, Lillian LaMonica. Hanos family interviews, photos, home movies, personal documents, and newspaper articles about the Ruggiero Boiardo estate, incidents, family and social events provided essential building blocks in re-creating the life of Richie the Boot. A heartfelt thank you to the Balestro family, Anthony and his sister Mary Balestro DelMaestro, for their interviews and photos. Several photos taken by Roger's uncle through marriage, Joe "Winky" Bruno Sr., were generously provided by his wife, Geraldine. Thank you! Family information provided by Boiardo niece Agnes Manfro DellAcqua and restaurateur Thomas Pannullo added helpful insight into the Boot's life, his family, and his friends. Many thanks to the poet laureate of the North Ward, Michael Immerso, author of *Newark's Little Italy*; his critique of the *Godfather Garden* proposal and his enthusiasm for the project were not only generous and spot-on but a huge boost. A special thank you to the Livingston Police Department for allowing me to hang out in the station house, pick their collective brains, and take up their valuable time. Finally, a warm embrace to Rhonda Graber for letting me crash in the apartment above her garage, Daryl Devlin for her luscious eggplant parm, and Max Linnett for being my favorite wise guy.

IN THE
GODFATHER GARDEN

THEY GOT ME, JOE

The car was a five-passenger, four-door Lincoln dual-cowl Sport Phaeton, a jet-black sedan with running boards, twin side-mount spare tires, and bulletproof glass. It bolted down the south side of Broad Street at four o'clock in the morning in downtown Newark. The sedan suddenly jerked across the wide, empty boulevard and into the opposing lane, pulling to the curb on the wrong side of the street in front of the Broadmoor Apartments, a four-story brick and limestone building with a canopy over the entrance and a sign advertising one- and two-room apartments. Richie the Boot had been sitting in the front seat, alongside the driver, and he exited the car on the left side onto the street and walked around the back of the car to the sidewalk.

His nickname, the Boot, allegedly came from his occupation: Ruggerio Boiardo was a bootlegger and a successful one. Others said he was named after the motherland, where he came from, the boot of Italy. Newspapers reported that he earned the moniker by brutally kicking and stomping on his foes, sometimes to death. The Boot himself once told the FBI that he got the name because he was frequently summoned to telephone booths in order to conduct business and to take calls from female admirers: "Hey Richie the booth," which sounded like "Richie da boot"; the nickname stuck.[1] He also was called Diamond Ritchie for his taste in flashy jewelry and in particular a diamond belt buckle that he was known to

1

wear. (Ruggiero was anglicized to Richie, which was spelled with a "t"—
Ritchie—in his early bootlegging days.)

On November 26, 1930, the Boot, aged thirty-nine, was at the top of his
game. He had evolved from a First Ward milkman who learned to turn a
profit by selling contraband liquor on his rounds to proprietor of a vast
network of stills that supplied Newark with much of its illegal booze. He
also owned several popular speakeasies that were frequented by influential people—businessmen, politicians, and cops. He ran the second most
profitable numbers racket in the city, and he was the captain of a fearsome squad of hooligans, sharps, and cutthroats who robbed, cheated, and
murdered to make a living. The local press described these characters as
"young men with patent leather hair," occasional "employees in the city
license division," and boys "who plunked each other in the back"[2] while
inhabiting "the twilight zone of city life."[3]

The Boot led a double life. He was a Good Samaritan who funded some
of the construction of Saint Lucy's Church and contributed an elaborate
stained-glass window. He distributed silver dollars to children on the street
and provided much-needed loans and other favors to his neighbors and
friends. "Whole families in the First Ward fall back on him for support in
their times of need," reported the *Newark Evening News*.[4] During the depths
of the Depression, the Boot estimated he gave away $3 to $4 million to the
poor in Newark.[5] He hosted marathon civic feasts that lasted days on end,
with ticket proceeds going to the coffers of his Modern Political Club, a
storefront social club and hideout for his gang. The Boot was a Democratic
power broker in the First Ward. "Voters traditionally went for the candidate
Boiardo felt could do the most good for him and his organization."[6]

He also was a restaurateur who built spectacular eating palaces such
as the Sorrento and the Vittorio Castle, where he entertained politicians,
judges, gangsters, policemen, and celebrities such as Frank Sinatra, Frankie
Valli, Joe DiMaggio, Marilyn Monroe, Elizabeth Taylor with Michael
Todd, Jimmy Durante, George Raft, Connie Francis, Bud Abbott and Lou
Costello, Sugar Ray Robinson, and Carmen Basilio.[7]

The Boot had many friends and many enemies. He had been on especially bad terms with Abner "Longy" Zwillman, the top gangster in Newark; Zwillman was a flashy Jewish kingpin of the Third Ward who smuggled
premium-quality booze into Newark and Atlantic City from Canada,
operated the top-grossing numbers game in town, and briefly dated the
Hollywood sex goddess Jean Harlow. The Boot's boys hijacked Longy's
liquor deliveries, pistol-whipped his drivers, and challenged Longy's gang
in running gun battles that were characterized in the press as skirmishes
between Jews and Wops. The violence escalated so dramatically that Al
Capone came from Chicago to broker a truce. Capone was protecting his
own interests; his Chicago operations not only imported booze from Canada across Lake Michigan but also moved substantial truckloads of illegal
liquor through Brooklyn, New York, and from various warehouses and
ports throughout New Jersey. The Boot and Longy came to terms after two
sit-downs. There was now peace between them.

The Boot lived on Newark Street but kept a pied-à-terre in the Broadmoor. He took the Broadmoor apartment to hide out, not from Longy, but
from his wife. He fought often with Jennie Manfro Boiardo and had been
arrested for domestic violence years earlier. Their arguments usually were
over other women. The Boot was an incorrigible and possessive woman-
izer. After he found out that his girlfriend was "playing around" with Solly
DeLarno, a Newark man, DeLarno suddenly disappeared. Rumors spread
that the Boot was responsible. The Newark police never solved the case.[8]

The Boot was a "massive hulk" and "a fleshy man, considered good-
looking in a florid way."[9] He lived large, proudly wearing a diamond belt
buckle that was the stuff of rich prose in the local papers: "It contains 250
pure white cut stones forming the likeness of an eagle," the *Newark Evening News* reported, "and in the First Ward hideaways, where men whisper
secrets over a bottle of good red wine[,] they will tell you this eagle has
meaning not only in Newark, but likewise in New York's underworld."[10]

It was said the buckle was given to him by a New York gangster as a
gift, in tribute for his prodigious feats as a hit man. A story in the *Newark*

Evening News traced the buckle's lineage to Jacob "Little Augie" Orgen, a New York Jewish gang leader and bootlegger who wore the buckle as a symbol of his leadership.[11] Little Augie and his bodyguard, Jack "Legs" Diamond, were gunned down on a Lower East Side street in 1927 by Louis "Lepke" Buchalter and Jacob "Gurrah" Shapiro, who would later found the Mafia killer squad Murder Inc.[12] Legs survived and later became one of the most colorful gangsters of Prohibition. Little Augie died, and according to the article his buckle was passed on to Frankie Yale, a Sicilian whose last name was originally Ieole and who was otherwise known as Frankie Uale. After Yale also met his maker, "in the manner approved by gangdom—via the 'ride' route"—the buckle disappeared for a while. "It was about this time that Ritchie, who had come to be quite a power not only in Newark, but also among Brooklyn racketeers by virtue of his ability to handle liquor, came into possession of a buckle as like the Augie-Yale sparkler as the proverbial pea. The inference is that he picked up some of the scattered threads of the Augie-Yale leadership."[13]

Another version had it that the buckle was booty after the Boot whacked (mob vernacular for killed) its owner, a rival boss. The Boot said he bought the buckle himself, paying $5,000 for it. A story in the *Newark Evening News* reported that it was worth at least $20,000. The Boot often boasted that the buckle was his good-luck charm, that it had once saved his life by stopping a bullet.[14]

He was wearing the buckle that cold Thanksgiving Eve in 1930, as well as a five-carat diamond ring and a tie pin studded with fifteen diamonds. He also was carrying $207 in cash in his pocket, a check for thirty dollars, a ten-inch stiletto, and a revolver. Police also allegedly found a note in his pocket. "It was said to have been signed by a Third Ward gangster," the Newark *Star-Eagle* newspaper reported, "and gave warning that he was about to be killed."[15] The Boot was not wearing his bulletproof vest that night.

As the Boot stepped out of the Phaeton, which had been given to him as a gift by his crew, shots rang out. An Associated Press report that appeared in the *Asbury Park Press* later reported that the Boot was felled by "16 slugs from a machine gun to his body" with "10 of the bullets pumped into his skull."[16] A less sensational report in the Newark *Star-Eagle* reported that he had taken four slugs to the head, three in the left side of his chest and one in his right, and there were "eight other marks where slugs penetrated."[17] The *New York Times* carried the most accurate account of the shooting, reporting that the Boot was not hit by bullets or slugs but by pellets from a shotgun blast. The location of the wounds spoke clearly: the intention was to kill him.[18]

The Boot's enemies were not the only party out for blood. This side-bar appeared in the *Newark Evening News*: "Soon after word was spread around the First Ward that Ritchie Boiardo had been shot, undertakers in the neighborhood began negotiating for the privilege of handling his funeral. Behind this lay the knowledge that a funeral for a man in Ritchie's position in the gang world would mean vast expenditures to make the ceremony as impressive as possible."[19]

The reaction of the Boot's driver, Joe Juliano, who also went by the names Joe Julian and Joe Casey, was curious. Instead of aiding his fallen boss, Juliano bolted in the Phaeton, leaving the Boot sprawled on the sidewalk. The *Newark Star-Eagle* reported that two unidentified women saw the Boot's body "and noticed his diamond belt buckle glittering in the arc light," but according to the story they did not have access to a phone and as a result did not make a report.[20] The superintendent of the Broadmoor told police he heard only groaning outside—no gunshots—and believed it was a drunk, so he didn't respond. Some tenants in the building, according to the super, looked out their windows and saw the Boot's body lying on the pavement but also apparently didn't realize he had just been shot.[21] The Boot lay in a pool of blood for almost a half hour until a milkman on morning rounds stumbled on him and notified the Second Precinct police. A paddy wagon rushed the Boot to the city hospital.

Canvassing the neighborhood, detectives quickly focused their investigation on a shabby rooming house across the street from the Broadmoor.

The manager of the converted three-story wooden house—a woman with the colorful name of Mamie Fetters—escorted the cops to a second-floor apartment that faced the street and had been rented by a pair of men who registered under the name Anderson. She described the men as well dressed; one was short and heavyset with a flat nose, and both were "American born," which meant they were not Italians. Two chairs faced a partially opened window overlooking Broad Street. A double-barrel shotgun was found lying on a bed; one of the barrels was discharged, and the other was still loaded with a double-aught shell normally used for hunting game. The shell contained about eight or nine buckshot pellets.[22]

In some respects the assassination attempt appeared amateurish to detectives. The barrels of the weapon, a shotgun normally used for trap-shooting and more than twenty years old, were "paper thin" from overuse. As a result the choke was worn away, allowing the shot to spread out quickly, and accuracy was compromised. The target was at least one hundred feet away, and by the time the buckshot reached its destination it had lost velocity.[23]

Other details, however, suggested the hit was well planned and the work of an organized group. The men had rented the rooms several weeks in advance of the hit, digging in for a long surveillance as they waited for the best opportunity to strike. They also had an exit strategy. In the bathroom detectives found a rope tied to a radiator, coiled under a side window, ready for a quick getaway; however, footprints indicated the men ultimately beat a hasty retreat out a rear window to an extension roof, then to the ground and over a back fence to Broadway. There were no fingerprints in the room; the men obviously wore gloves.[24]

And there was the question of the Boot's chauffer. After fleeing the scene Juliano drove to Boiardo's home on Newark Street. Mrs. Boiardo told the police she was woken up by the sound of tapping on her bedroom window at around 4:25 A.M. and the voice of a man who whispered through the glass that her husband had been hurt. She went to the window, but no one was there. She told police she thought it was her husband "playing tricks with her" and went back to bed. A few minutes later Juliano was at the front door. He told her about the shooting. Mrs. Boiardo called local hospitals and found her husband at Newark City Hospital, alive but in critical condition.[25]

The police caught up with Juliano at the hospital and grilled him. Why had he pulled in front of the Broadmoor on the wrong side of the street, directly exposing his boss to the sniper's crosshairs? He replied that for some unknown reason the Boot had ordered him to pull up that way. Why did he speed away after the shooting? He didn't realize there was a shooting. He heard a loud popping noise and thought it was a truck backfiring. Detectives were not convinced; they ordered Juliano back behind the wheel of the Phaeton and they retraced his steps, returning to the scene of the shooting.[26]

Juliano apparently then changed his story; according to the *Newark Star-Eagle* he told detectives he had heard the sound of gunfire after he dropped the Boot off, and as he turned a corner, he looked back and saw the big boss lying in the street. He said he saw people standing around his body and assumed they were assisting him.[27] The *Newark Evening News* reported that Juliano told police that, after hearing the gunshots, he drove around for a few minutes, passed the Broadmoor again, and saw a man lifting the Boot from the street. Juliano then raced to the Boiardo home to tell Mrs. Boiardo her husband had been injured.[28]

Juliano testified that earlier in the evening he had driven his boss and a friend, a man by the name of Lawrence Rendis, to the Cameo, an after-hours club where the pair spent the entire evening into the early morning. Later, he had dropped Rendis off at his home on Cutler Street in the First Ward and then took the Boot to the Broadmoor. Juliano's story didn't hold water; dry agents (law enforcement from the Federal Prohibition Bureau) had spotted the Boot and his men that evening looking on as they raided a contraband "whiskey and champagne" shipment on the Keansburg docks on the Jersey shore. Detectives also discovered shotgun-pellet damage in the rear wheel well of the Phaeton, which contradicted Juliano's story that he didn't hear shots until after he dropped the Boot off.[29] The police booked Juliano, charging him with concealing a crime. He was eventually indicted as a material witness.

Newspapers around the country, from Ohio to Texas to San Francisco, picked up stories about the shooting. The exploits of gangsters like the Boot were popular fodder in the press at the time, and reports often relied on hearsay rather than fact. The *Asbury Park Press*, which reported that the Boot had been gunned down in a hail of machine-gun fire, also reported that he was mortally wounded and was "expected to die momentarily."[30] Another story, published in the *Newark Evening News*, reported that although the Boot would survive his wounds, one of the bullets severed a "tiny nerve" in his left arm "robbing Ritchie of the use of the arm for the present and probably permanently."[31]

The *Newark Evening News* ran a story filed by a reporter who was in the Boot's hospital room. It reads like a "policier."

> He lapsed into unconsciousness[;] . . . but at 6 o'clock he revived for a few minutes. Detective[s] Hilt and Arnold were at the bedside and Ritchie looked up.
>
> "They got me, Joe," he said to Arnold.
>
> "Do you know me?" asked the detective.
>
> "Sure you're Joe Arnold."
>
> "Who shot you?"
>
> "Don't bother me now. I'll see you tomorrow night."
>
> Again he lapsed into unconsciousness. When he revived later, his wife, a son, Anthony, sixteen, and a daughter Agnes, seventeen, as well as Detective Benson were at the bedside.
>
> "How do you feel," asked Mrs. Boiardo.
>
> "Not so good. I hope I die," Ritchie said.
>
> "Who shot you?" asked Benson.

Ritchie gazed silently at the detective for a moment and then closed his eyes.[32]

As the fallen gang lord lapsed in and out of consciousness, an incident occurred in his hospital room that was straight out of crime fiction, though it was real and would create problems for the Boot. There are several variations of this story, including one that was told months later in court by a detective who was present as orderlies began removing Richie's clothing, struggling to unfasten the diamond belt buckle. The orderlies "tugged on Richie's trousers," and the detective assisted, lifting Richie's body so that they could pull down his pants. A thirty-eight-caliber revolver dropped out of Richie's right-hand pocket to the floor. The detective searched the pants and found a ten-inch stiletto. He confronted the bedridden gangster, who drowsily acknowledged that the weapons were his.[33] Later the Boot would recant this admission.

The incident led to a unique criminal prosecution that would dominate the news and enthrall the public, energizing prohibitionists and other civic groups. The police and the courts intended to use the case to break the Boot's power once and for all, but, in the end, they achieved the opposite result, making him a notorious celebrity and elevating his standing in the ranks of the mob, which had just begun to consolidate into an organized network.

Richie the Boot Boiardo emerged from this assassination attempt a charmed outlaw who would outlive all his rivals and elude serious punishment, skippering a fearsome New Jersey crime crew for multiple decades, from Prohibition through the Cold War, into the troubled waters of the sixties and seventies, and finally into the eighties, during the end of the U.S. Mafia's reign. His influence would linger even longer, inspiring the creation of what Vanity Fair magazine called "the greatest pop culture masterpiece of its day," The Sopranos.[34]

For six long seasons of The Sopranos the show's creator, David Chase, kept silent about its genesis as if observing a solemn mob oath of omertà. After the last episode of his mob soap opera aired, Chase was sued for plagiarizing the idea for the show. While successfully defending himself at the trial, Chase finally admitted that his muse was "Newark's erstwhile Boiardo crew—the Mafiosi I had been most familiar with as a young man."[35]

In 1972, when the first of *The Godfather* films came out, the Boot hung a sign in his beloved vegetable garden on his estate in Livingston. It read "The Godfather Garden." The Boot never saw the film version of the Mario Puzo book, but his friend Ace Alagna, the owner and editor of the *Italian Tribune*, was hired as an extra in the first installment of the trilogy and told the Boot that his life—and his estate—resembled Don Corleone's. The Boot agreed and confided his feelings to a friend who informed the FBI:

> Boiardo has noted several similarities in the events in his own life and in that of the title character leading him to believe that the character was patterned to some degree from him. Boiardo has commented that both were shot as a result of trying to keep narcotics traffic out of their areas, but nevertheless, survived the shootings; both live in a secluded estate surrounded by a compound of other houses [redacted passage][;] both have a great interest in gardening; and while in *The Godfather* the title character had four sons and one daughter, Boiardo has four daughters and one son.[36]

The Boot's assertion that he was shot for attempting to eradicate drugs in his neighborhood may have been a case of wishful revisionism influenced by the popularity of the Marlon Brando character in The Godfather and the dominance of drugs in the sixties and seventies. Throughout his criminal career, the Boot was against dealing narcotics, but, at the time he was shot, illegal booze, not drugs, was the prime mover of the criminal economy, and as we shall see, the Boot was engaged in running battles with many ruthless, cold-blooded competitors in the alcohol trade. Bootleggers of the twenties and thirties were constantly at war. Each man was a soldier who had to be consistently vigilant and brutal to survive. The Boot was a warrior in this subculture; he made his bones there and became one of the most feared and respected men of his time.

CHAPTER 1

DIAMOND RITCHIE

None has composed a more adventurous
song of renown, one that delights!
I will sing of the new Ruggiero,
blessed with all virtues, who surpassed
all other men the world has known.
— *Matteo Maria Boiardo,* Orlando Innamorato, *247*

Ruggiero Boiardo was born in 1890 in Naples, according to his birth certificate, and was raised in the town of Marigliano in the province of Naples. His recorded birthdate is December 8, which may not be accurate, as it is also the date of the Feast of Immaculate Conception. The Boot was placed in an orphanage as a child; Catholic orphanages often assigned the dates of important holy days to children whose actual birthdates were unknown. His biological parents also were unknown. The Boot later claimed that he was the illegitimate son of an Italian nobleman who was a descendant of the great Italian Renaissance poet Matteo Maria Boiardo, the author of *Orlando Innamorato,* an epic poem chronicling the heroic adventures and loves of the knight Orlando. Knighthood, horsemanship, heraldry, and chivalry became an obsession of the Boot, who considered himself, like Orlando, a warrior and "man of honor." He kept a framed portrait of the poet prominently displayed in his home.[1] A leading character in Boiardo's epic is named Ruggiero, a valorous knight who also was orphaned at birth.

Maria Carmine Favarulo, a peasant, and her husband, Antonio Esposito, adopted young Ruggiero when he was six years old. He apparently kept his last name instead of taking the name of his new family. He emigrated with

Maria Carmine from Italy to the United States when he was eleven. The transatlantic trip took nineteen days; they arrived in New York on December 18, 1901. His father had preceded them to the New World in May of the same year.

At the turn of the century there was a tremendous demand for immigrant labor in the United States, especially for workers in the railroad industries. Although contracted labor was outlawed in 1864, during the late nineteenth and early twentieth centuries, the *camoristi*, or Italian padrones, continued to arrange labor contracts with peasant immigrants, paying their passage and then, upon their arrival, exploiting their labor and living arrangements. Ruggiero and his parents were lured to the United States by work and the chance for a better life and were subject to the padrone system. They were sent to Chicago, where Ruggiero was put to work herding cattle on and off trains in the city stockyards.[2] By age fourteen he was working with a railroad company that sent him out with construction gangs in the Dakotas, Montana, and the Northwest; he was sleeping in boxcars, "living the rough and ready life," according to the *Newark Evening News.* "He was already an overgrown fellow and quite capable of taking care of himself with his fist or his tongue."[3] "I was not born with a silver spoon in my mouth," the Boot often said later. "I was born with a wooden spoon, and I worked hard."[4]

In 1906 the family broke apart, apparently over a disagreement about young Ruggerio's upbringing. Maria Carmen took her son to Newark, where she had relatives in the First Ward. Italians were drawn to Newark at the turn of the century by railroad work; tracks connecting Newark to Jersey City were being laid across the marshes by the Pennsylvania Railroad.[5] Padrones secured work gangs from the pool of newly arrived immigrants. They settled in the First Ward, opening bakeries and other businesses. By the time young Ruggiero arrived, the ward boasted the fifth highest concentration of Italians in the country and was teeming with Italian-owned macaroni factories, bakeries, shoe-repair shops, barbershops, and nearly one hundred saloons. Many of these saloons had large halls that were used for meetings and entertainment. Italian social clubs and fraternal and mutual-aid organizations were as plentiful as saloons. The mutual-aid societies were membership organizations that collected fees and provided health benefits as well as social events for members.

Factory workers and laborers made up the majority of the First Ward population; they had a ten-hour work day and earned about twelve to seventeen cents an hour. The average annual income of an Italian household was $600. Although the First Ward was part of a mid-size, industrial American city, the neighborhood was essentially provincial. Its tenements were crowded with large, extended families. Neighbors in the tenements had been neighbors in the same villages in Italy. It was an intimate world "where almost everyone was poor, where very few secrets were kept, and where every front stoop served as a village piazza."

Ruggiero got work in a leather factory in Newark and later as a construction mason/plasterer. In 1912 he married a local girl, Giovannina Jennie Manfro, who gave birth to their first child, Agnes, a year later. Ruggiero Jr., who later would go by his middle name, Anthony, was born in 1914. That same year the Boot was convicted of marital domestic violence and sentenced to one-year probation.

In 1920, Boiardo had his next brush with the law. He was found guilty of operating a gambling house and was fined $52.05. Later that year, his wife gave birth to a daughter, Carmenella. She would die eleven months later from complications of bronchopneumonia. At the end of 1920, the Boot, at the age of twenty-nine, became an American citizen.

The Boot's encounters with the law continued in 1921, when he was arrested for helping Tommy DiGiacomo, aka Tommy Jacobs, who owned a speakeasy, leave the scene of a crime. DiGiacomo had fought with his wife and pushed her out of the second-floor window of their apartment. The Boot spirited his friend away in a car.[6] She survived, and the Boot was held as a material witness. Also that year, while driving in his car, the Boot struck Antonio Romeo, an eight-year-old boy, breaking his left leg and crushing his skull. The boy died, and Boiardo was arrested. He claimed the boy ran from the curb directly in front of his car. Several witnesses stated that "with a little more care in driving, [the Boot] might have avoided the accident."[7] The Boot was charged with manslaughter; he was convicted on January 12, 1922, and served twelve months in the Essex County Penitentiary in Caldwell. While he was in prison, Jennie gave birth to another daughter, Rosina.

Richie Boiardo's fortunes were about to change, dramatically. The Volstead Act, the law banning the sale of alcohol, was enacted in 1919, but New Jersey remained a wet state one year after Prohibition legislation swept the country. The state's large urban immigrant population, including a mix of European Catholics and Jews who were more liberal about alcohol use than the rural Protestants who spearheaded Prohibition, refused to accept the new dry rules, and influential German American beer barons who owned major breweries in Newark put pressure on politicians to oppose the amendment. Jersey finally ratified in 1920, saloons were shut down, and yet the state stayed wet, illegally.

Speakeasies began popping up in many American cities, especially in port cities like New York and Newark, where boats carrying contraband alcohol from Canada and Europe could dock and offload, often under cover of darkness. The 130-mile-long coast of New Jersey, with its hidden landing havens, was ideal for bootlegger speed boats running in their goods from schooners and steamers. From these hidden ports, trucks dispensed their goods to Manhattan, Chicago, Newark, Jersey City, Philadelphia, Baltimore, and Washington.

Only the most affluent speakeasies sold imported liquor, and at high prices, while most illegal saloons in poor immigrant neighborhoods sold homemade wine and beer and also moonshine (produced in pot stills, or alky-cookers) and hootch, which was prepared from nonbeverage alcohol. Immigrant families set up home breweries in basements, backyards, and garages. Some of these mom-and-pop operators graduated to the big time and began making liquor for a living. During Prohibition, the federal Prohibition administrator for New Jersey, Colonel Ira L. Reeves, declared that "Newark, New Jersey, was a manufacturing center for the booze trade."[8]

Not simply an effort to stop the consumption of alcohol, Prohibition was a government attempt to legislate morality, a social program designed to curb immoral behavior and the alien customs of immigrants who were flooding into the United States. Ironically, Prohibition achieved the opposite result; it spawned a homegrown outlaw subculture of flappers, jazz speakeasies, and gangsters.

And, later, as the Great Depression kicked in midway through the so-called noble experiment, a significant number of men and women who could not find employment pursued lives outside the law in order to survive and prosper. As banks failed, unemployment rose, the stock market crashed, and a majority of Americans were living below the "minimum sustenance level." The richest 1 percent owned 40 percent of the nation's wealth, and the middle class consisted of 15 to 20 percent of all U.S. citizens.[9] The First Ward was hit hard by the Depression, but bootlegging cash flowed heavily, and many young men took to the streets to earn a living.

In New Jersey and the greater metropolitan area, Prohibition laws and federal agents were viewed as merely a nuisance, while local and state law enforcement for the most part either looked the other way or helped facilitate the illicit liquor business. Protection money was paid out to local politicians and law enforcement. In some instances, police cars escorted bootleg deliveries. Jersey stills were reported to be generating huge amounts of alcohol "from Ocean and Monmouth counties for metropolitan consumption."[10] Gang hijackings and turf wars along with beatings and shootings for protection tributes were widespread.

Bootlegging, like any business culture, had its organizational structure, its executives, and its rules of conduct. Prior to the establishment of organized crime, which began around 1929, the bootlegging subculture operated in an ad hoc, true laissez-faire fashion, yet it still followed a basic code. The key difference between the code of conduct in legitimate business and in bootlegging was this: disagreements between competitors that could not be settled through mutual agreement were ultimately settled not in a court of law but through intimidation, violence, and bloodshed.

Boiardo began his involvement in bootlegging in the early 1920s. At the time he was working as a milk delivery man with the Alderney Dairy Company. While making milk deliveries to speakeasies in the First Ward, Boiardo learned that many of them served "hair-tonic booze," or drinks whose ingredients included alcohol used in hair dressing and cologne cut with prune juice and caramel to mimic the color and taste of whiskey and rye. Manufactured under the wartime food-control law, nonbeverage alcohol cost $240 a barrel. Saloon keepers diluted the barrels with water and sold small glasses for thirty or forty cents, making significant profits.[11]

Boiardo arranged to purchase hair-tonic alcohol from John Serpico, a barber who in August 1901 had also emigrated from Marigliano. Boiardo then resold the nonbeverage alcohol to speakeasies throughout the First Ward. He soon quit his milk route and set himself up as a distributor.

By 1925 Boiardo had aligned himself with the First Ward bootlegging ring headed by Frank "Chichi" Mazzocchi, who took to calling himself the Rum King of Newark. Mazzocchi and his brothers Domenic and John owned a speakeasy in the ward called the Victory Café—which housed a boxing gym, a bowling alley, and a political association—and operated alky-cookers in rural areas throughout northern New Jersey. They hired the Boot to manage them. The Mazzocchi gang also engaged in stickups and heists. The Boot, Mazzocchi, and another gang member, Sam Angelo, were arrested late one night in 1925 outside Hausman & Sons, a shoe store on Springfield Avenue. The men were armed and allegedly preparing to rob the shop.[12] They were convicted of carrying concealed weapons and served six months in the Essex County Penitentiary. While the Boot was serving his sentence, Jennie gave birth to their youngest child, Phyllis.

After getting out of the pen, the Boot, who was thirty-six years old, focused on running alky-cookers for the Mazzocchi mob in rural New Jersey while setting up his own operations by purchasing or leasing cheap farmland that was being foreclosed as the economy began to collapse, leading to the Depression. The isolation of these properties, many of them in the Mendham area and East Brunswick, helped to conceal the activity, and it was easy for the mob to keep one step ahead of the law by hop-scotching from one abandoned farm to another.[13]

The mob also ran alky-cookers in the city. One of the most profitable, said to be owned by the Boot, was located in a garage in the back of a tenement house on Wood Street in the First Ward; it employed people from the neighborhood. At the time it was rumored to be the largest in Newark, a half-dozen gleaming 100-gallon pots that produced 100 five-gallon cans of pure alcohol per hour.[14] The pot still was basically a stainless steel container in which the brew was heated while a coil of copper tubing called a condenser converted the vapor coming from the pot into a liquid. Vapors escaping from the still were highly flammable. The Boot, like many bootleggers, did not use an electric heating coil to heat his pots; he used an open flame. Often when it got cold outside workers closed the windows and shut the doors, killing ventilation and trapping the odorless and highly flammable alcohol fumes inside.

On October 25, 1927, fumes ignited and 100 five-gallon cans of alcohol exploded, blowing the roof off the garage and shaking tenement houses within a three-mile radius. Thirty-seven-year-old Sam Angelo, who had been arrested with the Boot and Frank Mazzocchi for casing the shoe store, and twenty-one-year-old Carmine DePalma staggered from the building, their clothes in flames.[15] Firemen struggled to keep the inferno from spreading to tenements on the block. Angelo and DePalma died, and the Boot, not normally sentimental about people dying, was deeply saddened, according to his daughter Rosina.[16]

Two years later, the Boot suffered another disaster in his own alky-cooker, located in the garage next door to his house on Newark Street. The place had been raided by police and was being dismantled by Prohibition department laborers—described as "coloreds"—who created a spark with either a crowbar or a tossed cigarette, causing the explosion of a pair of 100-gallon stills, 75 five-gallon cans of alcohol, and 5 fifty-gallon drums.

A flaming river of alcohol rolled out to the street scorching parked cars, and the blast hurled three "dry-force" workers, employed by the Federal Prohibition Bureau, twenty feet in the air. One was killed, and the others were critically injured. The Boot was arrested and charged with receiving stolen property. Authorities alleged that 1,250 gallons of the alcohol in the garage had been stolen in a holdup of the offices of the Frelinghuysen Avenue National Oil and Supply Company.[17]

Following his arrest and conviction for gun possession in 1925, the Boot began distancing himself from the Mazzocchi mob. Around 1928, he finally broke with them and formed his own gang, taking a handful of Mazzocchi hoodlums with him. The Boot built on relationships he had made while running with the Mazzocchi mob and established a firm foothold of his own in the First Ward both in the rackets and as a political power broker. He opened prosperous speakeasies in the backrooms of social clubs with names like the Ritchie Association and the Modern Political Club. He used these as a base of operations to expand into other vices like gambling and running an Italian lottery, a numbers betting game that was a favorite of Italian immigrants and laborers who could bet as little as a penny on a winning combination of three numbers. The daily game winner was often determined by lottery numbers published in newspapers in Italy, where lotteries were legal.

The Boot ruled his small domain as a benevolent dictator; performing charitable acts for his neighbors while setting down strict rules for his mob, who were forbidden from engaging in prostitution and drug trafficking. The Boot was a smart politician; he understood that as long as he promoted the mild vices of penny gambling and bootlegging, ordinary citizens and the police would tolerate and even welcome him in the neighborhood, but the "dirty" businesses of narcotics peddling and whoremongering would not be condoned. On occasion the Boot made a display of his virtue; according to one legend he personally tracked down two pimps who were operating in the First Ward, beat them up brutally, and forced them out of town.[18] He also reportedly chased out several drug-dealing mobsters from New York and Philadelphia.[19]

At the same time he pushed to expand his influence beyond the First Ward. He forged alliances with other racketeers and was believed to have established strong connections in New York, especially in Brooklyn, where it was said the Boot had taken over control of the powerful Augie-Yale gang after Frankie Yale was murdered by Alphonse "Scarface" Capone. "There are those in the First Ward who firmly believe Ritchie rules this Brooklyn faction as well as the First Ward gang. They say the diamond buckle in his possession is not the only sign of this. Ritchie is said to prefer to rule whatever Brooklyn territory he may have from Newark because he is much safer here than if actually in the field."[20]

Yale was ambushed on a Brooklyn Street by a machine-gun-toting squad led by Frederick Burke, a hired torpedo (hit man) from Chicago who also led the crew behind the Saint Valentine's Day Massacre.[21] Although Capone was vacationing in Florida at the time, it was clear he ordered the hit.[22] Yale was one of Capone's early mentors; after Capone moved to Chicago from Brooklyn, they continued a business relationship, with Yale shipping alcohol from New York to the Windy City. After many of these trucks were hit by hijackers along the route, Capone suspected Yale had double-crossed him. Capone planted a spy in Yale's organization, James D'Amato, who was discovered by Yale and murdered. Capone retaliated.[23]

The death of Yale left a leadership void in Brooklyn that the Boot apparently tried to fill. He had long been acquainted with the Brooklyn boys because his mash farms and still operations in rural East Brunswick, New Jersey, neighbored bootleg farms owned by Brooklyn combines. And it is likely that the Boot either helped facilitate Yale's cross-country shipments or participated in his alleged double-cross of Capone. In either case, the Boot appeared to be aligned with an anti-Capone faction of the Brooklyn mob.

The Boot's first top lieutenant and torpedo was Ralph Russo, aka Johnnie Russell, a fearless ex-con with a strong appetite for violence. Russo came from a large Italian immigrant family that produced two other Boot soldiers who were younger, John "Big Pussy" Russo and Anthony "Little Pussy" Russo; they earned their nicknames for their reputations as cat burglars, who broke into homes and escaped the police by scaling walls and fences.[24] Ralph and John were impeccable dressers and former amateur boxers who were in great physical condition and had movie-star good looks. Anthony was the runt of the litter, short in stature and in temper; he was a mere teenager during the gang's early years but played a significant role much later. The Russo brothers were a close-knit, loyal, and deadly trio who played an important role in the rise of the Boot during Prohibition and later helped solidify his position as a major figure in organized crime.

The Russo family emigrated from the province of Naples, Italy, through Sao Paolo, Brazil, to the United States around 1906. Antonio Russo Sr., a cobbler working from home, and his wife, Lucia, a cook for a private family, at first lived in New York but eventually settled with their brood in the heart of the First Ward of Newark. They relocated several times within the ward, originally on Drift Street, then Sheffield, and finally on Garside Street, all within a few blocks of each other. Based on federal Census documents and newspaper accounts, by the time Lucia Russo turned forty-six in 1930, she had a total of fifteen children, including Teresina, Vincenza, Carmine, Luigi, Ralph, Michele (Michael), Giovanni (John), Salvatore, Anthony, and Carmela. The five older children either remained in Brazil or were on their own, not living in the household. Antonio Sr. died around 1922, at an early stage in the younger boys' upbringing. As a consequence their mother had to quit her job to care for the family.

The Boot knew the entire family from his early milk-delivery days and was acquainted with the father through his shoe-repair business. After Antonio Sr.'s death, the Boot assisted the family by providing them with food and money and work for the boys. At first, Ralph worked as a shoe-store salesman, and John as a helper for a nearby blacksmith who made wagons. Salvatore became an electrician and Michael a barber in the First Ward.

Ralph Russo's life of crime began at an early age as a truant from school. Unable to control his disobedient behavior, Ralph's frustrated parents committed him to a city home. He became an amateur pugilist fighting under the name of Johnnie Russell. The Boot recruited him and his younger brother John during their teens, and the brothers quickly learned the many facets of the trade: highway robberies, truck hijackings, bootlegging, swag processing, the Italian lottery, and strong-arm enforcement.

In 1924, Ralph was placed on one-year probation for receiving illegal booze. On February 6, 1925, while on probation, he committed an armed robbery of a jewelry store on Grand Street in New York City. According to newspaper accounts,[25] Ralph, who was eighteen, and his accomplice, Anthony "Money" Alfone, twenty-six, botched the job. The store owner fought back; Alfone hit him in the head with a pistol, and both men fled. With the owner in hot pursuit, the entire neighborhood jumped in on the chase, knocking over pushcarts and peddler's wares along the way. Shots were fired. In the confusion, a third, unknown, thief strolled into the unguarded store and robbed a half dozen diamond rings. Ralph and Alfone were arrested by the police and held without bail.

Ralph was sentenced to several years in New York's Sing Sing Prison and was released in 1927. Soon after his release he and five other accomplices broke through a basement wall of a Newark cafe and stole several kegs of wine. The owner, who lived upstairs on the second floor, fired shots killing one of the intruders. Ralph was later arrested; he confessed and was sent to Sing Sing again.

While he was in prison, Ralph's younger brother John stepped up and became the Boot's key lieutenant, playing an important leadership role during the gang's turf war with the Boot's erstwhile partners, the Mazzocchi clan. The polarization between the Boot and his former associates intensified after Frank Mazzocchi aligned himself with Abner "Longy" Zwillman's Third Ward gang. Chichi also established close ties with Al Capone and the Chicago boss's Brooklyn cronies.

After the Boot and the Mazzocchis parted ways, the Mazzocchi crew began muscling in on the Boot's operations, headquartered at the Ritchie Association, the Boot's social club, which was located at Crane Street and Summer Avenue, just a few blocks from the Mazzocchis' Victory Café.

Mazzocchi gunsels hijacked the Boot's gambling and bootleg customers and his booze shipments. Mazzocchi underlings Joseph and Phillip Rossi (aka Ross or Rosso, original name Grosso; Phillip also went by the name Young Dilly) ran a drug ring out of a First Ward saloon on Eighth Avenue in open defiance of the Boot's ban. The Mazzocchi crew, about ten gang members strong, was itching for a fight.[26]

In the summer of 1929, open warfare with Mazzocchi's crew erupted in the streets of Newark and in some outlying neighborhoods. The first casualties were an unidentified man whose body was found burned beyond recognition in a car left in a city dump; a gambler named Joseph Tricoli, who was shot to death on a lonely road in Eagle Rock Reservation; and a bootlegger named James Lemon, who was gunned down in Garfield. Although the gang affiliation of these men was not clear, police believed the murders were connected to the feud between Boiardo and Mazzocchi.

What followed, however, was very clear: a bold assault on Mazzocchi's gang by the Boot's men. The incident began in front of the Victory Café. Two armed men began chasing a pair of unarmed Mazzocchi hoods, Agostino Dellapia and Vincenzo Follo. The foot chase covered several blocks. The quartet raced past the Second Precinct police station and continued to a corner where Dellapia and Follo split apart. One gunman stopped and fired, hitting Dellapia, who dropped to the sidewalk. The gunmen then chased after Follo. "They fired two shots when an unidentified woman, who had been sitting on the steps at 6 Stone street, rushed to the sidewalk to protect her children who were playing there. She was in the direct line of fire and the gunmen stopped shooting."[27] The chase was joined by a third gunman in a car that careened around the corner; the driver leaned out of his window shooting, and he hit Follo.

The police finally took notice, and they spilled out into the street just as the car passed their precinct house. They found Dellapia slumped on the sidewalk, still breathing with two wounds in the chest, two in the abdomen, and another in the back. Follo was hit three times in the chest. Both men died. Although their killers were never apprehended, police authorities believed the Boot's men were responsible.

Another deadly encounter between the rival gangs occurred on December 4, 1929. Joseph Rosso, brother of Young Dilly and a key Mazzocchi lieutenant, was gunned down a block away from the Victory Café. Big Pussy, only twenty years old at the time, and another Boiardo hoodlum named Frank Nappi later confessed to the hit. At the time, Big Pussy had no convictions. Nappi had several priors for robbery and was previously stabbed during a hold-up. In an earlier dispute in June of the same year Rosso had shot Nappi in the leg, permanently crippling him. There was bad blood between them, a score that needed settling.[28]

According to Big Pussy's testimony, the hit was well planned. He had stolen a getaway car a few days before and parked it just blocks away from the Victory Café. On the night of the murder, Big Pussy went out looking for Rosso, dropping in at Ciminio's Pool Room on Seventh Avenue. Rosso was drunk. The men argued. Rosso said, "I'll cut you up and get the both of you before Christmas. I'll show you who's going to run the First Ward. I'll cut you before the night is over."[29]

Big Pussy told authorities he left the pool hall, with Rosso in pursuit, and dropped into the Victory Café, near his stolen car. As he took a seat at a table, Rosso arrived. "Just to make things look good Rosso bought me a cup of coffee there," said Big Pussy. "While I was drinking it Rosso put his finger to my cheek and whispered, 'that's where I am going to mark you.'"[30] Big Pussy brushed off the threat, left the cafe, got into his car, and waited. Rosso eventually followed, walking up Seventh Avenue. Big Pussy drove by and shot Rosso in the leg—as payback for crippling Nappi—and "in the abdomen for good measure." He left the scene quickly and dumped the stolen car.[31]

Following a tip, the police immediately raided the Ritchie Association, and twenty-nine men including the Boot were taken in for questioning. The police also found three revolvers. The newspapers noted that the Boot was wearing "a belt buckle studded with diamonds valued at $5,000, and a diamond ring worth an equal amount. Boiardo declared he knew nothing of the murder."[32]

The Boot and seven others were held as potential conspirators in the murder. After a long night of questioning, Big Pussy confessed to planning the murder and shooting Rosso. Nappi confessed to helping plan the murder.[33] In court, Big Pussy pleaded *non vult*, or no contest; in other words, he did not admit his guilt but submitted to the court for sentencing. He was sentenced to thirty years. Nappi was convicted of conspiracy but received only three years. Although the Boot was indicted as a material witness and was suspected of being the one who ordered the hit, all charges were eventually dropped against him. According to unidentified FBI sources years later, "It has long been rumored among the hoodlum element that Boiardo Sr. was responsible for the death of Rosso" and that Big Pussy took the "rap" for him. "Because of this, Boiardo Sr. has long favored Russo and has seen to it that he has been well off both financially and in position."[34]

In 1930, Ralph Russo was finally released from prison just as his younger brother John was convicted of murder. The Boot put Ralph back to work as soon as he was released. Shortly afterward, perhaps not coincidentally, the Rum King, Frank "Chichi" Mazzocchi, was gunned down, also in front of his Victory Café, which had changed its name to the Victory Political Association after the Rosso murder. While Mazzocchi, twenty-eight years old, was having a conversation with the driver of a car parked in front of the club at 10:30 in the evening, a dark green sedan quietly pulled up behind and "a typewriter accompanied by ukulele music played"—in gangster parlance the drum holding bullets in a submachine gun was called a ukulele and its fire was described as the sound of a typewriter.[35] Mazzocchi staggered back into the club. "They got me" he said, collapsing.[36] He was hustled into a car, which had a flat tire that had been punctured by the spray of bullets, and was driven to Saint Michael's Hospital, the vehicle limping across town. In his hospital bed, in critical condition with four bullets lodged in his neck and abdomen, Mazzocchi was questioned by police. He refused to name his assailants. The gangster died after an unsuccessful attempt to save him with a massive blood transfusion.[37] The shooting of Mazzocchi occurred seven months before the assassination attempt on the Boot and was believed to have led directly to the Boot shooting.[38]

Five months after the attempt on the Boot, a Mazzocchi hood who was allegedly one of the bungling hit men in the Boot shooting was murdered. Young Dilly Rossi (Joe Rosso's brother) was killed at his Ringside Athletic Club on Eighth Avenue by a shotgun blast that nearly decapitated him.[39] Heroin was found in his pockets, and an autopsy discovered 130 hypodermic needle marks on his body.[40] Twelve hours after Young Dilly's murder, the police discovered the body of Adam Dresch, a former Newark cop turned gangster. He was bound and floating in the Passaic River after being shot six times. Authorities theorized that Dresch may have been the other would-be assassin of the Boot.[41]

Frank Mazzocchi's brothers, John and Domenic, found themselves left in charge of a dwindling crew whose members either were killed or had defected to the Boot's gang. Finally, on March 6, 1932, John Mazzocchi was taken for a ride. His body was found in the backseat of an abandoned car in a desolate section of Belleville with a single gunshot wound in the back of his head.[42] At the time police were informed that John had dropped out of bootlegging and owned a confectionary and cafe where he maintained an illegal lottery business.

According to Public Safety Director Michael Duffy, commenting on the demise of the Mazzocchi gang: "There were ten active members and a number of lesser lights, and they dealt in alcohol throughout New Jersey and New York. The other mob was Ritchie Boiardo's, more powerful after the Mazzocchi murders because some of the Mazzocchi boys joined up. There were Jerry (Sweat) Rullo, Angelo (Gyp) DeCarlo, Charles (the Blade) Tourine, Joseph (Ding Bat) Parillo, and a good many others."[43]

CHAPTER 2

THE LONGY WAR

Till here, I've told you of the fights
and boundless blows between these knights,
and all their terrible attacks.
Now I must soar above the sky,
because two barons meet in arms
who make me tremble in my mind.
Lords, listen—if you like—a while
about two knights whose wills were fire.
　　　　　—Matteo Maria Boiardo, Orlando Innamorato, *218*

The press and the public speculated long and hard on the identity of the party responsible for the attempted assassination of the Boot. "None of Ritchie's gang is above suspicion of planning the murder of their leader," the *Newark Evening News* reported. "There are also said to be men who would like to see Ritchie out of the way because of certain women who favored him with their regard."[1] Other likely suspects included the Mazzocchi brothers, Willie Moretti, and even Al Capone.

The number-one suspect, however, was Abner "Longy" Zwillman, a man sometimes referred to as gangster number two, reputed to be the second most powerful mobster of his time right behind Lucky Luciano.[2] Longy was younger than the Boot by almost fifteen years but he had a head start. While the Boot was still working as a milkman and was married with three young children, Longy was already making rounds selling fruit and vegetables and illegal lottery numbers from a pushcart in the streets of the Third Ward, a largely Eastern European–Jewish immigrant neighborhood. Longy was the son of Russian immigrants.[3] His father sold poultry on Prince Street, the heart of the Jewish quarter, to support a family of seven children. He died when Longy, the oldest child, was twelve, leaving him and his four brothers and three sisters to fend for themselves. Longy's nickname allegedly derived from a corruption of "der Langer," German for "the tall one," which is what the Third Ward merchants took to calling him. In his early teens he was six foot two and was described as dark-skinned and broad-shouldered, with a head of dark hair neatly parted in the middle.[4] He was handsome, strong, ambitious, and dissatisfied with business in his home ward; he began pushing his cart up Clinton Hill, an upscale neighborhood, and soon found that he could make better money by taking lottery bets from his new customers for a local gambling operator than by selling produce. He eventually muscled in on his employer, grabbed his customers, and set up his own gambling operation.[5]

While the Boot was still delivering milk and working for the Mazzocchi gang as a part-time manager of their alky-cookers, sixteen-year-old Longy was running a solid numbers racket and building a protection ring with a group of his school pals, including James "Niggie" Rutkin and Joseph "Doc" Stacher. They called themselves the Happy Ramblers, a street gang innocent in name only, as they found themselves summoned whenever Jewish street vendors and storeowners around Prince Street were harassed and robbed by Irish thugs from the neighboring Eighteenth Ward. The Ramblers fought these interlopers with their fists at first and later would dispatch them much more efficiently with guns.

In 1923, Longy, at age seventeen, had a legendary run-in with a street hoodlum named Leo Kaplus, who had been roughing up his numbers runners and had threatened to kick Longy in the balls.[6] Longy personally tracked Kaplus down to a Newark tavern and shot him in the leg, although legend has it he was deliberately hit in the testicles. In any case, the incident made an impression on other gangsters; Longy was seen as one tough hood, to be feared and respected among Jewish and Italian gangs. Waxey Gordon, a New York bootlegger who owned illegal breweries around Newark, took notice and hired Longy and his men to protect his operations.

Longy also caught the attention of Joe Reinfeld, who owned a speakeasy on High Street and Eighth Avenue in the North Ward that was patronized by Italian immigrants, gamblers, loan sharks, and local community leaders. Reinfeld stocked his inventory with liquor that was clandestinely imported from Canada; he needed muscle to safeguard shipments that came in through Newark's port.

Reinfeld, a Polish-Jewish immigrant, had established a relationship with the Bronfman family, who owned the Seagram distillery in Montreal. Sam Bronfman himself started out as a bootlegger in Saskatchewan.[7] After authorities forced him out of the province, Bronfman moved to Montreal to go legitimate, buying the Seagram company and its Waterloo, Ontario, distillery. After several distilleries were merged, Seagram became the largest producer of spirits in the world. The Bronfman family controlled all aspects of their business: distilling, distribution, and export. They also imported liquor from England, which they exported to the United States on schooners that sailed down Rum Row along the northeastern coast. They formed the Atlas Shipping Company, a front company that also made clandestine deliveries to U.S. bootleggers. Atlas controlled warehouses in Windsor and Newfoundland.

In 1930, when Canada banned liquor shipments to the United States, Bronfman moved his warehouses to Saint Pierre and Miquelon, small islands in the Atlantic Ocean near Canada, and established the Northern Export Company, a Seagram distribution facility that catered solely to U.S. bootleggers, including Reinfeld. Because St. Pierre was a French protectorate, Bronfman could ship to the United States while avoiding Canada's observance of Washington's ban on the direct export of alcoholic beverages to the states. Seagram also had warehouses in the West Indies and Mexico that served the U.S. market.

Sam Bronfman developed an elaborate process for moving illegal shipments into the States from the north. Canadian customs agents were put on the company payroll to stamp bills of lading for shipments, and the company forged landing certificates from foreign ports; shell corporations, fictitious names, foreign bank accounts, and other money-laundering schemes were used to conceal their imports and enormous bootleg profits. In 1930 Atlas deposited over $3 million into the distillery's bank. Another shell company banked $8 million.

Reinfeld met Sam Bronfman in 1920, a year after Prohibition was enacted into law, and he soon became Bronfman's largest U.S. partner. Together they devised ingenious ways to move merchandise from Canada into the United States, using Newark and the Jersey coastline as the main point of entry. The Bronfman's whiskey-laden freighters routinely anchored at night twelve miles off Sandy Hook, safely beyond the three-mile limit of U.S. jurisdiction. Small speedboats would intercept the freighters, transfer cargo, and carry it ashore, delivering the goods to safe houses along the coast. One of Reinfeld's "rum schooners" was raided off the coast of Atlantic City after rival bootleggers who had their headquarters in the Ritz Carlton in the resort town tipped off the Coast Guard.[8] At the height of its operations Reinfeld's organization moved twenty-two thousand cases of booze a month.

In the wealthy shore town of Deal, just south of Sandy Hook, Reinfeld developed a unique technique using a rubber hose that pumped liquor from vessels with copper-lined tanks into oak barrels stored in three adjacent safe houses on the beach under cover of darkness. Red signal lights on the safe houses indicated the drop-off points. Twenty-five thousand gallons of Canadian whiskey could be pumped into the trio of homes in a matter of hours.

Reinfeld imported about 40 percent of all bootleg liquor in the United States during Prohibition, according to a U.S. Senate investigation, and Newark was the booze-smuggling capital of the States during much of this period.

Reinfeld, who lived on the same street as the Boot, had contacted Longy Zwillman looking for muscle. Not just any muscle. Joe wanted one of his kind. Jewish entrepreneurs were making inroads during Prohibition. Two of the most powerful gangsters were Meyer Lansky and Benjamin "Bugsey"

Siegel, both Jewish, who made a name for themselves by creating strategic alliances with Italian mobsters Lucky Luciano, Frank Costello, and Joe Adonis. Reinfeld's business needed protection from hijackers; he hired Longy and his boys to truck Canadian whiskey from the coast to Newark and New York. For the task, Longy purchased a fleet of surplus WWI armored trucks, which ran past a gauntlet of obstacles up the coast from as far south as Atlantic City, through the pine barrens and into grimy, depressed northern cities like Bayonne, Jersey City, Elizabeth, and Kearny, where corrupt cops exacted protection payments and local mobsters put out their hands for a touch. Longy's caravans ran from Newark's port, across dark swampland roads where hijackers lurked, through the industrial Ironbound neighborhood, past the warehouses of competing bootleggers.

The Ironbound, officially the Fifth Ward, was a narrow, working-class neighborhood that was penned in by the iron tracks of railroads and checkered with small factories, many of them ironworks and foundries. The neighborhood also was called Down Neck, allegedly for its tapered shape. Sitting on the edge of the sluggish Passaic River and the swampy meadowlands, between downtown and the port, the Ironbound was like a border town, a place people passed through but where they did not stay long. It was Newark's version of Vegas but without the glamour—wide open with illegal gambling joints, speakeasies, and lots of gang activity. There was one speakeasy for every six blocks in the neighborhood. Also very much like Vegas, the Ironbound was not the fiefdom of any one gang; in fact all of Newark's various mobs had agreed to coexist here. It was a sort of neutral zone populated by Italian, Irish, and German immigrants, but the Italians predominated.

In 1927 Longy shrewdly tapped a couple of young Ironbound toughs to help him move his trucks through this last stretch, Gerardo "Jerry" Catena and his younger brother Eugene (or Gene). Both Catenas had a reputation in their neighborhood, the Fifth Ward, for thievery, strong-arm enforcement, extortion, and cold-blooded murder. Gene once shot and killed a Lyndhurst fireman during an argument in a speakeasy. Jerry was more reliable and less impulsive than his brother; he was clever and brutal, and that impressed Longy, who promoted him to be his personal driver. He rose in Longy's ranks like a corporate middle manager, promoted because of his consistent job performance and unwavering loyalty. Under Longy's tutelage, Jerry would eventually mature into a low-key, resolute power broker. He would become more of a businessman than a hoodlum.

Longy was a solid role model for Catena. While working as a hired gun for Reinfeld, he set up his own small bootleg operation in the Third Ward and quickly emerged as a distributor in his own right.[9] His lottery business had grown to become the largest in Newark, and he expanded into extortion, infiltrating retail-worker unions in department stores and settling strikes by taking cash payments. He set himself up in an office in Newark's posh Riviera Hotel. When he turned nineteen, Longy forced Reinfeld's hand; he demanded to be a partner. Reinfeld caved, settling for a fifty-fifty split in the business and equal negotiating status, which allowed Longy to confer directly with Bronfman. According to the IRS, the combine would rake in about $40 million over the course of five years.[10]

The criminal pharaohs across the Hudson contacted the emerging Jewish gangster to establish a Jersey connection. Lucky Luciano, Meyer Lansky, Joe Adonis, Frank Costello, Bugsey Siegal, and Lepke Buchalter, who were beginning to cooperate with each other instead of battle, reached out; it's likely that the connection was made through one of Longy's associates, Guarino "Willie" Moretti.

Moretti was born in Italy in 1894; he emigrated to the United States with his parents and was raised on East 108th Street in Harlem.[11] He grew up with Frank Costello as his neighbor, and they remained lifelong friends. For a time he was a prizefighter, and, like the Boot, Moretti worked as a milkman.[12] A garish dresser who favored hand-painted ties, Moretti stood only five feet four but was intimidating nonetheless. He became Costello's muscle on the streets of Harlem and was the model for the character of Luca Brasi, the bodyguard of Don Vito Corleone in Mario Puzo's *The Godfather*.

With Costello's blessing, around 1930 Moretti moved to Hasbrouck Heights, New Jersey, just across the Hudson River from Manhattan, and began building his own gambling network and rum-running business in Bergen and Passaic counties; his headquarters were in Cliffside Park at the Marine Room, a casino within the Riviera Club, a popular nightclub on the Palisades north of the George Washington Bridge. He also owned a home in the exclusive Jersey beach town of Deal and conducted his bootlegging business there in between entertaining guests such as Dean Martin, Jerry Lewis, and Frank Sinatra, whose first wife was a cousin of one of Moretti's lieutenants.

Moretti was reportedly one of Sinatra's first financial backers and arranged bookings for the then-unknown crooner in Jersey clubs. Band leader Tommy Dorsey later signed the rising star to an onerous long-term contract. When Sinatra wanted out and Dorsey refused, Moretti allegedly forced the stubborn band leader's hand by jamming the barrel of a gun into his mouth. Dorsey sold the contract back to the singer for one dollar.[13]

After moving to Jersey, Moretti had several early run-ins with the Boot. According to FBI reports, Moretti attempted to run a prostitution ring in the First Ward, and the Boot bounced him out. Around 1930, the Boot expanded his bootlegging and hijacking operations into Passaic County, Moretti's turf and headquarters of the Garfield Express Company, which moved liquor from Jersey ports to speakeasies and was owned by New York hoodlums Louis "Lepke" Buchalter and Jacob Shapiro, both friends of Moretti's. The Boot's crew was systematically hijacking Garfield Express shipments. Informants told FBI agents that Moretti warned the Boot to stop his incursions and hijackings.[14] The stubborn Newarker apparently refused, and Moretti allegedly arranged the ambush on Broad Street that nearly killed the Boot.

The Marine Room, Moretti's club in Cliffside Park, was backed by Zwillman as well as Luciano, Lansky, and Costello, and it became a watering hole for tribes from both sides of the Hudson, including other heavyweight Jersey mobsters such as Albert Anastasia and Joe Adonis. The powerful New Yorkers wanted a piece of the lucrative bootlegging action in Jersey, and these intimate gatherings at the Marine Room turned into negotiating sessions aimed at figuring out how to share the bounty.[15]

These meetings would serve as dry runs for the first national organized-crime conference, which took place in Atlantic City in May 1929, hosted by the resort's resident crime lord and politician Nucky Johnson. In attendance was a powerhouse gallery of rogues whose names were ripped from the headlines: Al "Scarface" Capone and Greasy Thumb Guzik, both from Chicago; King Solomon from Boston; Nig Rosen and Boo-Boo Hoff from Philadelphia; Moe Dalitz and Chuck Polizzi out of Cleveland; Abe Berstein of Detroit's Purple Gang; John Lazia from Kansas City; and Charles "Lucky" Luciano, Meyer Lansky, Frank Costello, Joe Adonis, Louis "Lepke" Buchalter, Johnny Torrio, Dutch Schultz, Frank Erickson, Vincent "the Executioner" Mangano, Frank "Don Cheech" Scalise, and Albert Anastasia, all from New York.

The Atlantic City conference marked the establishment of what was called by the press the National Crime Syndicate, a confederation of Italian and Jewish gangs with clearly demarcated territories of operation and rules of conduct headed by a commission of the leaders of the top crime families, who resolved disputes among the membership.[16] The idea was to minimize gang violence and publicity across the country in order to focus simply on doing business and making money. Luciano was the main architect of the syndicate, and Longy reportedly played a role as a key strategist.[17]

Coming out of Atlantic City, Longy was on a roll; he was in favor with a crowd of Jewish and Italian thugs including local gunsels such as Sam Katz, Joe "Doc" Stacher, Jerry Catena, Nick Delmore, Dominic "the Ape" Paselli, Johnnie "Coke" Lardiere, Joe Stassi, and Carmine Battaglia, along with big shots from other states. Longy was called the top gangster in New Jersey, the "Al Capone of Newark" by the press and the FBI,[18] and was considered untouchable by other gangsters.

Longy also was held in high regard for a relationship he began with actress Jean Harlow in 1930. The mob-connected Hollywood agent

Marino Bello introduced them, and the affair brought Longy in contact with Howard Hughes, who had the actress under contract, paying her only $250 a week.[19] Longy arranged for Hughes to release her and negotiated a better deal with Columbia Pictures. The arrangement led to a starring role for her in *Platinum Blonde.* The actress had become famous for offering to prove to the press that her hair was naturally platinum by lifting her skirt. Long after the affair ended, Longy reportedly kept a collection of her pubic hairs, which he proudly displayed to fellow gangsters.[20]

Unlike his peers—and enemies—the Boot was not impressed by the mob's darling. To him, Longy was fair game. The Boot was a confident upstart who had a reputation for wearing flashy clothes and jewelry and generally "looking aces" and for being independent; he could be a thorn in the side of cops and mobsters equally, something frowned on by the leaders who gathered in the Marine Room and in Atlantic City. The Boot saw Longy as a threat to his livelihood and a stumbling block to his ambitions, and he was not afraid to do something about it.

"A war between a Third Ward leader who is generally credited with being the boss of the lottery racket in Newark and a First Ward leader, who has taken it into his head to break in, is impending. That is the word that has gotten around to those who seek fortunes via the numbers."[21] The Boot's desire to expand his numbers racket was reportedly the motive behind the bloody war that erupted, but it was the conflict over booze that launched the first salvo.

Although it is impossible to pinpoint when the first shots in the war were fired, a pivotal incident occurred in the Ironbound. Longy's influence in the Ironbound evolved through his association with the Catena and Paselli families—two influential neighborhood clans. Patsy Paselli was a civic leader in the Fifth Ward; his twenty-five-year-old brother Dominic was a street tough known as the Ape, or Sully the Ape. According to the *Newark Evening News,* Dominic "had heavy black hair on his head and body[; his hair] coupled with his supposed ferocity won him the name of the Ape. Long arms gave added point to the cognomen."[22] He lived in the heart of the Ironbound on Adams Street, and his neighbors were afraid to talk to him. The Ape was a freelance beer runner and hijacker who played both sides, sometimes working for the Boot and sometimes for Longy, depending on who was hiring on any given day. He also was an extortionist and strong-arm thug; he had his own retainers to protect businesses like the Market Grill, a "colored" cabaret on the corner of Market Street and Jackson Avenue.

The Boot meanwhile had established an alliance with the Ironbound's Antonio Caponigro, aka Tony Bananas, who was given this nickname because his father was a fruit vendor. Bananas had a reputation for being a wild man, unpredictable and deadly. Collaborating with Caponigro, the Boot ran a lucrative still in an Ironbound warehouse just off Ferry Street, the main artery in the Neck and the principal thoroughfare for bootleggers passing from the port to downtown. Longy's booze trucks flowed through Ferry Street traffic, melting into a steady stream of legitimate deliveries of produce, manufactured goods, and raw materials from the port.

The Boot's mob began hijacking Longy's beer trucks in the Ironbound, allegedly without the Boot's knowledge or consent. When he found out, according to a *Newark Evening News* article, "it was Ritchie's custom to have the beer returned or a cash equivalent offered and thus, the beer-runner's theory goes[,] good feeling was preserved."[23]

There are many apocryphal stories and legends surrounding the war between the Boot and Longy; one version suggested the Boot's men began the war by "swaggering through Longy's Third Ward fiefdom, harassing bartenders, threatening saloon owners, holding up numbers runners." According to this tale, told by one of Longy's "muscle men," the Boot attempted to force a Third Ward speakeasy owner named Hymie "the Horse" Klein, a longstanding customer of Longy's, to buy his liquor instead of Longy's.

> This fat little fuck walks into Klein's place today. . . . He has a card he slaps on the bar and tells the Horse that's his price list. The Horse gives

me the sign, so I walks over and asks this guy what's happening. He tells me to mind my own fuckin' business. I tell him this is my business, and if he don't get his fat ass out of the place, I'll throw him through the window. He's alone, so he just looks at me and walks out. I pick up the card. It has Richie the Boot's name on it.[24]

The Boot's men allegedly returned that night and raked the bar with submachine-gun fire; they followed up a few days later, ambushing one of Longy's booze trucks and executing a young boy in cold blood, according to another Longy associate who claimed to be an eyewitness:

I heard a shot, then breaking glass. It sounded like it was coming from my truck. Then I heard a scream—and some more shooting. I ran out and there was the kid, hanging half out the door with a hole where his eye used to be. The bastards killed him, then they turned a Tommy on the truck. They just shot up half the cases I had.[25]

On September 16, 1930, just blocks away from a clandestine liquor warehouse on Rome Street in the Ironbound that was managed by Doc Stracher and was said to be owned by Longy and Reinfeld, two cars filled with gunman crossed paths. Johnnie Russell, aka Ralph Russo, one of Boiardo's key soldiers and the elder brother of John "Big Pussy" Russo, was riding shotgun in one of the vehicles with Dominic "the Ape" Paselli, whose allegiance at that moment was with the Boot, or so it seemed. The other car was filled with Longy's men. Russo and the Ape were reportedly casing the Rome Street warehouse in preparation for a break-in. Longy's men intercepted them. Bullets flew between the vehicles in the middle of the day on the heavily congested corner of Lafayette and Pulaski streets in the heart of the Ironbound.

Decades later, the Boot gave FBI agents a completely different account of the incident. He claimed his crew was bringing into Newark a load of beer supplied by Dutch Schultz, the Bronx gangster, and Longy's men hijacked the shipment.[26] Schultz's real name was Arthur Flegenheimer;

he changed it, he said, so that it was short enough to fit into a newspaper headline. The Bronx gang lord was an unpredictable, independent operator who did not readily abide by the unwritten laws of the mob. He trespassed on other hoodlums' turf and made more enemies than friends, especially fellow Jewish gangsters like Arnold Rothstein and Meyer Lansky, who disdained his unsophisticated taste in clothes and his crude way of doing business.[27]

Schultz must have recognized a kindred soul in the Boot, who likewise was considered uncouth and undisciplined by his Italian associates. The two men reached across state borders and gang territories and engaged in some business, and apparently Longy would have none of it. Some years later, Schultz would make a bigger play for a piece of the action in Newark, and as a result he never left the city alive.

In the Ironbound fracas the Ape received a superficial wound on the back of his right hand; initial press reports indicated it was a bullet wound.[28] He admitted himself to Newark General Hospital on North Twelfth Street, in the Second Ward, explaining to the hospital's owner and chief physician, Dr. Charles Gnassi, that he had injured himself while trying to crank-start a car. After being admitted, the Ape told his brother that he feared he would be "put on the spot," or shot, in retaliation for the incident with Ralph Russo.[29] The remark seemed to suggest that he was responsible in some way for the gunfight, that perhaps he had intentionally driven Russo into the ambush. However, Russo was too seriously wounded to put anybody on the spot. He had taken a bullet to the head and apparently had been left for dead on the street. A stranger came to his rescue, picked him up, and drove him to Saint Michael's Hospital.

The Boot responded immediately, attacking "members of Longey [sic] Zwillman's Third Ward gang," according to the Newark Evening News. They were cornered in a garage near Zwillman's Third Ward Political Club. The Boot's men roughed up the crew and robbed them of several thousand dollars. "War was threatened between the gangs," the News reported. "There was a fear that killings would result."[30]

Another version of the story in the same paper stated that the Boot was personally involved in the ambush, and Longy was there too. According to this version, the retaliation was triggered not by the shooting of Russo but by conflicts in the illegal lottery racket:

> The report is that the first Warder known in sporting circle[s] as Ritchie paid a surprise visit to the Waverly Avenue headquarters of the existing "lottery monarch" one Longey, on Tuesday, to inform the latter of his intention. With him he took a following of lieutenants. Underworld gossip is that the invaders lined the surprised racketeer and his crowd against the wall. Emphasizing his words with more than his finger, the man who would muscle in told the man who was in to get out of the lottery racket at once and stay out, or words to that effect. The Third Warder was told he was making enough in the booze racket. Ritchie wound up by warning the man against the wall that he would be among the missing if he did not take the warning. It is said that the visit cost the Longey crowd $300.[31]

Longy's gang struck back, with Jerry Catena and Carmine "Big Yock" San Giacomo, his principal gunmen, spearheading dozens of shootings. "Hardly a week would go by without some major shooting incident," an FBI informant claimed.[32] The situation got so out of hand that the Boot, "whose North Ward gang was experiencing a series of setbacks by the Zwillman mobsters, went to New York to Charles Lucky Luciano to secure additional gunmen with which to wipe out the Zwillman group."[33]

Newark police responded to the mayhem by launching an all-out assault on the bootleggers, beginning with a raid on Longy's Rome Street warehouse; based on other tip-offs the gang squads hit a massive still in the Second Ward owned by the Boot and another in the First Ward owned by a former policeman "whose affiliations with the Third Ward mob are never questioned."[34] The press described these raids as dry-cleaning operations by a rejuvenated police department.[35] An article in the *Newark Star-Eagle* reported that the hammerings from the gang squads "reduced the number of [the Boot's] alleged body guards and forced him to adopt a bulletproof vest."[36] The raids made a significant dent in Newark's bootlegging traffic, with costly losses on both sides.[37]

Meanwhile, another overture was being made to Luciano, this time from the Longy side. Louis Quinto, a member of the Zwillman organization who reported to Catena, went to Lucky and persuaded him to serve as a peacemaker rather than as a partisan of one of the factions. The Longy War was spinning out of control and threatened to spread, forcing gangs to choose sides and disrupting the illegal booze trade that was becoming so lucrative. According to an estimate by United States Attorney Amory R. Bucker in 1926, the national bootlegging industry was raking in almost $4 billion annually.[38] The war also had the potential to destroy Luciano's ambitious plan for the mob families to cooperate, an initiative launched at the Atlantic City conference.

Al Capone, who had ordered the Saint Valentine's Day Massacre in Chicago a year earlier, made the first move to broker a truce between the parties. He personally met with the Boot and Longy at the Robert Treat Hotel to settle matters.[39] Capone was close to Longy's friend Willie Moretti and predisposed to favor the demands of the Jewish gang lord, who was a powerful boss with national recognition among other crime bosses. At this time, the Boot was still a minor player in control of a small territory, the First Ward. The Boot, however, held his ground against Capone and Longy. He wanted a bigger piece of the action; he wanted to split the control of alcohol in Newark down the middle, fifty-fifty. Longy and Capone were not willing to do that, and the negotiations failed.

Luciano finally intervened, calling another meeting, which took place in late September 1930. Jerry Catena served as a peacemaker from the Zwillman camp. An Italian, Catena was an ideal ambassador for the Jewish kingpin; he spoke the same language, literally, as Boiardo and the other Italian gang leaders. With Luciano leveraging his significant influence, the Boot and Zwillman finally settled their differences. Concessions were made by both sides to sort out their numbers-racket territory and booze-distribution issues.

The Boot was emerging as a political power outside the mob and inside; conceding to Luciano was a strategic move that aligned him with the Italian gang leadership in New York. He had stood his ground and won, and his ego—like his waistline—burst at the seams. The Boot was anything but modest; he celebrated the truce by throwing a grandiose, two-day marathon "Peace Banquet" in honor of himself at the Nuova Napoli restaurant in the First Ward starting on October 5, 1930. It was a gesture that seemed designed to offend the temperance-minded sensibilities of the public and to tweak the noses of his enemies.

The press had a field day. Reporters filed stories that crackled with witty, cynical observations. And there was a lot of grist for their biting prose, starting with the guest list—gang members, policemen, and politicians all in one room, including Congressman Paul Moore, Democratic Assembly candidate John A. McKenna, Democratic chairman of the First Ward Joe DeBenedictis, and a former federal law-enforcement official identified as U.S. Commissioner George Sommer, who, before retiring, apparently had been responsible for collecting bail posted by arrested bootleggers. "A huge sign bearing the important message 'Ritchie Bancett' hung in a blaze of light in front of the restaurant facing Sheffield Street, inviting stragglers (many who dared not refuse) to come in and pay respects to Ritchie. He was there nattily attired in a blue suit, greeting everyone."[40]

Sporting his diamond belt buckle, "a scarf-pin heavily encrusted with diamonds and a ring that looks like a baby spotlight used in theaters," the Boot had arranged for the party to last for two days, telling the press that he had so many friends he couldn't accommodate them all in one night, including a delegation of out-of-towners whose cars lined the avenue outside.[41] The Boot identified some to reporters: Tom Tato, whom he described as a cousin of Al Capone, and "Frankie of Omaha, Jerry Bruno of Harlem, Patsy of Chicago and Tony of Indianapolis."[42] When a reporter asked for more detail on names, the Boot shrugged and admitted that was all he knew them by. His wife and children also made an appearance. "Instead of being a Wild West affair, with guns lumping the guest's hip pockets, a reporter found a peaceable and extremely happy group of First Ward business men, busily engaged in inhaling miles of spaghetti and all the things that go with it. There were no shootings, no killings and no voices raised in anything but glee."[43]

The Newark "gang squad" that had launched an all-out assault on the Boot and Longy dropped by for a few minutes, apparently on business, and quietly left, while other uniformed police officers arrived and lingered and were generously fed. Two patrolmen who left with packages of food for their precinct house were later investigated by the district attorney. Everyone paid six dollars for the privilege of consuming "several thousand yards of spaghetti" and of toasting the prince of the First Ward, the "Supremo Patrono."[44] Toward the end of the event on the second day the guests presented the host of honor a shiny new Lincoln Phaeton with bullet-proof glass as a token of their esteem.[45]

The *Newark Evening News* reporter interviewed a guest named Johnnie Evans, who only a few days before had been arrested for packing a loaded revolver and was loud in his praises of the Boot.

> "You don't see any gunmen here, do you?" asked Johnnie. "Look at that group over there. All businessmen. Biggest grape merchants in Newark and the fathers of large families. There's another guy[;] . . . he's in the milk business, and the fellow next to him's a baker. No racketeers, businessmen. Friends of Ritchie. They know what a swell guy he is and what good he does around this ward. Why he'd get up at night to help a poor widow in trouble! He's a prince!"[46]

An appearance by the Third Ward monarch Longy Zwillman was expected; the Boot assured the throng that he and Longy were the best of friends and business partners, and he promised reporters a photo opportunity of him shaking hands with Longy. "Or burying the hatchet, but not in each other's head."[47] The highly anticipated guest of honor didn't show until after ten o'clock on the second night of the feast, arriving with an entourage of ten of his men. Longy spent an hour with the Boot, huddled together at a table conversing in low tones while champagne bottles were opened around them, "peculiar popping noises ... not guns ... sounding."[48]

Most guests agreed to have their pictures taken with the Boot, including Congressman Moore, who was overheard telling guests that "he believed Ritchie to be a fine gentleman and ... that if they stuck by him they would be all right."[49] Moore's subsequent defeat in a reelection bid was blamed on the photo. Longy, however, gruffly refused to stand with his host for a portrait. Instead he slipped under a stairway to avoid the cameras. "Isn't it enough for me to be here and shake hands with him?" Longy barked at a reporter.[50]

The party wound down after Longy left. A *Newark Evening News* article summarized the event: "The Ritchie-Longie [sic] feud is over—on the surface at least."[51] Another story in another paper was perhaps more prescient: "Everything was decidedly peaceful. Like the calm before a storm."[52]

The calm would not last long. One month later, on November 4, the Ape was gunned down on Frelinghuysen Avenue, a bullet passing through his cheek and another grazing his head; he was able to summon the help of a friend who returned him to Newark General Hospital, where he registered under a false name, John Caruso, for treatment and told Dr. Gnassi this time that he received the injuries in a fall from an automobile.

Normally, hospitals were required to notify the police when a shooting victim was admitted, but Newark General was not a normal hospital. It was a private, unlicensed institution that catered to a criminal clientele. Dr. Gnassi shrewdly prospered through Newark's bootleg wars. Basically a converted three-story home just north of the First Ward, the hospital was like a battlefield surgical unit, filled with casualties of the local street skirmishes. Dr. Gnassi treated his patients secretly, without reporting gunshot or knifing victims as was required by the city police department.

The Ape never talked about who shot him, and local newspapers were left to speculate. According to one theory the Ape was freelancing for himself, attempting to muscle in on the grape-racket extortion of New York racketeers, and was shot by a rival gang.[53] The *Newark Evening News* interviewed friends and associates who said the Ape owed someone $3,500 and couldn't repay the debt. It was also reported that the Ape was preparing to hijack a Boiardo liquor drop on Frelinghuysen Avenue when he was shot.[54] Since Longy and the Boot had just buried the hatchet one month earlier at their peace banquet, the Ape may have acted alone and violated their truce. Yet another theory was the Ape was "put on the spot" for the Ironbound shooting of Ralph Russo.[55] Although it was originally believed that the Ape was working for the Boot when Russo was shot, the First Ward gang may have suspected that the Ape had double-crossed them and had acted as a finger man for Longy, setting up Russo for the ambush.

The *New York Times* reported that Ape's wounds were dressed at Newark General and he was told he could go home. Instead, he insisted on staying "apparently in fear of his enemies . . . and he was assigned a room on the second floor."[56] The next day, two men dropped in on him; "they stayed for a considerable period," and hospital staff heard a loud argument in the room, but the men eventually left without incident.[57] Jerry Catena was later identified by nurses as one of the Ape's visitors, and it was reported that they caught a glimpse of a gun protruding from his coat.[58]

Two more men returned in the early evening; one was described as five feet ten, heavy built, wearing a blue coat and brown hat, and the other five feet nine, slender built, with a gray cap. They entered the Ape's room unannounced. Three gunshots immediately rang out. The Ape was hit in the temple and the back of the head, the third bullet went wild. The Ape died instantly. Hospital staff saw his killers rush out of the hospital. Later, the police rounded up a handful of suspects, all of them members of the Boot's gang. Jerry Catena also was brought in for questioning and held as a material witness to the murder.

Since the shooting of the Ape occurred just a few weeks before the assassination attempt on the Boot, some assumed that there was a connection—that the Boot was bushwhacked in retaliation for the murder of the Ape, who may have been working at the time for Longy. This was an unlikely scenario. After the Longy meeting, the Boot's reputation was on the rise, and he would not have been targeted for the murder of a lowly street hood, especially one with doubtful loyalties like the Ape. It was more likely that the murder of the Ape did not break the pact between the Newark bosses but instead achieved the opposite result, sealing the agreement, in blood. In view of this possibility, Catena may have visited the Ape to question him and confirm that he had broken the truce by attempting to raid one of the Boot's booze deliveries, and Catena may then have granted the Boot permission to send his torpedoes to whack the errant hood.

Dr. Gnassi was indicted on various criminal charges, from operating a hospital without a license to concealing crimes. Newark police alleged that Dr. Gnassi's failure to report the Ape's gunshot wounds led directly to his cold-blooded assassination. In the indictment against Dr. Gnassi, the department claimed that had his condition been reported they would have placed him under guard at another institution. Just a few months earlier, the hospital had treated another wounded holdup man, Walter Alberti, who was shot by a New York policeman. In order to pay Alberti's hospital bill, the bandit's friends robbed five gas stations in the neighborhood. The police charged that if Gnassi had reported Alberti's gunshot wounds, the robberies would not have occurred. It was also reported by the press that Gnassi purchased a "ridiculous" amount of legitimate alcohol for alleged medicinal purposes. Dr. Gnassi withdrew from the hospitals storage "4,800 pints of whisky and 300 gallons of alcohol" for alleged patient use over a short five-month period.[59] Although Gnassi was eventually acquitted of charges of concealing crimes, the state put him out of business by shutting down his private little charnel house, Newark General Hospital.

A principal suspect in the Ape murder was Ralph Russo. He was arrested on an open charge along with Harold Corbett, Ernest Fiumara, and Tony Bove, all gangsters associated with the Boot. Eventually, however, eyewitnesses could not positively identify the men, and the charges were dropped.

CHAPTER 3

I'M NO CRYBABY

Blood squirted from his mouth and nose.
He choked and fell down in the forest.
The young Ruggiero turned to others,
and no one can describe his fury.
Some men fell stunned and some fell dead.
                    —*Matteo Maria Boiardo,* Orlando Innamorato, *531*

When the Boot's thirty-eight-caliber revolver fell to the hospital floor, after the attempt on his life, prosecutors had a case against him. It was an unusual one that appeared to be putting the victim of a crime on trial, rather than the perpetrators; the men who tried to assassinate the Boot were never found, at least by the authorities. The police were convinced the Boot knew who was behind the shooting. In his hospital room they gave the seriously wounded gangster descriptions of the men who had allegedly shot at him; the Boot shrugged and said he didn't know who they were and that he "had no enemies that he knew of." He feigned naiveté, shrugging, even after police suggested that it was for his own good, and his safety, to name names.[1]

"If they want to finish me off, what can I do about it?" he said to them. "I'm no crybaby, I can take my medicine."[2] This angered the cops and outraged the good citizens of Newark, who were already fed up with rising crime in the city, which was caused in large part by the battling bootleggers. An editorial in the *Newark Evening News* observed: "The irony of the recent shooting of Ritchie Boiardo is that the victim was the first one involved against whom the police made a charge."[3]

Two indictments were handed down by the Essex County grand jury on weapons charges for the revolver and the knife—considered a concealed weapon—a few days after the shooting. The presiding judge declared, "Sometimes, at least, the law can act as fast as gangsters can. This will have a good affect on the community."[4] Investigators also seized books and records from the Boot's legitimate company, the Lucien Trading Company, which did business in perfumes, toilet waters, olive oil, and cheese distribution, and found that he had not paid taxes on $80,000 of personal income.[5] "According to government authorities, "[Lucien] was used as a blind for the diversion of industrial alcohol."[6] The Internal Revenue Service declared that there was enough evidence to also try him for income-tax evasion.

Bail on the weapons charges was set at $25,000. A surety company refused at the last minute to provide the bond; instead two friends of the gangster's—Thomas Cecere and funeral-home director Michael Megaro—put up $12,500 each, taking out loans on their homes. He was released from the hospital on December 5, 1930, with a half-dozen shotgun pellets remaining in his body. He posted bail in the Hall of Records and was whisked away in a car full of associates, with his wife following in another car.[7] The press reported he was going home, but he actually went to his sister-in-law's house to avoid detection by his enemies.[8] Two weeks later he was back in the custody of the police, held in connection with the murder of Thomas Tato, who was described in some newspapers as a cousin of Al Capone and in others as Scarface's East Coast rep. Tato had attended the Boot's victory banquet. He was found shot to death in an apartment on Thompson Street in the West Village of New York City. There was jewelry in the room and other evidence that a woman had been with him, suggesting the gangster had been lured to his death by a female decoy.[9] The Tato murder and the Boot's connection to it appeared to lend credibility to the theory that Capone had been involved in gunning down the Boot. The Tato case eventually was dismissed for lack of evidence; equally lacking in evidence was Scarface's alleged involvement in the Boot hit.

The Boot's lawyers sought and obtained an adjournment of his weapons trial, arguing that if he were moved from his home convalescence to the court, he probably would die. Doctors diagnosed a tetanus infection from a pellet that had punctured his left cheek and lodged in the roof of his mouth, causing his jaw to swell. He also suffered from a condition the doctors called "wrist drop," described by the newspapers as "a functional impairment of the movement of the wrist that prevents him raising the left hand." A slug that entered his neck caused "impairment of the muscles and is affecting the base of the brain."[10]

The trial was postponed two more times because of his condition.[11] The third postponement was to allow for an operation. The slug in his mouth was removed in a New York City hospital after hospitals in New Jersey, concerned about his notoriety and the possibility of another attempt on his life, "were not inclined to receive him."[12] Meanwhile, a key witness in the case, Frank Hand, one of the orderlies who undressed the Boot when the revolver and switch-blade were found, had died, and there was speculation that he had been "put on the spot" by the Boot's thugs. Prosecutors denied this theory.[13] Hand, who was sixty years old, had died after undergoing surgery for gallstones.

When the trial finally took place on February 18, 1931, it was an occasion of high drama, with the courtroom mobbed by spectators, security guards, and the Boot's soldiers: "The crowd grew with the hours. It became necessary to rope off sections on each side of the main court room entrance and to reinforce the roping with benches, backed in line."[14] The Boot's friends and fellow gangsters were thronged six deep around these benches. "They scrutinized passersby and hardly budged to allow [the prosecutor] to pass. . . . There was no violence, although many threats were directed at the photographers."[15] People brought their lunches wrapped in brown paper and newspapers; an elderly Italian woman sat in a corner with a rosary muttering prayers for the Boot; and a rumor circulated in the crowd that the defendant had slipped into the building in disguise, dressed as a woman. When he finally showed, the Boot shook hands with reporters and showed them the shotgun-pellet scars on his neck.[16]

The prosecutor's case focused on the testimony of several police officers who claimed that after the gun was discovered, the Boot admitted to them that it was his and said he carried it for protection. When the officers showed him the knife, the Boot also admitted it belonged to him. "I use it to open letters," he told the police.[17]

The Boot's lawyer, J. Victor D'Aloia, admonished the police for not finding the Boot's would-be assassins and for prosecuting his client instead. He suggested to the court, without making an outright accusation, that the gun was planted by the policemen who visited the Boot at his hospital bed. He grilled one of the officers, Deputy Chief Frank Brex, questioning why he showed up in the hospital room in the middle of the night.

"It was my duty as a police officer," Brex replied.

"Is that the best explanation you can give for going out at midnight to question this man?"

"It was a convenient time for me."

"Is that the best explanation?" D'Aloia roared.

"It's true," Brex said.

"Well," D'Aloia remarked. "We don't believe it to be true."[18]

A shouting match erupted between the officer and D'Aloia, and the judge pounded his gavel to maintain order; both men were censured. The Boot, who was wearing a dark blue suit, a green shirt, and dark green tie, briefly took the stand, denying that he had admitted ownership of the gun.

In his summation D'Aloia declared the affair was "the most perfect police-made case ever made in these United States." The prosecutor charged that the defense was trying to "throw dust and drag a red herring across the trail." "Don't you think from all the surrounding circumstances that this man carried a gun—a fully loaded gun?" the prosecutor rhetorically asked the court. Waving his arms toward the defendant he asked, "Does that type of citizen go around unarmed?"[19]

After two days of testimony, the jury found the Boot guilty of carrying an unregistered and loaded firearm. He was sentenced to prison for 2 ½ years. The judge threw the book at him, and the local newspapers applauded:

The people of Essex County do not approve of such as Ritchie Boiardo, gang leader. A representative group of citizens showed the general attitude when it found him guilty of carrying a concealed weapon. The state would probably have difficulty in convicting on such a charge an ordinary person who had been the victim of assassins, but such a demonstration as accompanied the Boiardo trial could hardly result differently. The state not only proved its case beyond a reasonable doubt, but it did so in such an atmosphere of thuggery that no other verdict could come from self-respecting freemen. The silent character witnesses represented by the defendant's bodyguard were as impressive as any the prosecution called. The verdict is inspiring to citizens generally and ought to have educational value for Boiardo's associates.[20]

Meanwhile, on the streets of the First Ward, and in the speakeasies and gambling houses across the city and the Hudson River and in many other American cities, the court of public opinion was deeply impressed by the Boot's tough-guy performance, particularly the fact that he did not rat anyone out, even though it was likely that he knew exactly who ambushed him.

While the Boot was in Trenton State Prison on the concealed-weapons conviction, he learned that the once-well-oiled machinery of his First Ward gang was beginning to creak and that his once-loyal lieutenants were looking to organize their own mobs. He decided to appoint a caretaker boss and, through his business connections in New York, selected Vicenzo Santoniello, aka Don Gigi, a Brooklynite who had just been released from Sing Sing after serving seventeen years for murder. "Ritchie wanted a strong man but not too strong. When he got out he wanted to be sure the substitute would not refuse to relinquish the reins." Don Gigi's installment was celebrated by a marathon fifty-six-hour feast at a First Ward restaurant; gang members pressured local businessmen to buy tickets.[21]

That summer the Boot, who was actively seeking parole, petitioned to transfer from Trenton to Crosswicks near Bordentown, a minimum-security work farm. He engaged the services of a psychiatrist and a psychologist to convince a classification committee that he was eligible for transfer. "The psychiatrist, who reported first, stated that [the Boot] was amenable, slightly unstable, fairly reliable. That was not so good. Then the psychologist tried his hand and gave him a better rating as amenable, stable and trustworthy."[22]

The Boot was granted the transfer and was assigned to work as a fireman, shoveling coal into the compound's heating furnaces, and as a gardener, tending the penal-farm flower beds. It was easy time, and the Boot took advantage, throwing picnics during the day and wine parties at night. His conduct was later investigated by a state Department of Institutions commission after it was alleged that he enjoyed "extraordinary privileges, even to the extent of . . . being permitted to visit his home in Newark."[23] At the time, rumors spread that the Boot regularly commuted between the Crosswicks farm and Newark and was frequently sighted around the First Ward.[24]

Lax supervision at Crosswicks also allowed the Boot to call the shots from the prison farm. Case in point: at Crosswicks, the Boot ran into an old acquaintance from the First Ward, Carmine DelGuercio, a First Warder who had a history of armed robberies and may have been a Mazzocchi soldier. "The meeting reopened an old quarrel." After DelGuercio was released and returned to his old stomping grounds, he was gunned down on the street by a passing car. Three shots were fired hitting him in the hip and the back, and the third missed, hitting an ashcan. DelGuercio survived, and although he refused to inform on his assailants, authorities were convinced the hit was ordered by the Boot.[25]

In the Boot's absence and with the Mazzocchi clan eliminated as a threat, Ralph Russo and his crew took advantage, going on a rampage of theft and extortion, forcing onerous protection payouts from business owners and shopkeepers, robbing local businesses, shaking down and terrorizing residents in the First Ward. The gang lived large while the Boot was away, operating out of several hideouts including Jerry Rullo's plush home in the Forest Hills section of Newark, overlooking Branch Brook Park. Police raided the nine-room house and found a five-hundred-pound safe that had been stolen from the Regent Theatre in the First Ward. The safe had been blown open with dynamite, but a strongbox inside containing cash "resisted the efforts of the crocksmen." They also uncovered large quantities of sugar, used in bootlegging, a German Shepherd guard dog that was coaxed into submission by a detective, and an eclectic range of personal effects: "A master's bedroom was luxuriously furnished in lavender satin with winking, cigarette-smoking French dolls strewn about. The gangster's library was lying on the bed. It consisted solely of a well-thumbed copy [of] "Al Capone, A Self-Made Man." All the latest electrical appliances were among the furnishings. There were two radios, a piano and portraits of Bach and Beethoven, as well as two merrily chirping canaries. A closet and an icebox were filled with food."[26]

The Boot was granted parole on November 23, 1932, after serving twenty months of a 2½-year term. He immediately took back control of his First Ward gang, put an end to the plundering of Ralph Russo and his boys, provided restitution to the owners and families who were victimized during his absence, and began to restore his reputation, which had been damaged by the reckless behavior of his unsupervised soldiers. He also began to prepare for the wet tide that was rolling in.

The anti-Prohibition movement had aligned itself with the Democratic Party, and its presidential candidate, Franklin Delano Roosevelt, ran for office on a wet platform, calling for a fast end to the "noble experiment." One of FDR's first acts as president in March 1933 was to sign the Cullen-Harrison Act, which allowed the sale of wine and 3.2 percent beer. Full repeal of the Eighteenth Amendment took place in December, when FDR signed the Twenty-first Amendment to the Constitution, rolling back the previous measure.[27]

Prohibition-era kingpins scrambled to stay afloat in the wake of repeal. The Boot scaled back on his alky-cookers, though he kept some operations running to slake the thirst of those who couldn't afford the high price of legitimate liquor, and he redirected his criminal focus to extortion, loan-sharking, and perhaps his most prosperous vice, gambling. He kept his gambling clubs well-stocked with bootleg booze. The Boot also attempted to aggressively branch out into other areas, such as infiltrating unions, dipping into their pension funds, and threatening companies with work stoppages unless they paid him off.

His torpedo Ralph Russo, not surprisingly, was more of a liability than an asset during this transition period. He and his partner Anthony "Money" Alfone were arrested for shooting undertaker Jerry Spatola Jr. at his home on Seventh Avenue. Spatola was a respected friend of the Boot's and the Newark community; he also was a close friend of Joe DiMaggio's. The undertaker was being harassed by shadowy characters associated with the Essex County Car Owners Association, a group that was organizing hearse drivers. One of Spatola's flower cars was sprayed with acid, and the driver of a car hired by the undertaker deserted a funeral cortege at a church. It turned out the association was the creation of the Boot. Spatola, who was injured in the shooting, was unable or unwilling to identify the pair in court, and the charges were dropped. The Boot later dissolved the association.[28]

On September 22, 1933, Russo, Rullo, Joseph Juliano, and the Boot were held as material witnesses in the murder of David Zipper, a New York racketeer who freelanced with the Boot's gang.[29] Zipper had allegedly been dealing in narcotics. His body was found hog-tied and stuffed in a grain sack in the trunk of a car. He had two bullets in his head. The car was discovered on the border of Belleville and Newark. In a scenario worthy of a Keystone cops comedy, a surveyor was brought in to determine which city had jurisdiction in the case. It was a macabre move, typical of law enforcement at the time, when gangsters had the cops tripping over one another trying to investigate yet another mob murder. In the end, it was determined that the car was two inches over the line inside Belleville. There was no evidence to hold any suspects, and no one was ever identified as Zipper's killer.[30] In June 1934, Russo and Rullo were in trouble yet again, arrested for several holdups around Newark and in Bergen County.

At this point it appears that the Boot's patience finally ran out. In May 1934, the Boot had begun a purge of his gang. Joseph Juliano was the first casualty, ambushed five blocks away from where the assassination attempt on the Boot had occurred. Juliano was shot in the groin, shoulder, and chest and left for dead. He miraculously survived and refused to identify his assailants. His silence spared him, and he eventually retired in self-exile to South Jersey. Decades later, on July 21, 1967, Juliano made a fatal mistake by returning to Essex County. His body was fished out of New York harbor; he had been "bound, shot and burned."[31] An informant told the FBI that the Boot had ordered the execution of his former chauffeur and confidante, who supposedly was collaborating with the police; the fact that Juliano had been suspected of playing a role in the attempted assassination of the Boot, thirty-seven years earlier, also may have contributed to his final demise.[32]

Jerry Rullo was taken for a ride two months after the first Juliano ambush; he was shot in the head with a forty-five-caliber bullet, and his body was discovered by two teenage boys in bushes on the side of a highway near New Providence, New Jersey. He was still "wearing an opal and diamond ring, a wrist watch and had money in his pockets."[33] Police officials said that Rullo was murdered because he had been "stepping out of line" from the Boiardo gang.[34]

Internecine strife within the Boiardo crew splashed across the front-page headlines, only to be eclipsed by a bigger story that suddenly arrived in town. Dutch Schultz, the iconoclastic Bronx gang lord who had become one of the most notorious and celebrated hoodlums of Prohibition and who had partnered with the Boot in moving beer into Newark, was executed at the Palace Chop House on East Park Street in Newark on October 23, 1935. Schultz had been staying at the Robert Treat Hotel, where both the Boot and Longy rented rooms, while he waited for a date at the Federal Courthouse in Newark, where he was to be tried for income-tax invasion. He was also in town, according to rumors, to put a stake in the ground and rebuild his operations after getting run out of New York by the cops. Although the Boot had worked with the Dutchman, he and Longy Zwillman were reportedly unhappy about the prospect of Schultz moving into their territory. The New York Times reported, "Schultz may have been killed at the behest of Newark gangsters, who resented possible attempts on his part to 'muscle in' on their territory."[35]

Lucky Luciano and Meyer Lansky were also unhappy about Schultz, who couldn't curb his taste for random murders of real and perceived enemies and couldn't keep himself out of the public eye. He was becoming a liability to the hoodlum high command, which wanted to make itself quiet and respectable in order to conduct business more efficiently and profitably post-Prohibition. Also, Schultz threatened to kill Thomas Dewey, a New York state prosecutor who was in relentless pursuit of organized-crime leaders; Luciano and his associates felt that such a high-profile murder would only make things worse, turning up the heat on organized crime. The Schultz hit was allegedly ordered by Luciano and Lansky, and because it was taking place on his turf, it was planned by Longy.[36]

Joe Stassi, who also went by the last name Rogers and worked for Longy as a numbers runner and all-around soldier, claimed Longy assigned him the task of managing the Schultz job. Stassi hired Charley "the Bug" Workman and Emmanuel "Mendy" Weiss, triggermen from Murder Inc., a group of Italian and Jewish hired guns and sluggers who performed hits for the National Crime Syndicate.[37] Murder Inc. was run by the Jewish American mobster Louis "Lepke" Buchalter, who was based in New York. When Buchalter went underground to elude the FBI—he was wanted on a narcotics charge—the syndicate handed his New Jersey rackets to the Boot for safekeeping. Not surprisingly the Boot, according to Stassi, also played a part in the storied assassination of Schultz, contributing two of his own soldiers. "Abe [Longy] was tight with Richie the Boot.... They had made peace, and it was decided Richie would provide the other men. We used Gyp DeCarlo and a guy, I can't remember his name, we called him Stretch. I gave them a rifle."[38] In Stassi's version of events Stretch drove the getaway car, but another version of the story identified Seymour "Piggy" Schechter, another Murder Inc. member, as the driver.[39]

Stassi's version of events went like this: Schultz and three of his men were having lunch at the Palace. Workman and Weiss burst in and started a gun battle. Workman didn't see Schultz, so he ducked into the men's room, where Schultz was washing his hands. Workman shot him. Meanwhile, Gyp entered the restaurant to back up Weiss, finishing off Schultz's posse with the rifle, a shotgun. Weiss and Gyp took off in the getaway car, and Workman slipped out the back of the restaurant. Schultz lingered for twenty hours; he died in a hospital bed and refused to identify his assailants.[40]

Workman was eventually caught, extradited to New Jersey, and convicted of the Schultz murder. He refused to name the other participants. Weiss was later executed in the electric chair for another murder, and Schechter was killed by his erstwhile associates at Murder Inc.[41] Neither DeCarlo nor the Boot ever discussed their alleged role in the murder. Two years after the hit the Boot and Longy were subpoenaed to appear before a Federal grand jury in New York that was seeking to apprehend Buchalter. Both men refused to testify about their relationship to the chief of Murder Inc.[42]

Four months after the Dutch Schultz murder, on February 18, 1936, the Boot finally dealt with his chief lieutenant and main troublemaker, thirty-one-year-old Ralph Russo, who was taken for a very long ride. Shot three times, he was found buried in a snowdrift by a farmer named Bosty Yecko in Imperial, Pennsylvania, just outside Pittsburgh. He was initially identified by the expensive overcoat he wore and a hat and belt with an R monogram. "The death that Ralph Russo had escaped in 1930, has overtaken him today," read the *Newark Evening News*.[43] Though he had been dead for just a few hours, police speculated that Russo had been shot somewhere else. He had been arrested thirteen times in his career, and the police suspected he also played a part in the Dutch Schultz hit.[44]

Informants who spoke to the FBI said Big Pussy and Little Pussy Russo were aware that the Boot had ordered the death of their older brother and they did not intercede, nor did they attempt to retaliate.[45] Big Pussy was serving time in Trenton State Prison for the murder of John Rosso;

Little Pussy was running full-time with the Boiardo crew. According to FBI informants, compared with other crime bosses, the Boot was notorious for eliminating anyone who posed a potential risk to the continuing existence of his operations, including members of his own crew.[46] The death of Ralph Russo was proof that for the Boot and for the Pussy Russo brothers, gang life came before family. In 1939, Big Pussy received a governor's pardon of his sentence. He was released after serving ten years of a thirty-year sentence in New Jersey's Trenton State Prison for the Rosso killing. He took up where he left off, once again becoming the Boot's right-hand man.

CHAPTER 4

FORTUNATE SON

All things that lie beneath the moon,
great wealth and earthly kingdoms—all
have been assigned to Fortune's will.
Brusquely she locks and unlocks door,
and when she seems most white, turns dark,
but war is where she seems the most
unstable, changing, hazardous.
Nothing else is as fraudulent.
— *Matteo Maria Boiardo,* Orlando Innamorato, *140*

Tony Boy Boiardo was baptized Ruggiero Anthony Boiardo; so that he wouldn't be confused with his father, he went by his middle name. His friends and associates took to calling him Tony Boy and "the kid," and throughout his life he lived up to the child-like monikers. He seemed always smiling and youthful, even in middle age. The *New York Times* described him as "a jolly, round-faced businessman in a rush to make money."[1]

Because he was the only son in an Italian family, it was not unusual that Tony Boy would continue in the family tradition, though it is not clear that the Boot intentionally groomed him to be the heir apparent. The Boot was a disciplinarian and wanted his son to get the education that he himself was denied as a young man. Once, in a fit of anger over Tony Boy's poor school grades, the Boot chained him to a post in the basement and left him there in the darkness for hours, according to his sister Rose. Jennie, his mother, heard his cries and sent his older sister, Agnes, to comfort him.[2] Jennie apparently knew better than to intercede directly herself.

The Boot could be especially hard on Tony Boy's mother, who took to drinking as an escape. During a heated argument with Jennie over his womanizing, she pulled out a gun and aimed it at him; the Boot picked up their seven-year-old daughter Rose and used her as a shield. Tony Boy was very close to his mother and was protective of her. Later, after his mother died, he disapproved of his father's many girlfriends.

Tony Boy and his sisters were well aware of what their father was capable; as they grew up on Nassau Street and later on Newark Street, they were exposed to guns in the house, the Boot's mysterious associates, and his trips to court and prison. Tony Boy was a child when the Boot was convicted of manslaughter; he visited the Boot in his hospital bed, at Trenton State Prison, and at the Crosswicks penal farm. He was just fourteen years old when he witnessed his first murder.[3]

Despite the Boot's pressure, Tony Boy's education was sketchy. In the middle of his freshman year at Newark's public Barringer High School he transferred to Seton Hall, a prep school, where he lasted only one semester. He transferred to Essex County Vocational School for a year and then back to Barringer, where he finally called it quits, dropping out in 1932 at the age of eighteen.[4]

In 1937 the Boot opened the Vittorio Castle Restaurant in partnership with Henry Abrams, alias Kid Henry, a former pugilist and convicted burglar. The partners signed over the restaurant to Tony Boy in order to obtain a liquor license, which the Boot and Abrams couldn't hold because of their criminal records, and Tony Boy was put in charge as host and manager. The Castle was well-named; the exterior was an undulating flow of towers and sturdy Flemish bond brickwork, tall arch windows, and a canopied turret entrance, like a medieval citadel. It commanded a busy corner of Summer Avenue and Eighth Avenue, the main thoroughfare in the First Ward. The dining room was a banquet hall that could seat a few hundred people; colorful frescoes, gilded sconces, and mirrors adorned the walls, and faux gold-leaf chandeliers hung from a twenty-foot ceiling. "The Vittorio Castle, built after Prohibition, was one of the most notorious nightspots in North Jersey, operating 24 hours a day, unmolested by authorities."[5]

The Boot, already well into his *Orlando Innamorato* period, which would last to the end of his life, held court in the Castle, entertaining politicians, gangsters, and celebrities, who came from New York City once they discovered the charms of Newark's own Little Italy.[6] In 1939, at his table in the Castle, the Boot gave Joe DiMaggio a four-and-half-carat emerald-cut diamond for an engagement ring for the slugger's first wife, B-movie actress Dorothy Arnold, whom he met on the set of the *Manhattan Merry Go Round*. She was nineteen, and he was twenty-three; they married later that year in San Francisco.[7]

An Alcoholic Beverage Control commissioner tried to shut the Castle down, arguing that the Boot and Abrams were seen frequenting the place, a violation of a state regulation prohibiting an establishment that served liquor from allowing "criminals, gangsters, racketeers ... or other persons of ill repute" on its premises.[8] The commissioner sent a letter to Tony Boy ordering him to keep his father and Abrams out of the restaurant, and the Alcoholic Beverage Control bureau subsequently disqualified the Castle's liquor license. The Boot applied for removal of this disqualification and obtained references from powerful people—Deputy Newark Police Chief Philip Sebold, Sergeant Edward McGrath of the department's morals bureau, Acting Police Captain Joseph Cocozza in the prosecutor's own office, several wealthy manufacturers and businessmen, and the pastor of Saint Lucy's Church. These men vouched for the Boot, claiming that his record was spotless and he was just "trying to earn an honest living."[9] At the time, the Boot had started a demolition company—Boiardo Construction—and had been subcontracted by the city to tear down an old amusement park to make room for public housing.[10]

The Boot's petition was successful, and the disqualification was lifted, but the incident created a scandal. The prosecutor's office launched an investigation into police department ties to the gangster and another investigation into the Boot's connection to an Italian lottery called the Rex B, a popular illegal numbers game played by working-class immigrants in the First Ward.[11] At the time, and apparently unbeknownst to his supporters and detractors, the Boot was also under investigation by a federal court for operating an alky-cooker in Galloway Township in Atlantic County that was raided in 1937; a 650-gallon still, liquor, and twenty-five thousand gallons of mash were seized. He was indicted on the still charge shortly after the Rex B lottery investigation was launched; he was found not guilty a few months later.[12]

Tony Boy was the man in the middle, fronting for his father. In photos of the many celebrations held at the Castle, Tony Boy is always seen happily glad-handing guests like Vittorio Castle regular Joe DiMaggio, obviously enjoying his role as host; however, the ever-smiling face hid constant anxiety.

On November 30, 1942, less than a year after the bombing of Pearl Harbor, Tony Boy enlisted in the U.S. Army Air Corp. He served at Mitchell Field on Long Island, the home of the Air Defense Command, which was responsible for developing domestic air defense, and he rose to sergeant of the guard, in charge of enlisted men at the base. Tony Boy was admitted to the base hospital after almost two years of service, suffering from migraine headaches, chronic rhinitis, sinusitis, food allergies, and "psychoneurosis, anxiety type, moderate, cause undetermined, manifested by tension, nightmares, anorexia, fatigue." He told doctors that he was constantly worrying about his family, especially his mother, and was angry at his sisters for neglecting her. "Patient very attached to mother, who has had three major operations in past five years." He said, "I dream about her funeral lots of times." He was taking ten to twelve aspirins a day and sleeping pills. On October 13, 1944, Tony Boy was honorably discharged for being "below prescribed physical standards for induction."[13]

The Vittorio Castle's liquor license was renewed under Tony Boy's name while he was still in the service.[14] When he got out, he divided his time between the restaurant and a variety of so-called legitimate jobs. He worked as a sales executive at the Harrison Oil Company, which his father owned. He later was named secretary-treasurer of the Mary Ann Park apartment building complex on Bloomfield Avenue in Caldwell. The

complex was built and managed by LaFera Construction, which subcontracted jobs to Boiardo Construction. Owner Joe LaFera was a close friend
of Tony Boy's, who invested $40,000 in the project when it was being built.[15]

The kid also claimed occupations as a clothes manufacturer, working
with Lanby Manufacturing in Newark; president of Trenton-based Tren-
Metal Inc. (formerly Kool-Vent Aluminum Awning Company of America),
a company owned by Jerry Catena; and a job at R&Y Novelty Company
in Newark.[16] He later managed the Sorrento Restaurant, another North
Ward eating hall built by the Boot after the Vittorio closed in 1952. (The
castle structure was used by Boiardo Construction as an office while it was
a subcontractor on the Columbus Homes, a public-housing development
that razed the heart of the First Ward in 1953.)

Tony Boy's résumé was eclectic and included a number of legitimate
activities. His principal occupation, however, was assisting his father in
the management of his gambling operations and post-Prohibition, pre-
tax booze empire. "Because of the Boiardo name, [his] upbringing, and
my grandfather's oversight, Uncle Tony really didn't have a choice," said his
nephew Roger Hanos. "My grandfather put his son out there to front for
him and the organization. My mother always said that she felt sorry for
my uncle."[17]

The Boot assigned his lieutenant Big Pussy as a mentor for Tony Boy; he
and Tony worked closely together and became good friends. Even before
his murder conviction, the Boot's daughters were infatuated with Big
Pussy; he was playful and friendly, and his good looks charmed them. The
Boot's daughter Rose had a serious crush on him and secretly sent him
letters while he was in prison up until her late teens. When the Boot found
out about the correspondence, he put a stop to it.[18]

Big Pussy had married Ann Schenck, a beautiful girl of German and
Norwegian ancestry and the daughter of a former Newark detective, and
Tony Boy was best man at the wedding. Rose and Big Pussy kept up their
friendship over the years, according to her son Roger Hanos. "Big Pussy
visited the Livingston farm on a regular basis. Sometimes he'd bring his

younger brother Little Pussy with him during the holidays. They would stop by my mother's house after visiting my grandfather for a cup of coffee and casual conversation."[19] Big Pussy's primary residence was in Wayne, and he owned a summer home in Point Pleasant, not far from his brother, who was based in Deal.

On October 22, 1946, Tony Boy's nightmares about his mother came true; she died at the age of fifty-three following a gall bladder operation and a desperate struggle with alcoholism. The Boot arranged a memorial service for his wife that the *Newark Evening News* described as "one of the most elaborate funerals Newark has seen in years."[20] Politicians and celebrities, including DiMaggio, showed up for the wake at the Megaro Memorial Home on Roseville Avenue; the crowd overflowed out to the front lawn, and the 750 floral pieces were estimated to be worth more than $10,000, according to the newspapers.[21] The next day a cortege of thirty-one flower cars and fifty limos carrying mourners crawled through the city to Saint Lucy's church.

According to conversations taped by the FBI between Tony Boy, Gyp DeCarlo, and Sam "the Plumber" DeCavalcante, the Boot was initiated as a caporegime, or captain, in the Luciano crime family in 1946, around the same time his colleague in crime Jerry Catena also became a "made" man.[22] Becoming a made man in the Mafia required making a pledge of life-long service to your crime family and devotion to it over blood relations. It also required swearing an oath of omertà, or silence, which meant promising never to talk about the family's business, inform on fellow members, or even admit there was such a thing as the Mafia, or La Cosa Nostra, Italian for "this thing of ours." The initiation typically involved a ceremony in which the candidate swore allegiance to a boss; with a knife the candidate shed some blood that was drizzled onto a saint's picture, which was finally set on fire in the initiate's hand.[23]

After the Atlantic City conference that established the National Crime Syndicate in 1929, Italian gangsters on the East Coast began consolidating their operations under five families—Luciano, led by Lucky Luciano, which later became the Genovese family under Vito Genovese; Mangano, led by Vincent Mangano, later to become the Gambino family under Carlo Gambino; Profaci led by Joseph Profaci, which became the Colombo family under Joseph Colombo; Gagliano, led by Thomas Gagliano, later to become the Lucchese family under Thomas Lucchese; and Bonanno, led by Joseph Bonanno.[24] The Boot came late to the party. He had been operating autonomously until then, although aligned with Longy Zwillman, and had become friendly and cooperative with Luciano following the armistice with Longy, who, being Jewish, could not become a made man, though he was an associate of the Luciano family with special privileges. (Rose Hanos remembered her father meeting with Luciano on several occasions in a park in Newark when her father took her out for a Sunday stroll.)[25]

The year the Boot was made capo, his boss, Luciano, was deported to Italy by the federal government and never returned. Frank Costello replaced Lucky as boss; the Boot reported to Costello, who was forced out in 1957 in a coup engineered by Genovese. Costello was gunned down by Vincent "the Chin" Gigante, a Genovese hit man; he survived and willingly stepped down. The Boot remained a Genovese capo to the end of his long life, and his son became his soldier, though it is unclear when Tony Boy was initiated into the crime family.

"I think Grandpa and Uncle Tony knew that once you are in this thing of theirs, there was no escape unless you had the smarts and as much money and legitimate investments as Jerry Catena and retired," observed Roger Hanos. "At the end, I don't believe my uncle or even my grandfather had the financial wherewithal or legitimate investments to cut all ties and retire. My grandfather was old school and an organization man—rich or poor—and would be carried out feet first like Catena said about himself. He was in it till the end!"[26]

Tony Boy married a local girl, Catherine Porreca, on April 30, 1950, and the event was even more spectacular than his mother's funeral. One thousand invited guests attended the reception; two thousand were packed into a church that had a seating capacity of 750; and gawking crowds swelled to fifteen thousand as dozens of limousines once again choked the streets of the First Ward around Saint Lucy's, where the nuptials took place. Jerry Catena and his wife were best man and matron of honor. The guest list included Ralph Villani, mayor of Newark; Hugh Addonizio, then a U.S. congressman; Congressman Peter Rodino; and Willie Moretti, the Bergen County mobster. The Boot hired a ten-piece band and ordered from the caterer a four-foot ice carving of a heart. Tony Boy and his wife then went on an around-the-world trip for their honeymoon. Everything was a gift of the Boot.[27] Years later, many comparisons were made between the Boiardo family and Mario Puzo's fictional creation, the Corleone family; however, in sheer size, expense, and bravura, Tony Boy's "glittering festival" easily dwarfed the lavish Corleone wedding scene that opened the film version of *The Godfather*.

CHAPTER 5

JERRY

My voice must soar to match my chant;
I need words more magniloquent.
My bow must sweep more rapidly
across the lyre; I must portray
a fierce and obstinate young man,
who almost brought the world to ruin.
— *Matteo Maria Boiardo,* Orlando Innamorato, *296*

Jerry Catena was an enemy, a friend, and a colleague of the Boot; beneath the surface, the blood between them ran cold. He was the right-hand man of Longy Zwillman and led the assault on the Boot's soldiers during the Longy War. He brokered the peace and later was the best man at Tony Boy's wedding and an honored guest at the Boot's estate. He was a partner of the Boot in many ventures, legal and illegal. He was an Italian American gangster who cut his teeth working for a Jewish boss, and later he rose to underboss and acting boss in the Genovese family.

Jerry Catena was a close-to-the-vest mobster, a behind-the-scenes operator who quietly became one of the most powerful crime figures in New Jersey and the country. One of the first white-collar mobsters, Catena rose to power efficiently and profitably, avoiding arrest and carefully maintaining a law-abiding reputation. He was a successful businessman as well as an organized crime figure.[1] However, during the FBI's drive to eradicate the mob in the 1950s, his name was included in Director J. Edgar Hoover's "Top Hoodlum Program" along with the names of the Boot and thirty-eight other crime leaders whose "underworld contacts extend throughout

the country."[2] Catena's Top Hoodlum file cites more than thirty-five informants and it runs more than 4,600 pages, larger than the files of most
marquee mobsters including Al Capone, Vito Genovese, Meyer Lansky,
and Lucky Luciano.

In 1963 Joseph Valachi, the first mob soldier to violate Cosa Nostra's
blood oath of secrecy, testified before a Senate investigating subcommittee;
he named names in the Mafia, exposing the existence of organized crime in
the United States. Valachi identified Catena as "the substitute boss" of the
Genovese family while Don Vito languished in prison on a drug charge.[3]
The Boot was named a major capo, placing him under Catena, and Tony
Boy was described as a button-man, or soldier. When he first heard that he'd
been named by Valachi, the Boot sarcastically dismissed him, observing that
his name rhymed with *pagliacci,* an Italian word for clown.[4] But it was no
laughing matter; thanks to the clown, the Boot and Tony Boy were subpoenaed to appear before an Essex County hearing on organized crime in New
Jersey. The Boot was questioned for an hour, and Essex County Prosecutor
Brendan Byrne told the press waiting outside the courtroom that he was
"cooperative." The Boot shrugged off the hearing, telling reporters he had
no idea why he was summoned and describing himself as a gardener. "Why
should I worry," said the Boot, glancing at a heavy gold watch on his wrist.[5]
Catena also appeared at that hearing, which was described by an Essex
County judge as "a general inquiry . . . designed as a deterrent measure."
Catena's testimony took only a half hour. Byrne also called him cooperative
but declined to say whether his testimony was productive.[6]

Gerardo Vito Catena was born on January 8, 1902, and grew up on
Van Buren Street in the Fifth Ward, or Ironbound section, of Newark. His
father, Francesco, emigrated from Salerno, Italy, to the United States in
1895, and worked as a hod carrier and mason. Catena completed grammar
school and went on to two years of high school at night, quitting at the
age of fourteen. His mother, Donata Speziale, passed away when he was
fifteen, leaving his father a widower caring for seven children. Jerry had
one older brother, Leonard; three younger brothers, Eugene, Frank, and

Anthony; and two sisters, Mary and Sadie. Although very little is known about his older brother and his sisters, his younger brothers were all connected in some manner to Catena's "business" dealings later in life. At a young age, Catena and his brother Eugene worked as laborers at the Port Newark shipyards.

"As a teenager, he spent much time at the Charlton St. School playground in the Third Ward, and it was here he met the late James (Niggie) Rutkin, Abner (Longy) Zwillman, Joseph (Doc) Stacher and some of the others who were to acquire fortunes during the free-and–easy era of the speak-easy."[7] Before becoming involved with Zwillman, Catena worked independently as a "bottle peddler," or bootlegger, during Prohibition.[8] In a 1939 FBI interview, Zwillman said that he had known Jerry for "approximately 12 years" and at that time Catena was making a living collecting bets on horse races—in other words, he ran his own "horse book."[9] Catena had multiple aliases in order to elude detection: Gerry, Jerry Cutana, J. Canteen, Gerard Catena, Gerald Catena, Jerry Catena, and Jerry Allen.

In 1936, Catena married Catherine McNally from Brooklyn. They raised five children in a fashionable home in the Newstead section of South Orange (daughters Patricia, Geraldine, Donna, Vicki; son Richard). He owned Jersey Shore summer homes in Deal and Belmar near Long Branch, close to the second homes of the Lansky, Zwillman, Stacher, and Boiardo families.

According to Catena's FBI file,[10] he had a string of early run-ins with the law, beginning in 1923, when he was arrested for shooting craps and gambling. He was sent away to Rahway Reformatory in 1926 for a robbery in Harrison and in the following year graduated to the Essex County Penitentiary, serving nine months for robbing a truck carrying a shipment of cigarettes. In 1934, Catena was arrested for bribing a federal juror; he was convicted and was sentenced to three months in a federal penitentiary and one-year probation. The case was the trial of Nick Delmore, who was charged with the gunshot murder of a Prohibition agent, John Finiello, at a bootleg brewery. After Catena's unsuccessful bribery attempt, the sole government eyewitness to the murder was executed, killing the prosecutor's case. Delmore was acquitted and eventually took charge of the gambling rackets in Union County, reporting to Catena.

During Prohibition, Catena was hired to assist Longy's gang in shepherding booze shipments from New Jersey ports to warehouses and speakeasies throughout the Northeast. He forged a strong relationship with Longy's Jewish gang and Willie Moretti, Teamsters Union officials, truck drivers, and port workers. He eventually became Longy's driver and lieutenant, and in that capacity he helped broker the peace that ended Longy's war with the Boot.

After the repeal of Prohibition in December 1933, members of the Italian and Jewish crime syndicate pooled their resources and capital to get a foothold in legitimate businesses and yet continued to support themselves with illegal gambling, loan sharking, extortion, labor racketeering, and other vice activities on a regional, national, and international scale. A chart created by the FBI in the 1960s,[11] mapping out the Genovese family tree, showed the Boot—alias Diamond Richie—near the top of the organization with a long list of soldiers working under him, including his son, Tony Boy, Settimo "Big Sam" Accardo, Thomas Campisi, Tony "Bananas" Caponigro, Charlie "the Blade" Tourine, Tony "Cheese" Marchitto, and other button-men. Catena was higher up the ladder. When Vito Genovese returned from Italy after World War II and took control of the family, Catena was assigned the role of family underboss, and Michele Miranda was made consigliore, or adviser, to the family.

Tony Boy bonded with Catena, partnering with him in a number of legitimate and illegitimate business ventures, and they also developed an active, mutual social and family life. The Boot encouraged the alliance. Home movies and photos of family weddings, picnics, horseback riding, and dinners shot at the Boot's estate in Livingston captured the close relationship that grew between these crime barons. Catena and Tony Boy shared an especially strong passion for golf and frequently played together at courses in New Jersey and Florida, such as the Braidburn Country Club in Millburn and the Knoll Country Club in Boonton; Tony Boy was a member of these clubs. An FBI informant reported that Jerry and Tony Boy played eighteen holes every Wednesday and Saturday morning at the Knoll, followed by a game of cards.[12] Catena became such a skilled golfer that he competed in pro-am tournaments. Tony Boy built a putting green at his new home in the suburbs; Catena had a driving-range apparatus installed in his backyard in South Orange.

The golf obsession was so great that many business meetings with their associates occurred at the Fairways Golf Driving Range on Prospect Avenue and Eagle Rock Avenue in West Orange. Willie Moretti, Gyp DeCarlo, and Tony Bananas were also avid golfers who played with them. Thomas Pannullo, a proprietor of a well-known Newark restaurant and a member of the Knoll Country Club at the time Catena and Tony Boy played there, reminisced: "Jerry was playing by himself one day and asked if he could join me. I had met Jerry, who had frequented my restaurant, Thomm's, in Newark. You would never know that he was connected with anything bad. He was such a gentleman, so friendly and well spoken."[13]

On November 11, 1957, the Boot's estate in Livingston was the location of a major organized crime meeting called by Vito Genovese and Jerry Catena. The meeting was a prelude to the historic Apalachin summit, which took place four days later. After Genovese took over the Luciano family from Frank Costello in a coup, he went after another rival, Albert Anastasia, boss of the former Mangano crime family, ordering his execution, which infamously took place in a Park Avenue barbershop on October 25, 1957. Don Vito then installed his friend Carlo Gambino as boss of the Mangano family, which became the Gambino crime family. The Apalachin summit was arranged by Genovese to officially confirm his leadership and to have himself anointed the most powerful crime boss in the country. The meeting also was intended to resolve gambling, casino, and drug-dealing disputes among La Cosa Nostra members. At least one hundred crime figures from across the country were invited to the upstate New York country house of Joseph "the Barber" Barbara, a northeast Pennsylvania mafia chief. Local Apalachin police raided the event and captured fifty-eight mobsters including Paul Castellano, Carlo Gambino, Joe Profaci, Santo Trafficante Jr., Genovese, and Catena.

The Boot did not attend the summit, but instead hosted the pre-Apalachin conference at his estate. The meeting may have been a planning session to prepare for Apalachin. According to an FBI chart tracking the ten major meetings of the Mafia in the United States between 1928 and 1957, the Livingston meeting was the second largest. The FBI report noted:

> On November 10, 1957, four days before the Apalachin meeting, approximately 30–40 large cars, including many Cadillacs, entered the property of Ruggiero Boiardo at Livingston, New Jersey. Boiardo resides in a castle like house set back from the road and nearly hidden from view by a high stonewall. He is a hoodlum with a long criminal record. . . . The cars arrived between 10 a.m. and 1 p.m., each car contained three or four men. The cars carried license plates from New Jersey, New York, and Pennsylvania.[14]

The Boot's grandson Roger remembered the event. "There were cars parked all up and down the driveway. This was a very unusual event because we never had such a gathering in the past, and we knew there was something special going on. The outside lights on the main house and up and down the entire driveway were on all night into the early morning, and there were people standing outside talking and guarding the entrance to the house. My mother vaguely recalls overhearing someone say, 'All guns have to be left in the garage.'"[15]

Catena, Genovese, and the other Apalachin attendees were indicted for attending the New York State meeting but not prosecuted. The *Newark Star-Ledger* reported that Catena's "neighbors could hardly believe that he was involved in the Apalachin conclave and that he 'took only two things seriously, his golf and his family.'"[16]

As Catena's star rose in La Cosa Nostra under Genovese, his original mentor, Longy Zwillman, was already in free fall. Longy was called to appear before the Kefauver Committee, which was investigating organized crime in 1951. Estes Kefauver, a U.S. senator from Tennessee, became chairman of the U.S. Senate Select Committee on Organized Crime and opened televised hearings on organized crime's infiltration into legitimate businesses. Longy avoided the committee for months by hiding out at the Canary Cottage, a former speakeasy in Florham Park with a nine-hole golf course, but he eventually showed up in Washington with his lawyer in late March, toward the end of the hearings, which forced the committee to rush his interrogation.

Longy testified about his stake in legitimate businesses, including the development of PATH trains into New York; he admitted he knew Luciano, Lansky, Costello, and Catena but claimed he was not involved in organized crime; and he admitted that he had been involved in bootlegging during Prohibition but did not give any specifics. "He admitted that he had previously been convicted on a charge of disorderly conduct in 1925 or 1926 and he admitted serving six months in jail on an assault charge. He refused to name his associates in the bootlegging business. He admitted he made purchases of liquor in his bootlegging days from Canada, but he refused to name the source of the Canadian whiskey."[17]

Longy told the committee that since Prohibition he had been "trying" to go legitimate. In the end, he skillfully managed to avoid a contempt of Congress charge while concealing compromising information about himself and his associates; however, the hearings unnerved him. He was worried that the television exposure compromised his standing with other crime figures. Months after the hearings ended, Longy's former partner Willie Moretti, who also testified before the Kefauver Committee, was murdered in a coffee shop, largely because of his candid, buffoonish performance at the hearings.[18]

Longy's worry continued in the following years. After he was the object of a federal grand jury probe into racketeering, the Internal Revenue Service filed $940,471 in tax liens against him and his family for unpaid taxes. On June 23, 1953, he was arrested for income-tax evasion; following a six-week trial, the case was dismissed. But the IRS continued to hound him.

Finally, the McClellan Select Senate Committee subpoenaed Longy in 1959 to appear at a hearing on organized crime and labor. An FBI wiretap had uncovered evidence that Longy bribed two jurors in his tax-evasion trial. Longy never made it to the hearing; he was found hanging from a water pipe in the basement of his West Orange mansion.

The press reported the death as a suicide, though the authorities were unable to account for bruises on his body and indications that his hands had been tied with wire. Rumors circulated that Longy had been executed on the orders of Genovese, and there was talk that Catena played a role. An article in the *New York Post* spelled it out:

> Catena, once chauffeur for Zwillman but an underworld baron in his own right for some years now, has been inching his way up in deal after deal. He gained additional control as a result of the murder [of] Anthony [sic] Anastasia. He moved higher when Vito Genovese suddenly found himself enmeshed in a long and dangerous narcotics trial. And his last major rival was found yesterday dangling from the end of an electric cord in West Orange, N.J. Zwillman didn't wait for the executioner's gun or the nocturnal visit to tell him he was dethroned. Zwillman killed himself.... A government official told the *Post* today that Zwillman had been resisting this ambition of his ex-chauffeur, and that Zwillman had learned he had been marked for execution by gunmen.[19]

A subsequent FBI report confirmed Catena's succession: "He was one of late 'Longie' [sic] Zwillman's chief lieutenants and appears to have inherited the Zwillman organization. Utilizes his brother, Eugene, as primary assistant and brother, Frank, oversees labor and gambling on Port Newark waterfront. Catena allegedly exerts influence over several unions in the Newark area and has been reported in on conferences with important political figures."[20]

Vito Genovese was convicted of selling heroin later that year and sentenced to fifteen years in prison. Catena was promoted to acting boss of the family and gained full control of the family's New Jersey operations.

He shared power in the family's national and overseas operations with Thomas Eboli, aka Tommy Ryan, a Genovese underboss, and Michele Miranda, a consigliore, who were part of a "ruling panel" formed by Genovese while in prison.

Don Vito's appointment of Catena was not well received by some of his brethren. Gyp DeCarlo was caught grousing in a bugged conversation that Catena "only wants the job because it makes him bigger than someone else"; DeCarlo suggested that Genovese did not hold Catena in "very high regard" but installed him on the family's ruling panel because Catena controlled "extensive financial investments in Las Vegas." DeCarlo was envious of Catena, the FBI memo concluded.[21]

He was not alone; an unidentified FBI informant's report claimed Miranda was unjustly passed over as acting boss because of his close relationship with Frank Costello. The informant stated that "he received the definite impression in recent contacts with knowing underworld people that Mike Miranda, Richie Boiardo and others are not truly loyal to Vito Genovese. The informant advised further that the reason Mike Miranda is possibly not loyal to Vito Genovese is that Genovese made Jerry Catena the boss when Miranda looked for and expected the appointment."[22]

The Boot worked with Catena, but a considerable gulf remained between the Jersey mobsters, perhaps the bitter fruit of their Prohibition battles. However, Big Mike Miranda and the Boot bonded. Miranda was born in San Vesuviano, Naples, in 1896 and became an enforcer for Luciano before being promoted by Genovese to consigliere. He frequently crossed state lines to visit the Boot, according to the FBI, which kept a tail on the Forest Hills, Long Island–based gangster.[23] In the mid-1940s, when Miranda was being sought for a murder, he hid out on the estate for a month. The Boot's daughter Rose recalled playing many hands of gin rummy with Miranda while he was on the lam in Livingston. Rose, in her early twenties, was an excellent gin rummy player, and Miranda was not happy that she routinely beat him.[24]

Early in Catena's career as acting boss, he was targeted for a kidnapping. The plot was uncovered by the Miami office of the FBI, which was tipped off by an unnamed informant who alleged that a gang planned to abduct Catena and a high-ranking, unidentified mob lieutenant of Genovese capo Michael Coppola while they vacationed in Florida. Both men were to be held for ransom offshore in a boat. The informant was the bag-man in the plot; he was supposed to pick up the ransom money and deliver it, but instead he squealed to the Feds and to Catena. The FBI never acted on the information, and the kidnapping apparently did not take place, although the FBI Miami office ruefully observed in a memo about the plot, "It is known that in some of the past previous kidnappings, which apparently took place . . . the victims have even denied these kidnappings for fear of their lives."[25] Subsequently, according to an FBI decoded communication, when informed, "Catena . . . was visibly shaken and requested his wife not be advised of the same."[26]

Catena inherited a vast criminal enterprise that required making policy decisions with all the other Cosa Nostra family heads. As one of the nine national Cosa Nostra commissioners, he had authority over Las Vegas profit-skimming operations, territorial issues, union extortions, Shylock loans, kickback schemes, protection, gambling, strong-arm enforcement, and swag operations. Jerry also had his fingers in Caribbean gambling and illegal distilleries in Antigua and the British West Indies.[27] Under Catena's leadership, the offshore gambling and alcohol operations of the Boot and some Philadelphia families were integrated into the Genovese empire, and the Boot's crew received monthly union kickback payments that they distributed to Genovese bosses.

Richie the Boot, Anthony Provenzano, and Gyp DeCarlo were Jerry's direct capos. His younger brother Eugene was his capo also. Catena limited his own exposure to mob underlings; he used his younger brother as his key representative for handling gambling in Passaic County, for overseeing the Port Newark area, and for Elizabeth union kickbacks. After Willie Moretti was assassinated in 1951, Eugene was placed in charge of his territories.

Although Eugene was relied on heavily by his older brother, he was unpopular; many fellow racketeers considered him rude and unpleasant.

Jerry was aware of Eugene's difficult personality, but he did not trust anyone else to carry out his orders. Jerry was contemptuous of other members of his immediate crew, complaining that they did not have "one brain among them."[28] Eugene's center of operations was a front called Best Foods, a purported brokerage firm handling Italian food products and other products sold by large food chains. Best Foods operated out of a converted brownstone mansion on Clinton Avenue, Newark. The Best Foods office was a base for Catena operations and a frequent meeting place; it also happened to be electronically monitored by the FBI, which also bugged the offices of Jerry's other legit business, Runyon Sales, a distributor of automated coin machines, jukeboxes, pool tables, slot machines, and pinball machines.

Eugene had extensive connections with city governments, retail food chains, and their unions. His crew included John Lardiere, aka Johnnie Coke, a former Teamsters business agent; Thomas Pecora, aka Timmy Murphy, a mob enforcer; and his brothers: Joseph "Joe Peck" Pecora, Teamsters Local 863's secretary-treasurer, and Edward Pecora, a Teamsters official in the Automated Sales, Servicemen and Allied Workers Local 575. Joe Peck was considered a formidable soldier; "informants in the past have indicated Pecora equal in stature to [Anthony] Provenzano as far as underworld authority goes."[29]

Eugene and his crew were implicated in the mid-1960s A&P detergent scandal. Allegedly, he was hired as a sales consultant for North American Chemical and, with the help of Irving Kaplan of the Meat Cutters Union Local 464 and Joe Peck, attempted to force A&P to purchase North American Chemical detergent.[30] A&P had tested the product, found it unsuitable, and refused to purchase it. Later, A&P stores in New York were firebombed, resulting in $7.4 million in damages, and two A&P store managers were murdered, prompting an investigation by a Senate organized-crime commission.

Anthony Provenzano, aka Tony Pro, vice president of Teamsters Local 560 in Union City and president of the New Jersey Area Joint Council under Jimmy Hoffa, reported to Jerry. A Clifton, New Jersey, resident, Tony

Pro was a former pugilist, truck driver, and union organizer with a fiery temper. *Time* magazine called him the "Ruler of the Newark docks."[31] His special skill was tampering with Teamsters pension funds and using the money for various Genovese family schemes, such as the attempt to create kickbacks from a deal with Saint Barnabas Hospital, which was in need of funding for a new facility in the suburbs. A declassified FBI document states that the FBI had investigated an allegation that Eugene Catena had helped Tony Pro and Hoffa orchestrate a Teamsters loan offer of $750 million to the medical center. According to their math, the loan would have netted them $750,000 in kickbacks.[32]

In June 1978, Provenzano was convicted of ordering the murder of Anthony Castilleto, a rival local member who challenged Tony during union elections. Harold Konigsberg, a Provenzano mob enforcer and extortionist, was convicted of carrying out the hit, despite the murder of a star witness. Tony Pro was also the FBI's prime suspect in the disappearance of labor leader Hoffa in 1975. After establishing an alibi in the Hoffa case—he was in the company of union leaders in Hoboken when the Teamsters boss vanished—Tony Pro took a break at his Hallandale, Florida, home, entertaining a reporter from *People* magazine, basking in the sun by the side of his pool with a gin and tonic and a cigar. "As much as I love the guy, Jimmy became an egotistical maniac," he told the journalist. "I'm a human being. I just want to be left alone. I don't do anything abnormal. I'm not a faggot. My great joy is my family."[33] He died of a heart attack at the age of seventy-one in 1988, while serving time in prison for the Castilleto murder.

Another key Genovese operative working under Jerry was Angelo "Gyp" DeCarlo, who had started his criminal apprenticeship working for the Boot during Prohibition. He was implicated by Joe Stassi in the assassination of Dutch Schultz. Early career achievements included arrests for counterfeiting, robbery, income-tax evasion, and violating federal liquor laws. Gyp crossed over to Zwillman's organization before the family switched from Luciano to Genovese. He became a Genovese capo, overseeing gambling

and extortion in Union and Monmouth counties, Newark, and Staten
Island. His crew of soldiers included Peter "the Bull" Landusco, Daniel
"Red" Cecere, and Joseph "the Indian" Polverino.

Gyp owned the LaMartinique Restaurant in Mountainside, a regular
haunt for the Boot, Tony Boy, the Catena brothers, Albert Anastasia, Zwillman, and John "Big Pussy" Russo. Roger Hanos recalls the Boot taking
him and his brother and sister to La Martinique on Saturday nights for
dinner. The Boot would bring his girlfriend, Edith Bencivengo, and some
of her relatives and a few of his non-mob-related friends. "He'd bring easily fifteen to twenty guests," said Roger. "At another table he would have
four to five of his boys sitting nearby. I recall seeing Andy Gerardo, Jimo
Calabrese, Toby Boyd, Lou Coke, but not Big Pussy or Little Pussy. My
Uncle Tony, aunts, or cousins never came with us. My parents didn't come
either. He just took us kids and the Penna family, who were caretakers of
my grandfather's estate."[34]

DeCarlo maintained his headquarters and held mob meetings in the
Barn, a nondescript building attached to La Martinique. The Barn was
bugged by the FBI, and DeCarlo was recorded holding court there, regal-
ing visitors with boasts about past murders and other mayhem. In 1969, a
federal court released an FBI taped conversation of a DeCarlo session that
was recorded while DeCarlo was working for the Boot. On it DeCarlo is
discussing with Tony Boy and Sam "the Plumber" DeCavalcante an early
hit on a victim identified as "Itchie." "There was me, Zip, and Johnnie Russell," said DeCarlo, referring to David Zipper and Ralph Russo. "I said,
'You gotta go, why not let me hit you right in the heart and you won't feel a
thing.' He said, 'I am innocent, Ray, but if you got to do it.' So I hit him in
the heart and it went right through him."[35] The tapes also revealed Genovese family connections with Congressman Peter Rodino, Newark Mayor
Hugh Addonizio, and other politicians.

DeCarlo was convicted of extortion and sentenced to twelve years in
prison in 1970. Two years later, his sentence was commuted by President Richard Nixon. His release was a surprise to state and federal

law-enforcement officials, and there were rumors that DeCarlo's friend
Frank Sinatra asked Vice President Spiro Agnew to intervene;[36] Sinatra
allegedly sweetened the request with a $150,000 political contribution.
DeCarlo died of cancer on October 20, 1973, at the age of seventy-one,
eleven months after his pardon. The Tony Award–winning musical *Jersey
Boys*, about the singing group the Four Seasons, includes a Gyp DeCarlo
character; he allegedly, in real life, helped Tommy DeVito, one of the Seasons, resolve a gambling debt.

"Jerry Catena," groused Little Pussy, in a conversation taped by the
FBI, "has more fucking money than God."[37] The FBI agreed, estimating
that Jerry's personal assets exceeded $50 million.[38] These assets included
many legitimate businesses, such as the Public Service Tobacco Company
in Hillside, a cigarette vending-machine company that he owned with
Longy Zwillman, Joe Stacher, and Michael Liscari, who was a close friend
of Luciano's. Legitimate ventures like Public Service Tobacco were successful because of illegitimate practices: the company's cigarette vending
machines were forced on restaurants and stores; owners were threatened
with violence if they refused. These methods made for serious profits.
According to the Kefauver Committee final report, issued in 1951, Public Service for the fiscal year ending November 30, 1949, had gross sales
of $1,421,881.38.[39] Jerry also owned a partnership in the People's Express
Company, a trucking firm that bought its trucks from one of Longy Zwillman's General Motors dealerships. After Jerry testified before the Kefauver
Committee about his ownership of the company, the bad publicity forced
him to sell his interests.

Jerry commuted to an office every day at Runyon Sales in Newark. The
company distributed vending machines in New York, New Jersey, and
Connecticut. Although Jerry was an owner of Runyon along with partners
Abe Green and Bernie Sugarman, he was not listed as an officer; however,
his brother-in-law James Brown was its treasurer. After he purchased a
controlling interest in Runyon in 1951, Jerry was listed as vice president
and then president.[40] Runyon also distributed juke boxes manufactured by

AMI and slot machines for Bally Manufacturing and Kenny Manufacturing. Jerry was caught on an FBI surveillance tape boasting that Runyon did about "$20 million a year in business, but the full potential far exceeds that."[41] Jerry also had an estimated 8 percent ownership stake in Bally's; the company bought him out when executives discovered that a Mafia leader was a stockholder of the company.[42]

Jerry also was a partner in G. & M. Trading, Mechanic Enterprises, World Wide Music, and the Passaic Music Company, and he held interests in the Murchison Oil Lease Company in Oklahoma, Automated Vending, Cada Realty Company in Newark, Marcal Pulp and Paper Company of East Paterson, and Tren-Metal (formerly Kool Vent Aluminum Awning Company of America), a company in which Tony Boy Boiardo held a 13 percent interest.[43] His FBI files reported that Jerry had a hidden interest in several Holiday Inns in Northern New Jersey.[44] Jerry also owned or had financial investments in significant real estate properties. One parcel was 106 acres of prime land on Route 22, which was rezoned to be a light industrial area. Its value increased ten times over the original purchase price.[45]

According to an FBI report, racketeers from New York and New Jersey held "gambling interests ranging from central and western Europe, through the Caribbean to Washington, DC and Las Vegas."[46] In Havana, Cuba, Jerry invested in the Riviera Casino with Florida crime boss Santo Trafficante Jr., Meyer Lansky, and others. Jerry frequently traveled to Havana, and the FBI monitored these trips. His Runyon partners Abe Green and Bernie Sugarman borrowed $50,000 each from the company to purchase Riviera shares during its construction.[47] Charlie "the Blade" Tourine managed a few of the Caribbean casinos. The Boot meanwhile had an ownership stake in the Capri Hotel and Casino with a host of other mob stockholders including Lucky Luciano. (The Capri and Riviera were built in 1957 and fell into the hands of the Castro regime in 1960.)

The gang's Las Vegas investments, managed by Catena's boyhood crony Joe "Doc Rosen" Stacher, included the casino profit-skimming operations of Zwillman, after his death, and of Frank Costello, who was imprisoned and facing deportation. Casino skims worked in several ways, often in combination. The basic method was to have an inside man with access to the casino counting rooms simply skim profits from the daily casino take. Another scheme involved extending gaming credit to an organized-crime member who was not expected to repay the loan, or games were rigged to allow gangsters or hired players to win. In all cases, mobsters infiltrated casinos, taking an ownership stake in order to place their people inside. These Genovese skim operations took place in the Sands Hotel, Fremont Hotel, Horseshoe Club, and Flamingo, and they lined the pockets of Meyer Lansky, Gyp DeCarlo, and the Boot. Gyp DeCarlo was recorded by FBI surveillance claiming that Jerry's take from his Las Vegas skims was about $120,000 per month, with the Boiardos receiving a smaller share. Another FBI informant's estimate of Catena's take was more generous: $150,000 per month.[48]

Jerry's organized-labor remunerations were substantial. In a decoded FBI radiogram, DeCarlo "indicated that Jerry probably receives income between one hundred and two hundred thousand dollars a year from labor union sources."[49] The unions infiltrated by the Genovese family included the International Longshoremen's Association, various Teamsters locals, liquor salesmen, and retail clerks.

The "strength of the mob lay in the connections it had with political officials and law enforcement personnel," the FBI observed in a passage in Jerry's FBI file. "[The Mafia is] a heavy campaign contributor to both major parties and to factions within both parties."[50] Jerry's ties to New Jersey politicians were widely known and hotly investigated by law enforcement during his tenure as the top Mafia figure in the state.[51] In 1968, after two former officials of the U.S. Justice Department testified before a legislative hearing on organized crime and described New Jersey as "the most corrupt state in the country and a playground for mob members,"[52] a special grand jury investigation into organized crime was launched under the leadership of Assistant Attorney General William J. Brennan 3d, the son of Supreme Court Justice William Brennan.

The grand jury, in cooperation with a New Jersey State Senate crime committee, investigated charges that six state legislators were in the Mafia's pocket. A seventh suspect, C. Richard Fiore, a Republican who represented the North Ward of Newark, which included the old First Ward neighborhood,[53] and who was chairman of the Assembly Committee on Law and Public Safety, was linked directly to Jerry. Fiore had complained to a Senate aide that the grand jury and the Senate investigations were putting "too much pressure" on the mob and "Jerry is unhappy about it." He also confided to the aide that he had become chairman of the Assembly crime committee to relieve the pressure. "I've got to stop these kinds of things," Fiore was quoted as saying. The aide could not prove the conversation took place, and Fiore was never officially charged. He was reelected to his Assembly seat the following year.[54]

A cryptic FBI memo dated April 20, 1962, reported that Jerry had attempted to buy influence in Trenton by making a contribution to the campaign of New Jersey Superior Court Judge Richard Hughes, who ran for governor in 1961.[55] A former federal prosecutor in the U.S. Attorney's Office for the District of New Jersey and a county court judge from 1948 to 1952, Hughes, a Democrat, won the governorship and served two terms. He became a powerful and effective governor. The FBI memo, a decoded radio message, included information supplied by an unnamed source, most likely an agent who was conducting surveillance on Jerry. The source indicated that Jerry was visited by an unidentified man—his first name is redacted in the document and his last name is listed as unknown (LNU)—to discuss a real estate deal involving a profit of $33 million dollars. LNU was "upset over some changes in arrangements" with the deal. According to the memo, Governor Hughes's name was brought up in the conversation, and LNU referred to a campaign contribution of $50,000. This apparently angered Jerry, who said to LNU, "A little knowledge is a dangerous thing." LNU apologized, and the source observed that it was clear Jerry was threatening the man for talking too much.

Although it is difficult to connect the dots in this conversation, it suggests that Jerry was attempting to influence a county or state decision regarding a land purchase by funneling money into Hughes's campaign war chest. The details of this deal are not known, and it is also unclear whether Jerry succeeded in influencing the Hughes administration or even whether Hughes himself was aware of the deal. There are no follow-up reports in the FBI file; however, on December 12, 1961, a month after Hughes's election, the Newark FBI office had sent a teletype to the home office in Washington reporting that an unnamed individual approached Jerry about influencing the Newark city council to approve a $21 million urban-renewal grant in Newark. Apparently, some city council members were hesitant to approve the grant fearing they would lose voter support. The unnamed individual insisted that "Catena could deliver the city council," the teletypes reported.[56]

Years later, at the 1970 extortion trial of Gyp DeCarlo, electronic eavesdropping tapes recorded in Gyp's office between 1961 and 1965 were admitted in court. In one conversation among fellow mobsters, Gyp boasted, "If Hughes gets in[,] ... [is] elected ... , we're all right." Governor Hughes reacted immediately to the release of the tapes at the time: "It is back fence gossip in which hoods brag to each other about how big and important they are. The unfortunate thing about tapes is that there is no protection for innocent people."[57]

Ironically, when the state grand jury began its investigation into organized crime in 1968, Hughes was deeply involved in the process. His administration proposed a measure that would grant immunity from prosecution to witnesses who testified against mobsters. He also supported a passed bill that legalized wiretapping. C. Richard Fiore, the Newark assemblyman linked to Jerry, opposed both measures.

In May 1961, there was evidence that Jerry and the Boiardos were competing for political appointments:

Anthony Tony Boy Boiardo and [name deleted] are quite upset at Jerry Catena for sponsoring [name deleted] in the position of Assistant County Prosecutor. [Assistant Prosecutor Joseph P.] Lordi is currently engaged in conducting a Grand Jury investigation of gambling in Essex County and is specifically directing his attention toward Boiardo's bookmaking operation. According to the informant, Lordi got the job as assistant prosecutor because Jerry Catena had appealed to Dennis Carey, a prominent county political leader.[58]

Throughout his FBI file, informants mention that Jerry repeatedly warned his soldiers and business partners that their telephones and offices were bugged and that his movements were being recorded. In 1969, Jerry was subpoenaed to testify before the New Jersey State Commission of Investigation and invoked the Fifth Amendment approximately eighty times. He was imprisoned for contempt in March 1970. His only statement before his release five years later was that he would "stay in jail for the rest of my life" and they would have to carry him out "feet first" before he ratted on anyone.[59] Jerry was not alone; eight other hoodlums had refused to talk to the state commission and were handed indefinite sentences: Gene's lieutenant Johnny "Coke" Lardiere; boss of the Philadelphia–South Jersey family Angelo Bruno; Nicholas Scarfo and Ralph Napoli, both Bruno associates; Nicholas Russo of Trenton; Robert Manna, reputed Jersey City rackets boss; Joseph Zicarelli; and Anthony "Little Pussy" Russo.

While Johnnie Coke was serving time, his wife, Carolyn, drank a bottle of Fresca soda that "contained enough arsenic to kill seven-hundred people."[60] She was able to call for help but died just two hours later at the hospital. Her death was deemed suspicious by law enforcement; there was speculation that either she was talking to authorities to obtain her husband's release or her death may have been a warning to her husband to keep his mouth shut. Ironically, Johnnie Coke, who was given his nickname because he grew up around the corner from a Coca-Cola bottling plant, filed an unsuccessful lawsuit against the Coca-Cola Company of New York for the arsenic poisoning of his wife.[61]

On April 10, 1977, while on a twenty-six-hour Easter furlough from prison to visit family, Johnnie Coke detoured to rendezvous with a prostitute at a motel in Bridgewater, New Jersey, but came face to face with a hit man carrying a twenty-two-caliber pistol with a silencer. The gun jammed, and Johnnie Coke said, "What're you gonna do now, tough guy?" The gunman then reached for a concealed thirty-eight-caliber gun in his pants leg and shot Johnnie Coke four times.[62] Genovese soldier Mikey "Cigars" Coppola was suspected in the murder; he fled and was on the lam for eleven years with his wife, living in San Francisco and New York. After his capture, he was tried and cleared of the murder because of insufficient evidence.[63]

CHAPTER 6

THE CLUB FREMONT
INCIDENT

There he encountered frightened troops,
men who did not know what to do.
He shouted, "You're contemptible!
Chased by a single cavalier!
Why don't you burrow through the mud
rather than let yourselves be seen?
Throw down your weapons! Go home! Sleep!
You don't know what shame—scandal—means!"
　　　　　—Matteo Maria Boiardo, Orlando Innamorato, *102*

Pasquale "Smudgy" Antonelli entered the Club Fremont on Friday, September 23, 1960, at ten o'clock in the morning. He was summoned by Tony Boy Boiardo, who used the Fremont for meetings and as a clearing-house for his numbers operations.[1] The Fremont was basically a bar and grill, open for lunch, never for breakfast. A morning meeting meant Tony Boy wanted privacy, for an important matter. Smudgy arrived at the Fremont unarmed, but he wasn't taking any chances; his wife accompanied him. She carried a pistol in her pocketbook.

The general consensus among mobsters was that Smudgy, a freelance numbers runner, was a punk and a thief and could not be trusted. He was known for being a hothead and instigating violent holdups; just two years earlier he had robbed a lumber company, pistol whipping one of the employees and shooting off the ear of another.[2] Informants who spoke to the FBI after the Club Fremont incident, however, stumbled over one another with conflicting stories about his relationship to Tony Boy. One said Smudgy had set up a rival bookmaking and loan-sharking business in Tony Boy's territory without permission and was about to get run out of town by the Boiardo mob. Another squealed that Smudgy owed Tony Boy money and was going to pay a penalty. Yet another informant claimed that Smudgy had been robbing Tony Boy's runners and was marked for a rub-out by the Boiardo mob. Yet another was convinced Smudgy wasn't robbing the Boiardos but he knew who was and Tony Boy just wanted to rough him up and grill him on the identity of the culprit. Finally, perhaps the most likely story: Smudgy was given a contract to kill the person or persons responsible for the stickups but he reneged, and when he showed up at the Fremont he was "belittled and slapped around a bit." Meanwhile, a panel truck was parked behind the tavern with three bags containing cement and lye to dispose of Smudgy's supposed victims.[3]

Smudgy's status was based on a muddle of insinuations and half-truths, but it was very clear what he represented—a challenge to Tony Boy's authority. According to FBI documents, the Boot began to turn over his rackets to his son around 1958. Tony Boy ran a decent lottery, offering same-night service on payouts to winners, but numbers games in other counties were stealing his business by raising the odds, paying 600-to-1 compared with Tony Boy's lowball 500-to-1 odds. He also sold "cut numbers," or "cut cards," more popular combinations like 777 that have reduced payoffs, for as much as 20 percent less in order to avoid the risk of a run on his lottery when those numbers were hit. And he was doing business with smaller numbers games, which he permitted in his territory by being the bank that laid the "edge off" large bets that they couldn't cover. Unfortunately, this combination led to his bank's being overwhelmed by winning numbers, and he had to borrow money from the Boot to pay them off.[4]

A more pressing concern: robberies. A gang of Puerto Ricans held up three of Tony Boy's lottery drops; one of the victims was his biggest bookmaker in the North Ward. Stickups created headaches and big financial losses for Tony Boy, and they looked bad. Tony Boy wasn't protecting his turf and his people. He ignored his bread and butter—the local rackets—and instead took trips to Nevada, Florida, Puerto Rico, the Caribbean, and Havana with the Hollywood actor George Raft, overseeing the Boot's growing portfolio of investments in various hotels, casinos, and other businesses in Las Vegas, Miami, Hallandale, and on the islands, including the lucrative Capri Hotel and Casino.

Around this time a *Newark Evening News* photographer snapped a photo of Tony Boy in a fedora, smiling broadly, well tanned and obviously pleased with himself.[5] Tony Boy reveled in these high-flying junkets, flaunting his glamorous connections. He was not in Newark anymore; he was in a glittering, exotic mecca of money, white sandy beaches, and beautiful women; he was an international jet-setter in the company of Hollywood royalty; and he had a goomar, a mistress, in New Jersey and allegedly another in Florida.[6]

The Havana casinos were at the height of their popularity and decadent splendor. It was a tantalizing, seductive scene, a hothouse of pleasure that made it easy to forget the grim streets that were the source of the Boiardo family wealth and standing and that were slowly falling out of their control while the heir apparent played. The Boot had a discipline problem on his hands with his fortunate son.

"Tony Boy is not well liked and probably will stay in power only so long as his father lives," read an FBI report based on interviews with mob informants.[7] One intelligence agent summarized: "Tony Boy is perhaps as heartily disliked as his father is respected."[8] The *Newark Evening News* weighed in on the subject: "As a young man Tony Boy was one of the most disliked residents of the old First Ward. Pampered by his doting father, Tony Boy lorded it over leaders of his father's organization as well as its lesser button men. Many of the 'boys' resisted desires to put Tony Boy in his place. Tony Boy was described as a wild young man behind the wheels of fast sports cars and at night spots."[9]

The FBI reported that "Boiardo's greatest worry is what will happen to his son Tony Boy when he dies. As soon as Boiardo dies, his son Tony

Boy will not have long to live[;] . . . there were so many people who hated Tony Boy that it was almost a certainty he would be killed as soon as the old man dies."[10]

"It is a well- known fact among the hoodlum element that [Tony Boy] is not well liked," another FBI report concluded, "and that this element is willing to 'make book' that Boiardo would not live more than ninety days after [the] 'old man' dies. Source said that in the past, [a] 'contract' had been put out on subject but the 'old man' stopped them."[11]

Gyp DeCarlo and Anthony "Little Pussy" Russo were caught on FBI tapes discussing how selfish and obnoxious Tony Boy was and that it was impossible to work with him, and they predicted—or threatened—that he would get whacked when the patriarch passed on. DeCarlo recalled Tony Boy boasting about killing "a couple of guys" without getting an okay from higher-ups in the syndicate, and he quoted Tony Boy as crowing: "If somebody fools with me too bad, then I'll go without an okay and I won't let you or nobody else know about it."[12] Gyp and Little Pussy bitched about Tony Boy and his bad attitude; Little Pussy went so far as to suggest that Tony Boy deserved to "get hit," a dangerous thing to say about the son of a Mafia don.[13] Little Pussy would eventually regret his ill-chosen words.

Others claimed, ironically, that Tony Boy was kept alive only because of his close friendship with Little Pussy's older brother.[14] After the Boot retired, Big Pussy, according to mob scuttlebutt, was made the real power behind the Boiardo organization. Russo had taken a big fall for the Boot—he was jailed for the murder of John Rosso in 1929—and he was adequately rewarded when he got out of prison. It was said that the Boot appointed Big Pussy his "number one man," torpedo, and liaison with other organized crime families.[15] He became a consummate and lethal organized-crime diplomat for the Boiardo organization.

The Club Fremont was on the ground floor of a three-story clapboard apartment building on a residential street in the Roseville section, a mixed neighborhood of Italians and Irish on the west side of Branch Brook Park. Roseville was considered an upgrade from the old First Ward; it had detached duplexes and single-family homes, though it was still densely populated. Residents were second-generation children of immigrants; they had outgrown the tenements and were starting to assimilate, heading up "guinea gulch"—Bloomfield Avenue—toward the suburbs.

The Italian clubs, or *circolos*, of the old First Ward were christened after honored places in the old country—the Teorese Club on Garside Street and the Atripaldese Club; they looked backward, nostalgically. The Club Fremont sounded Anglo, like Tony Boy's Braidburn Country Club, reflecting his aspirations. He didn't look back; he looked forward to a life among the nonethnic professional classes who lived further up the gulch in leafy Verona, where he resided now with his family at 75 Oakridge Road, in a four-bedroom, two-story brick Colonial with a finished basement, a garage, and a big yard.

At the Fremont there was a bar, small kitchen, and tables in the front, and a nice size party room in the back with tables, chairs, and a pool table. This party room was sectioned off by large accordion-type doors. Joe DiMaggio, Jimmy Durante, and Martha Ray were just a few celebrity friends of Tony's who stopped by for a social visit or slummed for the night at the illegal gaming tables at the Fremont.

On paper, the Fremont had been owned by Tony's brother-in-law Joseph Porreca, who later transferred ownership to a corporation trading as the Club Fremont Inc.[16] In practice, Tony ran the joint.[17] The morning Smudgy and his wife showed up at the Fremont at least four people were in the club—Tony Boy, Big Pussy, Jimo Calabrese, and the club's regular daytime bartender, Natale Lento. A first-generation Italian American, Lento was the only one among them who probably was not connected with the shooting incident that occurred that day. He was short and heavyset with a thick neck and a bullet head that gave him the look of a tough guy, but his thick-frame glasses softened his features. Lento was easygoing, but not very healthy; like Tony's mother he suffered from gall-bladder problems. He lived in a small apartment in Belleville above a cleaning store on the main drag, Washington Avenue, with his second wife, Loretta. He was fifty-eight years old, a hard worker, and the father of a grown daughter from his first marriage. He showed up early that day to set up the Fremont for lunch.

When the FBI later started beating the bushes up and down guinea gulch looking for information in the wake of the Fremont shooting, the chirping was noisy and discordant.[18] Informants not only gave inconsistent portraits of Smudgy, they also gave conflicting versions of the incident. In one, Smudgy and Jimo Calabrese were both summoned by Tony Boy as they were both suspected of ripping off the Boiardo numbers runners. According to this version, Smudgy and Jimo were led to the Fremont not knowing that Tony Boy and Big Pussy were waiting inside. This was an unlikely scenario as Jimo Calabrese had been a close, long-time lieutenant and alleged killer for Tony Boy and remained one well after the Club Fremont incident.

In another version of the shooting, Smudgy was the aggressor. He was operating his own private bookmaking and loan-sharking business in Tony Boy's territory and had been warned to stay out or be rubbed out. Smudgy defied the threat and continued to operate solo. Finally, after learning that Tony Boy was about to whack him, Smudgy turned up at the Club Fremont without invitation, on his own initiative, in a preemptive attempt to ambush Tony Boy.

Smudgy meanwhile had his story to tell, and it also appeared full of holes. Under oath, he told investigators that he was the only person with a gun, which he pulled out of his wife's purse as Big Pussy approached him. Big Pussy grabbed the gun, they wrestled with it, the gun went off, bullets sprayed the room hitting Big Pussy, Jimo, and himself.

The known facts are that Big Pussy was shot in the chest, Jimo Calabrese in the stomach, and Smudgy himself in the stomach and right shoulder. Four or five shots were fired, according to cops who arrived on the scene. Two thirty-eight-caliber bullets were found in the walls, and they matched Smudgy's gun, which was later found by the police.[19]

The hoodlums scattered. Jimo on foot, holding his hemorrhaging guts, hailed a passing truck and was driven several blocks to a gas station at Bloomfield and Third Avenue, where he made a call in a pay phone and then staggered back and collapsed to the floor of the booth. An ambulance whisked him away to nearby Martland Medical Center, where surgeons removed a bullet from his stomach and he was held under arrest, listed in fair condition.

Big Pussy was driven to Columbus Hospital; he "was either shoved or staggered out and up the hospital steps" as the car sped off, according to a report in the *Newark Evening News*.[20] In Big Pussy's wallet, hospital attendants found a gold police badge and an identification card issued by the Passaic police department identifying John Russo as an "Honorary Police Commissioner." The card was signed by Passaic's public safety director. Doctors thought they had a prominent public official on their hands, not a convicted murderer. (When the news hit the press, this badge created a scandal, and an investigation was launched into corruption in the Passaic police department.) Meanwhile, Big Pussy was in critical condition. Surgeons removed a bullet that had entered his chest, punctured his left lung, and remained lodged in his back. His left lung was so damaged that the doctors had to remove it.[21]

Bleeding profusely, Smudgy bolted the Fremont at the wheel of his 1953 Cadillac, drove fourteen blocks to Martland Medical Center, and burst into the hospital screaming for help. Smudgy's mother was a switchboard operator at the hospital; she collapsed when she heard that her son had been shot. Just before Smudgy was wheeled into the operation room to remove a bullet in his stomach, homicide-squad cops arrived and talked to him. Smudgy confessed immediately: "I shot the two of them," he said, and denied anyone had shot at him. While in the operating room, the cops found his gun "still hot" in his pocket with five rounds missing.[22] Smudgy was later charged with two counts of atrocious assault and battery, assault with intent to kill, and carrying a concealed weapon.[23]

Smudgy convalesced in the hospital for several months, escaping from protective custody on New Years Eve, 1961. He was quickly recaptured by police and was slapped with another charge, avoiding arrest. His bail was set at $10,000; he was eventually sent to jail.[24]

Tony Boy disappeared, without a trace. The cops at first had no idea he had even been there. Smudgy never mentioned him. Neither did Jimo or Big Pussy. Tony Boy's name came up only later, after Newark detectives began digging around. They learned that Tony Boy was not only in the club but had been wounded and shot in the legs, and might have used a gun too, popping off two rounds at Smudgy.

Two days after the Fremont fracas and just a few blocks from the club, one of Smudgy's close associates, Joseph Cartisano, was gunned down on the street while apparently casing the offices of the Columbia Exterminating Company, which was a reputed front for another Boiardo numbers operation. Cartisano was with a fellow tough guy, Sebastian Montouri, who was not hit. Cartisano survived.[25]

Tony Boy was on the lam. No one knew how he managed to escape the scene of the shooting, but according to family members he somehow turned up at his sister Phyllis's house on the Boot's estate in Livingston; the Boot had moved there from Newark in 1945 along with his entire family, including Tony Boy. Phyllis and her older sister Rose were there; they helped to stabilize his condition.[26] An informant told the FBI that Tony Boy was then driven to Pennsylvania, where a surgeon removed bullets from his legs.[27] He then moved again, apparently driven by Charles Delmonico, the son of Charlie "the Blade" Tourine, down to Miami, where he holed up in Delmonico's house.

The Club Fremont incident triggered a crisis in the Boiardo organization. Rumors circulated that the family's lottery operations had totally shut down after Tony Boy skipped town, and, with Big Pussy in the hospital in critical condition, no one was in charge of the extensive network of bookies, numbers runners, and loan sharks. Newark gamblers speculated that if Big Pussy was sent back to prison as a parole violator for his part in the shooting, Tony Boy was finished as family boss. The Boot, meanwhile, was enjoying his retirement on vacation in Italy with Edith Bencivengo, his girlfriend. The old man was forced to cut short his romantic interlude and return home. It was clear to local mobsters and gamblers that the old man had come back to clean up his son's mess.

The Boot told detectives that his son had left him a note saying that he was off to Puerto Rico on business. Following up on his tip, detectives searched airline passenger lists at Newark Airport, and they contacted police authorities in Puerto Rico. They found no trace of Tony Boy. It was obvious they were getting the run-around from the cagey patriarch. Meanwhile, Tony Boy's mother-in-law told the police she believed he had left for Florida two days *before* the shooting.

Jimo and Big Pussy were questioned by Essex County Prosecutor Brendan Byrne. According to FBI documents, the boys were coached first by an investigator in the prosecutor's office who was on the Boot's payroll. The Boot's inside man warned Big Pussy and Jimo that they had to tell "exactly the same story" or else they would be charged with false swearing and perjury, and he prepped them on how to answer questions from the prosecutor "in an attempt to prevent the true details from coming out."[28] Those details included the fact that Tony Boy was present at the incident and was involved in the gunfight. The FBI at the time was suspicious that the Boot's man inside the prosecutor's office may have been Joseph P. Lordi, the assistant investigator, because Lordi's appointment to the prosecutor's office was, according to an FBI informant, orchestrated by the Catena brothers.[29]

Less than two months after the Club Fremont incident, on November 8, Tony suddenly appeared, hobbling into Essex County Prosecutor Byrne's office. He explained to Byrne that he had injured himself in a fall on a dock in Miami, where he had been staying with his friend Charles Delmonico. Tony Boy said that he knew nothing of the shooting at the Club Fremont until he had recently heard that he was wanted for questioning. He said that he was traveling to Florida at the time of the incident, having left New Jersey on the evening of September 22, driving all night with his friend Delmonico, and arriving the next morning in Miami. Byrne questioned Tony Boy under oath for two hours. Tony Boy was cooperative; he even permitted a police surgeon to examine his injured legs; the doctor found scars on both of them.

He was not so cooperative one week later. On November 16 Tony Boy appeared before the state Superior Court and refused to answer two questions related to the shooting: Was he at the Club Fremont on the day of the shooting? And did he have any knowledge of the shooting? These were questions that he had answered under oath in the prosecutor's office. "Pleading possible self-incrimination, Boiardo told the grand jury nothing," the *Newark Evening News* reported. "Ordered to answer questions by superior court Judge Alexander P. Waugh, Boiardo kept mum." Tony told the court that he was keeping silent because his attorney Sam Kessler, who was out of town on a trip to Europe, had instructed him not to "say anything until he gets back."[30] Kessler's associate lawyer Benedict Harrington was in court, but he told Judge Waugh that he could not go against Kessler's advice. Tony's rationale, of course, cut much deeper: when Prosecutor Byrne had grilled him, Tony Boy was considered a possible witness in the case, but when the grand jury went after him, he was a prospective defendant. He had to protect himself, and so he took refuge in the Fifth Amendment.

Tony Boy was concerned that he was in danger of perjuring himself. If it could be proven that he was at the Club Fremont at the time of the shootings, or even in the area, he stood a strong chance of being convicted and sentenced to jail time for false swearing. And if it could be proven that he had used a gun and shot at Smudgy, he would face additional charges of assault with a deadly weapon and attempted murder. He couldn't afford any of that. In his many years in "this thing of ours," he had never been convicted of a crime.

His record was nearly spotless. A few years earlier he had been arrested for conspiring to run an illegal lottery, but the charges were dropped; he claimed he had been mistaken for another Tony. And then there was the publicity surrounding a car accident. He had driven off the road on South Orange Avenue in the wooded South Mountain Reservation. An Essex County prosecutor charged that someone had attempted to kill him by running him off the road. Tony Boy explained that it was nothing: he had had a few drinks at a friend's house, and he had swerved off the road by accident. He was very concerned about keeping up appearances and not doing anything that reflected negatively on his wife and children. (Meanwhile, he was very nonchalant about his drinking and driving, which apparently was not considered a very serious offense at the time.) He said that he was having a hard time "living down his own father's reputation."[31]

The Newark police department told the press that they had received reports that placed Tony Boy at the scene of the Fremont shooting and said that the gangster had been wounded.[32] Someone was talking, but who was it? Big Pussy and Jimo were beyond suspicion, and even though he faced assault and attempted murder charges Smudgy was keeping his mouth tightly shut. He had already covered for everyone, testifying that he was the only one with a weapon and the only one who had shot anybody.

Vito Torsiello, the club manager, was arrested and booked for concealing a crime and obstruction of justice charges, but he wasn't even at the club when the shooting broke out. The cops did arrest another man, Patsy Ferrante. It wasn't clear whether Patsy was at the club at the time of the shooting, but he was booked as a material witness "for his own protection," according to the police, with bail set at $5,000.

A few days after the shooting, Prosecutor Byrne announced a special Essex County grand jury inquiry to investigate gambling and racketeering. According to the *Newark Evening News*, the grand jury investigation was touched off by the series of Newark shootings, which law enforcement considered an outgrowth of gambling and loan-sharking activities—starting with the Club Fremont incident and including the drive-by Cartisano shooting. The *News* characterized the incidents as "a type of underworld double cross[,] . . . the robbing of lottery operators."[33] At the time Byrne secretly confided to the FBI that the grand jury was convened primarily to investigate the Club Fremont shooting and to prove that Tony Boy was there.[34]

On December 9, 1960, the court convicted Tony Boy of criminal contempt, declaring it had a "reasonable basis for apprehension of criminal involvement" when he refused to answer questions.[35] He was sentenced to thirty days in Essex County Penitentiary, where his father was first incarcerated for the death of an eight-year-old boy. The jail was just a few blocks away from Tony Boy's home in Verona. Kessler, his lawyer, was at his sentencing, and he told the jury that Boiardo had "reasonable grounds for apprehension that an attempt was being made by the prosecutor to involve him in the shooting or to lay a foundation for a false swearing charge."[36] Tony Boy was released that day on $1,000 bail.

On January 9, 1961, Patsy Ferrante, a material witness in the Club Fremont shooting, was found shot to death in a stolen automobile in Harrison. Ferrante, thirty years old, had been taken for a ride. Police speculated that Ferrante was involved in the holdups of gambling bookies and that Tony Boy had mistaken Smudgy for Ferrante. "Whoever fired the shots at the club was after the fingerman in the lottery holdups, police believe," reported the *Newark Evening News*.[37] The murder of Ferrante was seen by the prosecutor's office as rectifying the mistake, and the circumstances of his death made it obvious to gamblers and mobsters in the North Ward and beyond that the Boot was back in charge.

Tony Boy appealed his conviction in the state Supreme Court on March 20, 1961. His chances did not look good. According to FBI informants, the Boot instructed his son to ask Gyp DeCarlo for a favor. Tony Boy needed at least one judge on the court to rule in his favor, and the Boot believed Gyp had connections with the court. Tony Boy approached Gyp, whining that Gene Catena had refused to help him. He said Catena once had told him he would do anything for the Boiardo family, but when he received his subpoena Tony Boy went to Catena and "got no satisfaction."[38]

Tony Boy explained to Gyp that he believed Byrne was persecuting him, setting up the special Essex County grand jury inquiry just to nail him. According to an informant, Tony Boy suggested that Little Joe Benedictus, a Newark political figure and former associate of Gyp's, knew some of the judges and could help. Gyp was noncommittal, but he advised Tony Boy that he could beat the contempt charges if he kept his mouth shut; the minute he spoke up, the prosecutor would slap him with a perjury charge, said Gyp.[39]

After being hung out to dry by two friends and old associates of his father, Tony Boy did his own thing. He didn't follow Gyp's advice. On May

11, 1961, he appeared before the special Essex County grand jury and testified, telling the judges he was in Florida at the time of the shooting and
knew nothing about the incident. The presiding judge "took note of the fact
that Boiardo eventually answered the questions put to him by the . . . grand
jury but it was too late for Boiardo to purge himself [wipe out the contempt charge]."[40] The jury denied his appeal. Tony Boy began serving his
sentence in July 1961. In jail he complained of stomach pains and was
removed to the jail hospital. Other inmates complained he was getting
special treatment. The prison physician diagnosed a peptic ulcer condition
and noted that Tony Boy had a history of ulcer and gall-bladder trouble.[41]

On May 21, 1961, the Essex County grand jury returned thirteen indictments against ten men as a result of a ten-week investigation into illegal
gambling and loan sharking. According to the *Newark Evening News*, the
grand jury claimed to have uncovered a "huge gambling conspiracy in
Essex County, organized with military thoroughness and employing violence and fear." Superior Court Judge Waugh claimed the inquiry proved
that "such a criminal conspiracy exists in the county and may even extend
beyond the county."[42]

The grand jury charged that the "directors of the conspiracy have provided a table of organization comparable to any military establishment,"
and "territories have been allotted, authority delegated through intricate
means, discipline demanded and achieved by a set of morals foreign to
any normal standards, and secrecy made an integral part of the operation. Violence and fear permeate from the top down to prevent any dissi-
dence, and provide the cohesiveness that binds an efficient organization."[43]
The jury demanded a list of recommendations to stem the tide of this
elaborate conspiracy, including longer sentences and increased fines for
the convicted and enactment of a wiretapping statute to help investigators
find the culprits.

The indicted included Smudgy, Jimo Calabrese, John "Big Pussy" Russo
for the Club Fremont incident; Vito Torsiello for concealing a crime and
obstructing justice in relation to the incident; and Joseph LaMorte, a local

hood who was charged with conspiring to rob the Columbia Exterminating Company, a front for a lottery operation. Cartisano was named a co-conspirator with LaMorte and Sebastian Montouri, another punk who also was caught casing the joint. The prosecutor's office was confident, hinting that their case was built around the ironclad testimony of a mystery star witness. The trial was set for September 25, 1961.

Natale Lento, the bartender at the Club Fremont, was reported missing by his wife on September 11, just two weeks before the trial date. Lento had been quietly detained as a material witness to the shooting along with Vito Torsiello, the club's manager, because both men gave "conflicting stories of the events leading up to the shooting and to the shootings themselves." According to Prosecutor Byrne, who spoke to the press after Lento's disappearance, the bartender's testimony before the grand jury was responsible for the indictment on false swearing charges of Russo and Calabrese. He was the prosecutor's star witness.[44]

Lento was last seen behind the wheel of his 1958 black Chevrolet leaving his modest apartment on Washington Avenue in Belleville at seven in the morning on September 7. His wife was not sure where he was going at that hour; she said he had only fifteen dollars on him. The FBI assisted local law enforcement in a manhunt for Lento, following leads provided by a nest of informants. One reliable canary informed them that without a doubt Lento was "definitely gone" and that his disappearance was the work of none other than the Boot. According to the informant, the Boot had contacted Lento personally. He tried to persuade the bartender to recant his testimony, which obviously placed Tony Boy at the Club Fremont at the time of the shooting. The Boot offered to pay all of Lento's expenses and to take care of his family if he was sent to jail for changing his story.[45] Clearly, it was very important for the Boot that his only son stay out of jail; he was willing to spare no expense, to do anything to save his Tony Boy and to keep his organization intact.

For whatever reason, Lento, an ordinary man, unconnected to organized crime, turned out to be extraordinarily stubborn. Did he have morals? Did the Boot offend him? Or perhaps it was Tony Boy. After all those years of tending bar for the obnoxious, spoiled heir apparent, perhaps Natale Lento decided to do the right thing. He refused to cooperate with the Boot.

The FBI informant could not say who exactly iced Lento, but he did suggest that some men from Brooklyn may have been assigned to do it because the Boot had connections there, and it was better that someone from outside the neighborhood do the job.[46] The Boot was a professional; he knew how to whack a man with style and without leaving behind any evidence, and that was especially important in Lento's case because the victim was not a soldier; he was basically an innocent bystander.

Did the Boot suffer pangs of conscience knowing he made someone disappear who really did not deserve it? Probably not. The Boot apparently rescued his son and also had saved his organization, including key lieutenants Big Pussy Russo and Jimo Calabrese, finally placing himself back in the saddle, riding the white horse, in charge of his mob. The bartender's life was a small price to pay in this scheme of things.

On September 27, 1961, the New Jersey Alcohol Beverage Control commissioner revoked the Club Fremont's liquor license. Five years later, on January 6, 1966, Prosecutor Byrne's office dismissed indictments against Calabrese and Russo. The continued lack of cooperation from Jimo, Big Pussy, Torsiello, and Smudgy (who was the only one convicted in the case; he served four years in prison, was released in November 1965, and fled the state of New Jersey) and, more important, the disappearance of the key witness in the Club Fremont shooting, left the prosecutor without a case.[47] The Essex County grand jury inquiry into illicit gambling, loan-sharking, and some shootouts, initially announced with fireworks and big ambitions, finally simply fizzled out.

To this day, Natale Lento remains missing.

CHAPTER 7

CASTLE CRUEL

It gave heart to the cavalier
to find a strange adventure here.
Beyond the first door was another
and through it was a verdant garden,
in which a knight was standing, armed,
as if it were his work to guard
a sepulcher, which had been set
beyond the second portal's sill.

—*Matteo Maria Boiardo,* Orlando Innamorato, *454*

In the summer of 1939, the Boot bought twenty-nine acres on Rikers Hill in Livingston, about fifteen miles from Newark, with views facing west, away from the city toward farmland that rolled gently toward the distant Delaware River. The property sat on a geographical and social divide where, at the time, the suburbs ended and rural Jersey began.

Using materials salvaged from Boiardo Construction demolition jobs in Newark, including large blocks of stone from the old Post Office building, the Boot built a self-contained compound of four homes, an aviary, a barn, swimming pools, a hunting lodge, an orchard, picnic grounds, and tennis and basketball courts. In a panic during the Cuban missile crisis in the early sixties he also built a bomb shelter. (Ironically, the U.S. military became the Boot's first immediate neighbor when they built a Nike air-defense base right next to his estate in 1955, during the height of the Cold War. The base was a radar-control site that was paired with a launcher area in East Hanover, where Ajax and Hercules missiles stood poised to protect New York City from a Soviet strike.)[1]

In 1945 the family moved from Newark to the estate, which the clan took to calling "the farm." Tony Boy and his wife lived in the main house with the Boot for a few years, and then they moved to a modest house in suburban Verona and finally to the WASP-y enclave of Essex Fells, the home of the exclusive Essex Fells Country Club, the oldest country club in the state. Thomas Edison, the Chubb family, the Colgates, and the Mercks had been members. Theodore Roosevelt had played golf there, as had Sam Snead and many other top-ranked professionals. Tony Boy never became a member; in the sixties the club was hard to join, especially for arrivistes from Newark.

Three of the Boot's daughters, Agnes Crescenzi, Rose Hanos, and Phyllis Balestro, and their families lived on the farm; each had her own home. The houses were clustered in the back of the property, like a European hamlet. Each house had a cast-iron fountain in the front yard, forged in the Eiffel foundry in Paris, depicting herons with spread wings. The houses had solid walls, at least a foot thick; the exterior stone was backed up by an interior layer of cinderblock, which was coated with a thick crust of plaster; the houses were virtually impenetrable, bulletproof. Stone-block walls seemed to be everywhere on the farm, along with gargoyles and grottoes sheltering likenesses of saints, knights, and serpents.

The gardens of the compound were elaborate. Besides the Boot's beloved vegetable and flower garden, which was behind the main house, there was a statuary garden of painted busts of his grandchildren, including a likeness of Roger at sixteen, looking serious in a field of half-smiling faces frozen in mortar. The busts flanked a grand equestrian sculpture of the Boot in a jaunty porkpie hat in the saddle of a prancing white charger, a likeness of Chief, his favorite horse. He loved to ride through the property on Chief, sometimes emerging from the woods in suburban neighborhoods in Livingston and Roseland. Residents there still remember him trotting down streets with an entourage of men also on horseback.[2]

For the grandchildren, growing up on the Boiardo estate was like living in a fantasy land, a kind of Eden and a retreat from the rest of the world. It was hidden behind woods and protected by fences and gates. Roger Hanos grew up there with his younger brother, Darrel; his sister, Lillian; and his cousins Maurice Crescenzi, Michael Balestro, a somewhat quiet boy, and his older brother Mario Jr., who was gregarious. Their parents, Phyllis and Mario Balestro Sr., doted on the boys, buying them extravagant playthings such as a miniature motorized Thunderbird car, which the boys raced up and down the driveway. Years earlier their older cousins Frank and Richie Barile—the sons of the Boot's fourth daughter Mary, who did not live on the estate but often visited from her home in nearby South Orange—rode horses from the Boot's stable.

There were horses on the farm, peacocks and crown cranes, a herd of deer, ostriches, pigs, dogs, pigeons, and chickens. The Boot's grandchildren played in the aviary, running after the peacocks, making them screech—a noise that was described by neighbors as sounding like women screaming—and they fed the deer and the pigs in the menagerie. "Growing up in rural Livingston at the time was quite an adventure. We had woods, open fields, statues all over the place, and buildings that looked like castles," recalled Roger. "During the late 1940s and throughout the fifties and sixties the farm was a huge playground, a Disneyland for me and my cousins."[3] In the summer, the boys swam in the estate swimming pool, which was fifty feet wide and one hundred and forty feet long; it had a fountain in the middle and was surrounded by bathhouses and a grand Italian marble patio.

The Boot enjoyed treating his grandchildren to Saturday matinees at the Colony Theater in Livingston. He also threw parties for family and friends at the pool and on picnic grounds in the back near the woods, where there was a huge grated fireplace made of stone, picnic tables, and a big shelter with bathrooms. The Boot loved to have barbecues, but he never ate food from the grill or from a can. He was conscientious about his diet. He only ate vegetables from his garden and fresh cheese and meats from the butcher.

For the adults there was a chapel on the property and a family shrine with statues of just about every saint one could name. The Boot gave the impression he was religious, but he never went to church. He was superstitious, known to visit a psychic on occasion, and he dabbled in questionable health cures. To treat his arthritis he regularly visited a quack chiropractor who used a lounge chair equipped with vibrating springs that were wrapped around the patient. The Boot called him "Dr. Springy." The Boot also believed in reincarnation and that after he died he would return as a bird—a red cardinal.[4]

The Boot's daughters, however, especially Rose, Mary, and Phyllis, were religious. Phyllis sent her children to Saint Philomena's and Saint Raphael's Catholic schools and went to church every Sunday. Rose occasionally sent young Roger down to the main house to ask the Boot to join them at mass. The patriarch would come to the door and give Roger money, usually about twenty dollars, to put in the basket and with a wink and a nod would instruct him to inform his mother that he had already been to the early-morning mass, an obvious lie. The nuns from Saint Philomena's occasionally came to his house and requested donations for charity, and the Boot gave them what they came for, and then some. According to Rose, during one such mission the Boot was in a sly mood; he patted one of the nuns on her bottom as she walked out.[5]

For a few years, Marion, one of the Boot's girlfriends, lived in the hunting lodge back in the woods. After the Boot's wife died, he had many lovers. Marion was the most striking. She was an opera singer and pianist; she brought beauty and culture to the estate. The Boot's grandchildren loved her, and so did he, for many years. The Boot met her when she was seventeen and he was sixty-one. At first she lived in the mansion. Tony Boy was against the relationship; he didn't want her in the house. He argued with his father. To placate his son, the Boot set her up in the hunting lodge, but that wasn't good enough for Tony Boy. Marion was one of the reasons Tony Boy moved out of the Boot's house.[6]

Considering the business he was in, the Boot wasn't very high tech when it came to security on the farm. The main gate, which was automated, was always left open. The Boot explained to Livingston police that he had to keep it open because eleven cars a day passed through. The perimeter of the thirty-acre spread was either walled or fenced in or abutted the Nike base next door. There were no security cameras or electronic alarms; instead he relied on his muster of peacocks, which let out piercing screams at the slightest sound, and four huge Belgian shepherds named Leo, Chucky, George, and Bootsie. Three of the shepherds roamed freely.

Leo was the fiercest; he was stationed at the threshold of the main house, tied down with a heavy chain that stretched nearly across the driveway; there was just enough room for a person to walk by. He was so intimidating and powerful that even the Boot wouldn't take him for a walk on a leash. Roger and his siblings always tiptoed by Leo as they walked to catch the bus to school. When the Boot asked Roger to feed him, he would walk on tenterhooks, quickly drop the dog's bowl, and then run like hell. At night, the dogs could not tell friend from foe; they would attack any car driving up or down the hill. The tax assessor, a frequent visitor, and the police never stepped out of their vehicles. The Boot loved his dogs, but if they crossed him, he punished them brutally. When one killed a peacock, he tied the dead bird around the dog's neck and left the rotting carcass to dangle there for a week.

The security system was primitive and far from foolproof. One summer night in 1966, trespassers breached it. A group of high school kids from Wayne and Lyndhurst decided they wanted to see the "haunted house." They parked on Beaufort Avenue at nine-thirty at night, passed through the open gate, walked up the quarter-mile-long driveway, somehow avoided Leo and company, and approached the main house. When they saw a light on inside, they turned to go back and then saw a sudden flash of light and heard what they thought was a firecracker. A seventeen-year-old boy and sixteen-year-old girl were raked with birdshot in the arms and legs. They scrambled back to their car, found a doctor in Roseland, and notified the police. Their injuries were not serious.[7]

The reaction of law enforcement can only be described as overkill; then again they were dealing with an alleged cold-blooded murderer, no matter that he was also a grandfather. An Essex County grand jury was convened to investigate; Prosecutor Brendon Byrne dispatched seventeen officials from the state and county, including local police, to execute a search warrant. They confiscated three shotguns and a small supply of shells. The Boot, who always had a way with words and a great sense of irony even in the most delicate situations, told a reporter that he had owned guns for twenty years and these particular weapons were for "hunting rats, weasels, and birds."[8] There was no indication that the reporter caught the drift of his statement or detected any double meaning in his words, for in the underworld these same creatures are also commonly used as metaphors for snitches, traitors, and informants.

Byrne was determined to prove that the Boot had taken a potshot at the kids. Twenty witnesses were subpoenaed to testify, including all seven teenagers, who didn't see the shooter; Boiardo family members who were on the estate that night and refused to comment; and the Boot, who was questioned for three hours in court, denied knowing anything about the incident. Outside the courtroom, the star witness was surrounded by members of the press, and, as usual, he was as amiable and ironic with them as in the old days when he used to curry favor by handing out cigars, silver dollars, cookies, and candy to reporters. "'You can't live peaceful,' said the one-time alleged gang leader of Newark's old First Ward. Dressed in a blue-green iridescent suit, yellow shirt and yellow and red dotted matching silk tie and handkerchief, he added he could not live in peace 'because my name is Boiardo.'"[9] Three years earlier, the Boot had showed up at the Valachi-inspired grand jury hearings wearing a battered fedora and threadbare cardigan sweater, which he described as his "Sunday suit." This time he quipped to reporters he was wearing his "Monday suit."[10] The grand jury closed its investigation of the shooting a week later: "it could find no basis for action after hearing Boiardo and 19 other witnesses."[11]

Several months later, Peter Penna, the caretaker of the estate, told Roger that the Boot had been warned about the raid in advance and had instructed him to hide a significant cache of guns in the shrubs and gardens on the property. Roger was not surprised. There were all sorts of guns on the estate. The Boot always kept a .410-gauge shotgun in his garage, a forty-five-caliber German Luger in his kitchen drawer, and a thirty-eight-caliber snub-nosed revolver under a hat near his nightstand. The Boot later brought his grandson into a horse stall in the barn and told him to remove the false bottom of the hay trough, where there was a hoard of shotguns, pistols, and automatic weapons, many of them still in their original boxes. The Boot instructed Roger to hide them in the attic of his house. Roger was worried about all that artillery in his house, so he told his father. Months later, Roger checked on the arsenal and it was gone. His father said that he had gotten rid of the weapons. Roger never found out what happened to the guns, and the Boot never brought up the matter again.[12]

The centerpiece of the farm was a twenty-nine-room massive pile of stone described by the *New York Sunday News* as a "feudal baron's castle."[13] A walled parking lot designed for privacy was adjacent to the castle and an imposing flight of steps led to its front door. The roof was red-tiled, and its ornate spires and chimney reached above the trees. The Italian maxim *Buono Prossimo Si Divide Buone Cose*, which translates as "Good Neighbors Share Good Things," was etched in stone at a side entrance. A ground-floor den or family room was decorated with Early Renaissance–style frescoes and Raphael-inspired artwork that depicted mythological themes in the manner of the French academic painter William-Adolphe Bouguereau. In a return to the exterior medieval motif, bronze statuettes of knights on horseback sat on the mantel above a grand fireplace with a profile of an ancient warrior chiseled into gold-painted stone, along with an aphorism that was a rewording of a verse by the Renaissance philosopher Sir Francis Bacon:

> Rare Meat Rye Bread to Have, Good Old Wine to Drink
> Good Books to Read, Good Friends to Have
> Good Fireplace to Have, Good Wood to Burn

The Boot entertained guests in his basement-level "cardinal bar," which was decorated with murals of castles and drawings of his favorite bird, the red cardinal. The battlements and half-round towers of a castle were built into the wall as a frame for the mirror behind the bar and were embellished with lights. A huge kitchen was also on this floor, outfitted with stainless steel restaurant appliances, copper pots, and acres of pantries. Within the kitchen a salvaged bank-vault door served as the entrance to a massive liquor and wine cellar. A grand marble stairway led upstairs and wound its way through three flights into other frescoed chambers, heavily draped and lit with crystal chandeliers.

The Boot's esthetic tastes ranged from medieval to Early Renaissance and Baroque to the French Academic school (he owned a colloid reproduction of a Bouguereau painting), but his heart was in the Middle Ages, especially the world of men in armor. After Prohibition, he had managed to return to his motherland and no doubt was exposed there to the history and culture of the period through art and architecture, but it's not clear that he ever actually read the literature. He adopted the great poet of chivalry and romance Matteo Maria Boiardo as his ancestor for one obvious reason—the shared name—but he also obviously felt a kinship with the poet and his preoccupation with violence, romance, and sex. Matteo Maria Boiardo's noble lineage also attracted the Boot—the poet was a Renaissance nobleman, courtier, and politician, a captain of Modena and Reggio. The Boot was a captain too, but he also believed that he was a king. He once told an FBI informant as much: "Boiardo regards himself as a king and stated that when they jailed kings of countries in the old days, they were still kings when they came out."[14]

Tony Boy indulged his father in this fantasy. On a trip to Italy he hired a Florentine company—the Istituto Araldico Coccia—to research the family genealogy. He presented his father with the findings, a one-hundred-page bound book that traced the family tree: "It seems that the Boiardo were the lords of the land and the municipality of the castle." It reproduced a Boiardo family coat of arms consisting of a flag with an upside-down V and a sixteenth-century Armet-style knight's helmet. And, no surprise, the volume concluded that the Boot was indeed related to Matteo Maria

Boiardo; the Boot and his family were described as the latest generation and the "modern Boiardo who live in the New World":

> In that day of 1890 a good man was born, a true Italian, Ruggiero Boiardo. To him the Italian colony of New Jersey owns [sic] the example of honesty, moderation[,] the teaching of industry, the love of the mother-country. . . . Our line will continue so that the name of the Boiardi will always shine in the world, under any sky and any latitude, flag of a race that behaved with honor, fought with faith and continued traditions so that they were never abandoned.

The History of the Genealogy of the House of Boiardo also included a back-of-the-book bonus—an astrological profile. The Boot was a Sagittarius:

> You are born equestrienne [sic], literally and symbolically, riding through life and experiences, rarely looking back, loving adventurous undertakings and the bracing breeze of lively encounters with nature and humanity. You have inexhaustive [sic] talents both wondrously open and hidden, fountains of joy, zest for living; yet are prone to peculiar procrastination, incomplete ventures, lack of discipline.[15]

Matteo Maria Boiardo's enduring masterpiece, *Orlando Innamorato*, is an epic journey through fields of corpses, castles, monsters, and beautiful women, most of them goddesses, fairies, or demons. Orlando was himself a literary descendant of Ulysses, the Greek warrior who searched for his wife, Penelope, battling monsters and Penelope's suitors along the way. Orlando was an Italian knight who searched for his sweetheart Angelica and battled monsters, Angelica's suitors—other knights—and whole armies.

One of the central motifs of the work, contained in one long canto, is the "Castle Cruel," a deceptively wondrous place where travelers are welcomed and then fed to a monster that lives in a sepulcher within the castle. Ranaldo, a fellow knight of Orlando and competing suitor of Angelica, arrives at Castle Cruel, kills the monster, assumes everyone in the castle is complicit, and massacres all its residents, including the queen of the castle, who tumbles to her death from a window. Scholars have interpreted this story as an allegory teaching a moral lesson, which, simply stated, is that justifiable violence perpetuates a vicious cycle in which the guilty and the innocent become victims; such acts are not just but cruel.[16] It is a noble canto and a lesson that the Boot perhaps did not read—or understand.

In the sixties, the vicious cycle continued as the FBI went on an aggressive attack against the Mafia, infiltrating their ranks and clandestinely—and often illegally—taping conversations among its most important members. From 1961 through 1965, the bureau targeted Gyp DeCarlo, the Boot's fellow capo, and Sam "the Plumber" DeCavalcante, a friend and sometime associate of the Boiardo crew; he was the boss of a New Jersey crime family that was independent of the Five Families—Genovese, Gambino, Lucchese, Bonnano, and Colombo—and was often called the sixth family. The feds had hoped to use the recordings in a criminal-conspiracy case against these men, but the recordings were executed without a warrant and were not admissible in court. The judge instead released them to the press, and the fallout for the mob, and the Boot in particular, was devastating. The Boot was back in the headlines again, in a very big way.

In 1967, editors at the influential publication *Life* magazine pored over the FBI material and launched their own investigation into the "brazen empire of organized crime, the alarming growth of a multibillion-dollar cartel founded on corruption, terror, and murder." A striking tabloid story kicked off the series of articles; the story was illustrated with a technicolor photo spread under a headline that screamed: "Macabre Home of a Capo, Monument to Mob Murder." The article was all about Richie the Boot. "He is a significant figure in organized U.S. crime and his estate, literally, is one of its monuments." The *Life* article was lurid and fascinating, claiming that the Boot not only murdered people on the farm but also barbecued them in the backyard. "The number of victims incinerated" on the property was considerable, *Life* reported, and it quoted Little Pussy, who was caught in a casual chit-chat with Gyp: "Stay away from there. So many guys have been hit there. There's this furnace way up in the back. That's where they burned them. On the grate." Pussy boasted that he personally dragged one victim "to the furnace by a chain tied to the dead man's throat."[17]

The *New York Times Magazine* followed up with another sensational piece, reporting that Little Pussy and Gyp had described the Boot as a "nut" who not only roasted his own victims on the spit but also provided grilling services for other mob bosses, including New York boss Thomas Lucchese. Little Pussy claimed that Lucchese's boys handed the hapless victims to him and "we'd take them up."[18] He said the furnace was way up in the back of the property.

During a session that was secretly taped in his office at the Martinique Restaurant, DeCarlo told Little Pussy about an earlier conversation he had had with Tony Boy, who boasted about how he and his father killed a man they called simply the "Jew."[19] The transcribed tapes of the original recordings appeared in the January 12, 1970, edition of the *Newark Evening News*:

> BOIARDO: How about the time we hit the Little Jew?
>
> DECARLO: As little as they are they struggle.
>
> BOIARDO: The Boot hit him with a hammer. The guy goes down and he comes up. So I got a crowbar this big, Ray. Eight shots in the head. What do you think he finally did to me? He spit at me and said you [obscene].
>
> DECARLO: They're fighting for their life.[20]

Little Pussy scoffed at Tony Boy's version of the hit, claiming, "The Boot ain't in the thing." Little Pussy then went on to explain in his rambling, fractured syntax, characteristic of the illiterate gangster, that he had killed the Jew with the assistance of his brother Big Pussy and Tony Boy.

> I go to Johnny (John Russo, Pussy's brother) and the kid (Tony Boy)— walk in—say "anytime, watch it" you walk in the front door that you open; it opens a certain way—Johnny and the kid are there. I come—I got the Jew. I picked the Jew up in front of the Grotto [a club owned by Tony Boy] in the afternoon. I ride him up, real nice, talk with Harry 'cause I need an O.K. Ride him up, take him up there, real nice, go

through the door. I got the pistol, I walk in then—we're supposed to talk over a deal. Now just Johnny comes from behind the door, hits him on the head with a butt, the guy goes down. As he goes down, the kid drops his pistol, the kid's got a pistol, the kid goes for the pistol. He says "You (obscene)." Gonna put a pistol at him. I grab for the pistol. I get it just in time and then when I hit him, the kid grabs the pistol from Johnny, then Johnny hits him with a crowbar in the head. As he's gettin' up, I hit him. Now the guy is gettin' up again. As he's gettin' up, I hit him. I hit him and I picked him up. I got a chain and put it around his throat, got the—didn't need too much—picked him up. I lugged him and I put him in the garage. Threw him in the back of the car. I . . . brought . . . him in the tank— and then they were done with it. Everything was . . . set. . . . Good hot fire[,] . . . matches and everything, you know.[21]

The "tank" referred to the furnace on the Boot's property. Law-enforcement authorities were never able to determine the identity of the victim.

A chatty Little Pussy also was caught on tape talking to DeCarlo about other killings that allegedly took place at the farm. "Do you know how many guys been hit up there? Three guys for Tommy Brown [Lucchese]. Neil Oreander (phonetic), he hit the guy for Oliver at the farm. He hit Billy. There was Johnny, Billy and Al and his daughter; they hit his daughter there, all of them. He killed a doctor up there."[22]

Investigators believed "Billy" referred to William "Billy Jinks" Cardinale, a Boiardo gang underling, self-styled barber, bootlegger, and union racketeer, who disappeared from his home in Keansburg, New Jersey, on January 30, 1951. His new Chrysler sedan was found abandoned in a ditch with his glasses on the front seat. "He was blind without his glasses," his wife told a reporter.[23] Billy Jinks was never found.

According to FBI documents, the Boot was enraged over the allegations and complained bitterly about the invasion of his privacy that resulted. He denied that there was a furnace on the property. He told an informant that he "would not use his own home for illegal purposes or to have people killed. He learned long ago, especially during the days when stills were used, that you never use your own home for any such purpose."[24]

The *Life* magazine article marked the height of the Boot's notoriety. Not since the glory days of Prohibition had he received so much attention; back then he welcomed the publicity, it had made him many friends. When he was gunned down on Broad Street, a thousand people crowded Saint Lucy's Church to pray for his recovery.[25] He was beloved and admired and was considered a hero after risking his life to rescue the body of Felicia Celentano, a godmother of one of his daughters. The Boot had just gotten out of prison and was attending Celentano's wake in her house when an electrical fire started and engulfed the room. The Boot snatched her body from the coffin, placed her safely in another room, and then assisted the injured.[26]

In the fifties and sixties, the Boot was portrayed as a monster in the press and had few fans even among fellow hoodlums, although he was flattered by a letter from a twenty-two-year-old Miami girl who sent her picture and asked to be invited to the farm. The Boot was tempted to invite her, but he was wary that she "had been persuaded by the FBI so that organization could get someone in his house."[27]

Newfound fame brought the Boot more uninvited guests. Trespassing photographers and reporters walked up the driveway; small planes and helicopters buzzed overhead; curiosity seekers scrambled through the bushes to get a glimpse of the Mafia don; and pranksters threw cherry bombs over the wall on the Fourth of July. Roger once spotted a stranger coming up the long driveway. He was young and determined; even after Roger warned him several times that he was trespassing and should leave, the man kept coming. "Wow, this is a beautiful place," he said as he got closer. Roger ran to the main house to call the police. The Boot and Pete Penna were inside. The Boot said, "No, don't call the police; let him come up." Roger called anyway. The Livingston police arrived. It turned out the man was a door-to-door salesman. He was escorted off the property. A few weeks later Pete Penna, the caretaker of the farm, laughed about the incident and told Roger that the Boot wanted to shoot the man.[28]

CHAPTER 8

LOOSE LIPS

Listen and hear what I advise,
you who pursue the courtier's path,
if you don't capture Fortune fast,
she'll fret, she'll turn aside her face.
You have to keep your eyelids raised,
don't cringe before a threatening gaze,
ignore what other people say.
Don't worry whom you serve: Okay!
—*Matteo Maria Boiardo,* Orlando Innamorato, *320*

When the cat was let out of the bag, and the tapes were released, it probably came as no surprise to anyone, especially the Boot, that his soldier Little Pussy was caught talking behind his back, telling tales about a furnace on the farm. Pussy had a character flaw that was as big as the pink Cadillac convertible that he liked to cruise around in, top down, radio blasting, exuding the crude allure of a natural-born bully. Little Pussy couldn't control his mouth; it was constantly flapping. Unfortunately for him, the FBI seemed always to be listening. While most of the Boot's mob kept a very low profile, especially his older brother Big Pussy, who was quiet and deliberate, Little Pussy was a cop magnet who often effortlessly stumbled into range of one of their listening devices. When the FBI illegally wiretapped the office of Gyp DeCarlo at the Barn, his office in Mountainside, in 1961, a parade of hoodlums were caught on tape, but few were as entertaining, informative, and self-destructive as Little Pussy.[1]

On February 26, 1963, Little Pussy was recorded telling DeCarlo that Tony Boy was "a bad kid" and that the Boiardos were "weasels," and he called the Boot "the most treacherous . . . in the world."[2] And when the FBI bugged the plumbing company of Sam DeCavalcante in another part of the state from 1964 to 1965, Little Pussy again fell into their trap. "You oughta put him down," Pussy had the temerity to advise DeCavalcante about a fellow mobster named Lou Larasso. "Does this guy resent the moves you made or what? You're the boss! He ought not treat you like you're dirt."[3] Years later he was caught again on tape, chatting up Las Vegas police sergeant Philip Leone, boasting that he offered to eliminate Jimmy "the Weasel" Fratianno, a mob informer, for Tony "Pro" Provenzano, the man suspected of killing union leader Jimmy Hoffa: "That's what I said to Tony Pro," said Pussy. "I said, we'll whack him. I mean it. . . . We'll whack him right then. I said no problem."[4]

Little Pussy was an old-school wise guy, a stout little Caesar—five foot seven, his weight hovering around 175—who stomped about, bragging and blustering his way through the underworld. He had a taste for Rolexes, gold chains, and making a show of bringing out a wad of cash. When the Boot's daughter Rose and her friends won a new car in a raffle at Saint Lucy's church, Little Pussy pulled out a money clip and peeled off several thousand dollars on the spot and took the vehicle off their hands.[5] "Pussy Russo," said Kevin McCarthy, chief of the U.S. Organized Crime Strike Force, "was a figure from a bygone era, when mobsters could afford to be flamboyant."[6]

FBI files on Little Pussy show that he also blundered in chatting up the bureau. He once admitted to an agent that he was a bookmaker and then quickly backpedaled and apologized for his career choice, explaining that persistent stomach troubles and back injuries made it impossible for him to get a regular job. Another obstacle to legitimate employment, not mentioned by Little Pussy to investigators, was the fact that he was essentially illiterate; he could barely read or write and depended on others to take dictation. "Write it down and everything," he told a corrupt Las Vegas cop in a conversation taped by the FBI. "I don't write. I don't know how to spell or nothing. Yeah, write it down on one of my cards."[7]

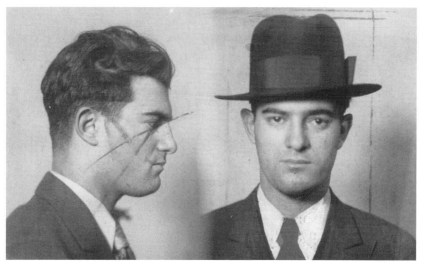

Mugshot of John "Big Pussy" Russo, arrested for the murder of Joseph Rosso, 1929. (FROM THE COLLECTIONS OF NEWARK PUBLIC LIBRARY)

The Boot incarcerated on a concealed-weapons conviction after the attempt on his life. He is at Crosswicks penal farm, where he allegedly threw wine and rum parties with other inmates, 1931–1932. (COURTESY ROSE HANOS)

The Boot at Crosswicks penal farm, winter of 1931–1932. (COURTESY ROSE HANOS)

The Boot toasts Joe DiMaggio at the Vittorio Castle, June 29, 1939. Seated at the table left to right: unknown, DiMaggio, the Boot, Peanuts Ceres; standing left to right: Jerry Spatola, Tony Boy. (FROM THE COLLECTIONS OF NEWARK PUBLIC LIBRARY)

The Boot and friend Luigi on a boat trip, circa 1936. (COURTESY ROGER HANOS)

The Boot marries off his fourth child, Rose, September 29, 1943. (COURTESY ROSE HANOS)

Tony Boy on the town with his friends, at the Chanticleer, Millburn, 1943. Left to right: Mr. and Mrs. Agoglia; Tony Boy and girlfriend Helen; Rose and Turk Hanos. (COURTESY ROSE HANOS)

WEDDING DINNER OF MR. & MRS. ARGER HANOS
AT VITTORIO CASTLE NEWARK N.V. SEPT. 29, 1943.

Big shots at the Vittorio Castle for the wedding reception of Roger's parents, Rose and Arger "Turk" Hanos, September 29, 1943. At the front table, clockwise: Joe "Doc" Stacher (back of head only); Mr. and Mrs. Sam Katz; Jerry Catena and Kay, his wife; Mary and Longy Zwillman; Carmine Battaglia, a capo and associate of Catena's; Joe Stassi, aka Joe Rogers, who claimed the Boot, Longy, and DeCarlo planned and executed the hit on Dutch Schultz at the Chop House in Newark. The Boot stands with the bride at the far back of the room on the right next to a potted plant; Tony Boy stands in uniform on the left near the doorway. (COURTESY ROSE HANOS)

Richie the Boot, circa 1944.
(COURTESY ROSE HANOS)

Tony Boy in uniform with his
proud papa, the Boot, at the
Vittorio Castle, circa 1944.
(COURTESY ROSE HANOS)

The Boot rides Chief, his prize stallion, on the farm, circa 1948. (COURTESY ROSE HANOS)

The Boot and grandchildren on the farm, circa 1949. Left to right: Lillian Hanos LaMonica, Roger Hanos, Maurice Crescenzi, the Boot, and Tony Boy Boiardo in the background. (COURTESY ROSE HANOS)

The Boot's mansion, circa 1955. (COURTESY ROSE HANOS)

Marion, the Boot's mistress, with the Boot, Phyllis Balestro, and Rose Hanos at a bon voyage party; the Boot sent his daughters and his mistress on a whirlwind trip to Europe in 1954. (COURTESY ROSE HANOS)

Roger sits in the lap of bad-boy actor and part-time gangster George Raft at the Boot's mansion, 1956. (COURTESY ROSE HANOS)

Roger and his confirmation sponsor, John "Big Pussy" Russo, 1959. (COURTESY ROSE HANOS)

The Boot and fans at Sammy's Restaurant, Mendham, circa 1960. (COURTESY ROGER HANOS)

Reminiscing about the past, circa 1960. Left to right: Charlie "the Blade" Tourine, George Raft (back at the farm after being thrown out of Cuba by Fidel Castro), Rita Penna, Phyllis Boiardo Balestro. (COURTESY ROSE HANOS)

Tony Boy leaves court after a hearing on the Club Fremont incident, 1960. (FROM THE COLLECTIONS OF NEWARK PUBLIC LIBRARY)

A typical Sunday afternoon swim party for family and guests at the main pool on the farm, circa 1965. (COURTESY GERALDINE BRUNO)

Jersey Boys meet Jersey boys at Lillian Hanos's wedding, 1966. Left to right: Frankie Valli, John "Big Pussy" Russo, Tommy DeVito, the Boot. (COURTESY JANET HANOS)

The Boot and his Belgian shepherds on the farm, circa 1969. (COURTESY ROSE HANOS)

Richie the Boot and his girlfriend Edith Bencivengo at Roger's wedding, May 31, 1970. (COURTESY ROGER HANOS)

Angelo Chieppa and his wife, Eleanor, at Roger's wedding, May 31, 1970. (COURTESY ROGER HANOS)

The Boot tends to his tomatoes, circa 1974. (COURTESY GERALDINE BRUNO)

In the Godfather Garden with Richie the Boot, 1974. (COURTESY GERALDINE BRUNO)

Roger Hanos and his grandfather Richie the Boot toward the end of the Boot's life, 1982. (COURTESY JANET HANOS)

Roger Hanos at the Boot's grave in Holy Cross Cemetery, North Arlington, September 2008. (COURTESY ROGER HANOS)

Little Pussy was a public nuisance as well. Roger Hanos and his brother, Darrel, occasionally ate dinner at Little Pussy's Surf Club in Long Branch. Roger recalled that his grandfather's button-man would conduct meetings at a table in the restaurant, out in the open. One evening, Little Pussy noisily confronted a man sitting at the bar. "Pussy swore and cursed at him," said Hanos. "He accused the man of being an FBI agent and told him to get the fuck out. And he threw something at him."[8]

During Prohibition, Little Pussy's role in the Boiardo gang was minor; he was only a teenager. His father had died when he was six years old. He was thirteen years old when his older brother John went to jail for shooting John Rosso, and he was twenty when his oldest brother, Ralph, was executed by the gang. Little Pussy's first arrest occurred in 1940, when he was twenty-four years old, for a motor-vehicle violation—he was caught carrying falsified car-registration papers.[9] Until then he had stayed well under the radar of law enforcement, although he and his brother Big Pussy had already established a reputation as thieves.

But by the 1940s and 1950s, the Pussy brothers graduated from simple burglary and hijackings to loan-sharking, counterfeiting ration stamps, bookmaking, and running card games for the Boot in the First Ward. Ration-stamp scams were a moneymaker during the war years; the U.S. government issued stamps restricting the purchase of scarce goods such as sugar and gas. The stamps were as good as money, but easier to forge. Gangsters printed fake stamps and sold them or kept them for their own use, especially for sugar, which was used to make illicit alcohol. The stamps were also easily stolen and resold. Although the end of Prohibition made liquor legal, the war made booze scarce and expensive, allowing bootleggers to stay in business well beyond the glory days of the speakeasy by supplying cheap and plentiful homemade booze to fill a thirsty demand.

Because of his loyalty to the Boot and Tony Boy along with the respect he had gained within the Genovese family, Big Pussy assumed the role that his older brother, Ralph, once had as the Boot's lead lieutenant. Throughout his relationship with the Boot and Tony Boy, Big Pussy was the primary enforcer, bag man, and point person for the family's gambling, union-kickback, and casino-skim ventures. On the Boot's behalf he also worked with other mob-family bosses throughout New Jersey and New York. He frequently was dispatched to "iron out or settle mob gambling or business disputes."[10] He partnered in loan-sharking, gambling, and extortion with other mob leaders such Thomas Pecora, aka Timmy Murphy; Joe Paterno; Tony "Bananas" Caponigro; and Vincent Craporatta, aka Jimmy Sinatra.

According to the FBI, Craporatta, a Bruno family associate, and Big Pussy ran several gambling operations, primarily bookmaking, lottery, and crap games in the Ocean County area.[11] Their Jersey Shore bookie and gaming set-ups took place at J.P.'s Tavern and Sharpe's Lodge in Lakewood. He also continued to play a role in moving stolen property with his trusted underling and strong-arm man Anthony DeVingo, who operated a legitimate store called the Big Deal Outlet.

In 1964, Big Pussy became part owner of Toppeta Motor Car Sales in Newark. Although the dealership appeared to function as a mob meeting place, legitimate business also took place there, and Big Pussy apparently was a good car salesman; Chrysler rewarded him with a junket to Mexico City in 1965, and the vacation was no mere weekend boondoggle: he spent an entire month south of the border on the car manufacturer's dime.[12]

Up until the late 1970s, Tony Bananas and Big Pussy, with the Boot's oversight, managed several gambling ventures in key territories in the Caribbean, New York, and New Jersey. Bananas was known for his arrogance, violent temper, and his ability to carry out cold-blooded hits. He and his brother-in-law, Alfred Salerno, were also involved with the Boot in the illegal alcohol racket well after Prohibition ended. Many years later, on April 18, 1980, Bananas, who eventually became the Bruno family consigliere, was found shot, stabbed, and beaten to death in a body bag in the trunk of a car in the Bronx. His killers stuffed $300 in his mouth and his rectum, indicating that he was greedy. His brother-in-law, Salerno, was found executed nearby. These murders allegedly occurred as a result of

Bananas's involvement in the unsanctioned execution of Angelo Bruno, Philly's top mob boss, on March 21, 1980. It was reported that Bananas ordered the shotgun death of Bruno while Bruno was sitting in his car.[13]

After he got out of jail on the Rosso murder rap, Big Pussy managed to avoid any major problems with law enforcement. He used his underlings wisely and discreetly when carrying out his work for the Boot. His right-hand enforcer was Anthony DeVingo, who grew up in the First Ward in a strict Catholic environment with his eighteen siblings. Despite his religious background, DeVingo was a quick student of crime, mentored by Big Pussy in the fine art of swag procurement, strong-arm enforcement, and murder. DeVingo was an unorthodox mobster, even by Boiardo-gang standards. He was a witty storyteller with a flamboyant streak; he turned his home in suburban Roseland, a sleepy town next to Livingston, into a showplace of kitschy statuary.[14] And he took his gang life home with him, enlisting his wife, Annette, in illegal activity. She handled his loan-shark records, a highly "unusual" situation according to prosecutors who busted the husband-and-wife team in 1984.[15]

The difference between Big Pussy and his younger brother, Little Pussy, was like night and day. Whereas Big Pussy worked quietly in the background, not attracting heat, Little Pussy was all foreground and an easy target for law enforcement. On July 5, 1945, when he was twenty-nine years old, Little Pussy was arrested and charged with operating one of the largest ration-stamp counterfeiting/distribution rings on the East Coast along with Settimo "Big Sam" Accardo, Domenic Jackson Amattucci, and several other top mobsters. He was found guilty and sentenced in 1947 to one year in jail and five years' probation. He served his time in the Federal Correction Institution in Danbury, Connecticut, and was released in February 1948.[16] When he got out, he found that his standing in the Boiardo mob was greatly diminished.

That same year the Boot had turned the day-to-day street leadership of his crew over to his son, Tony Boy, and the heir apparent did not trust Little Pussy. According to FBI informants, Tony Boy felt that his numbers

runners were mishandling gambling operations and holding out on payments to the family, and Little Pussy was apparently targeted as a scape-
goat for these problems.[17] With his father's blessing, Tony Boy took over
Little Pussy's loan-sharking and bookmaking operations. Powerless to do
or say anything, Little Pussy complained to his older brother, who was
deeply respected by the Boot and his son but was apparently unable to
intervene on his kid brother's behalf.[18]

Tensions between Tony Boy and Little Pussy escalated; in the late 1950s,
the Boot attempted to diffuse the tense situation. Vito Genovese's driver,
Vincent "the Chin" Gigante, was arrested and jailed for the attempted hit
on Frank Costello, leaving a vacancy. Becoming the driver of a don like
Vito Genovese was a plum position in the mob that often led to bigger and
better things within the organization. The Boot arranged for Little Pussy
to take the job, and almost immediately the newly minted chauffeur managed to rub Don Vito the wrong way. Little Pussy had whacked someone—
the "Jew," who was reputedly incinerated at the farm—without asking his
boss's permission:

[RUSSO:] So now what happens is this. After the guy is going up . . .
burning, I turn around. I get in the car. I bring it to Harrison and the
kid [Tony Boy] follows me. I think everything is alright. The following day, I get a call. Vito wants to see me. I go all the way to New York.
He says, "I know what happened." He says, "You dirty [expletive].
I oughta choke you in this car. That [expletive] Catena been down
to the people, come up in front of Albert [Anastasia] and Frank
[Costello] and everything and tell a story that they just got rid of
a Jew, and Pussy got rid of the car in Harrison and I make believe I
know what it's all about, [that] I gave the O.K. and everything—And
on that day you were near me." I said, "Wait a minute, Vito, I don't
know what you're talking about." I said, "Talk to the Boot. If you
don't want me to drive you no more, I'll get out and go home." I said,
"If you want to know anything, you go talk to the Boot."

DeCarlo: Did you tell him you had an O.K.?

Russo: Why, you know it. That's why I told him to see the Boot. I say
to the Boot, "What's this about [you] usin' me? I hear Jerry made a
remark about the hot car, the guy's body and everything about me
droppin' the car off. What did you say to Vito? I told Vito to come
and see you. I don't know what it's all about."[19]

According to Little Pussy, the Boot responded: "Don't worry, let me handle it.
They embarrassed Vito, and Jerry's putting the heat on him in front of Albert
and Frank."[20] Apparently, the Boot made everything right. Little Pussy wasn't
fired, although, in any case, his chauffeur gig was short-lived. Don Vito was
sent to prison on a drug-smuggling charge in 1959 and never returned.

Little Pussy was then dispatched to North Miami to handle the Boot's
growing gambling operations in Florida. The pugnacious soldier thrived in
Florida; he set up extensive gambling interests in North Bay Village, Palm
Beach, and throughout the Miami area. Bookmakers and numbers opera-
tors in Miami paid him for protection. According to an FBI informant,
Charles Tourine, aka Charlie the Blade, and Little Pussy operated gam-
bling concessions at Harbor Spas in Miami, the Mayflower Hotel in Palm
Beach, and the Play Lounge in Miami. Pussy also had a financial interest in
Ciro's Restaurant in North Miami Beach, a popular mob hangout.[21]

In Florida, Little Pussy associated with Santo Trafficante Jr., the mob
boss based in Tampa. Although they discussed the possibility of organizing new gambling activities in the Miami area, Trafficante ultimately nixed
the idea; he felt the move would generate too much heat. Possibly as a
result of the breakdown in these negotiations, Little Pussy got involved
in a violent argument with Trafficante's attorney at the celebrity table at
Dean Martin's restaurant, North Bay Village, in Miami in March 1969.
Little Pussy was drunk and unruly. A fight broke out, and Trafficante and
another associate had to break it up.[22]

With the permission of Vito Genovese, who was directing affairs from
his prison cell, the Boot pushed for control of mob activities in the northern

half of the Jersey Shore and added the territory to Little Pussy's portfolio with the backing of Angelo "Gyp" DeCarlo, who also ran operations
in the beach towns. At the time, business was not booming at the Shore,
and the Boot was basically exiling Pussy to the mob equivalent of Siberia.
The Boot was becoming increasingly disturbed by Little Pussy's inability
to manage his affairs without attracting attention. Pussy, however, made
the most of the move and quickly consolidated gambling, loan-sharking,
political protection, union influence, vending-machine distribution, and
construction contracts in Monmouth and Ocean counties. DeCarlo took
a 50 percent cut of Russo's Shore operations, and the Boot took another
25 percent, leaving Little Pussy with the remaining 25 percent, an arrangement that frustrated him and caused more strains within the crew.[23]

At the Shore, Pussy lived up to his extravagant reputation, buying a
house at 17 Monmouth Drive in Deal, a block away from the ocean in
the most desirable section of a very exclusive resort town. The FBI estimated that the house cost Russo between $85,000 and $90,000. (The
4,000-square-foot home still stands on a 25,500-square-foot lot and is valued today at approximately $3.5 million.) He became a partner in Donato
Construction Company in Red Bank and invested in a drugstore, race
horses, the Green Grove Manor, the Surf Club, and the Paddock Lounge.
He held interests in the Piano Bar, Squires Pub, Joseph's Restaurant, the
Adventure Hotel, and the Harbor Island Spa, all of which were in Long
Branch. The spa was an exclusive health and diet resort catering to an
affluent clientele; Jackie Gleason and standup comedian Jack E. Leonard
were frequent guests.[24] While establishing his beachhead at the Shore, Little Pussy commuted to Florida and continued to take care of the Boot's
interests there.

But the man who became known as the Boss of the Jersey Shore was
disgruntled and didn't hesitate to make his feelings known, especially his
contempt for the spoiled heir apparent. When Gyp DeCarlo remarked to
Little Pussy, in conversations taped at the Barn, that Tony Boy had been
aware of the mob's killings since the age of fourteen, Little Pussy said that

he would like to see the kid "get hit." Gyp suggested that could happen once the Boot passed away. He also gossiped with Little Pussy about Tony Boy's close relationship to Jerry Catena. According to Gyp, Catena never trusted the Boiardos, and there was a mutual loathing between Catena and Tony Boy despite the fact that on the surface they appeared to be the best of friends. "I don't get the picture between the kid and Jerry," said Little Pussy. "I know Jerry don't like this kid, and he don't like Jerry." Gyp explained that Catena had told him he was "doing it for a reason." The Boot had asked Catena to keep his son close. "This old man is afraid of dyin' for what might happen to his kid," Catena explained to Gyp.[25]

Little Pussy's loose lips also helped confirm FBI suspicions that the Boot was involved in the disappearance of Anthony Strollo, aka Tony Bender, a New York capo under Genovese who lived in Fort Lee, New Jersey, and controlled bars and nightclubs on New York's East Side and in Greenwich Village. Strollo was a chameleon capo who gave his allegiance to the highest bidder. He started working with Salvatore Maranzano, defected to Luciano, then to Genovese, then to Costello, and back to Genovese, for whom he became underboss for several decades. Finally, he switched one more time, joining a conspiracy of big names—Luciano, Meyer Lansky, Carlo Gambino, and Costello—who believed the powerful Don Vito was running amok and had to be taken down. The conspirators successfully framed Genovese on the petty drug charge that put him in prison but did not put him out of business. The ever-resilient Don Vito ran his mob through Catena, the Boot, and others from his prison cell. It was from there that he gave orders to eliminate his Judas, Tony Bender.[26]

Bender left his Fort Lee home on the morning of April 8, 1962, telling his wife he'd return shortly. He never did. A year later, Little Pussy discussed Strollo's fate with Gyp, recalling a conversation he had with Sam "Momo" Giancana, then the Mafia boss of Chicago, about a meeting Giancana had had with the Boot. Giancana had been chiding the seventy-nine-year-old patriarch, questioning his crew's relevance, asking whether he or Little Pussy had killed anyone lately. According to Little Pussy, the Boot

responded by unequivocally claiming that he had personally killed Tony
Bender. Based on the conversation between Gyp and Little Pussy, the FBI
concluded, "Apparently Boiardo tried to give the impression that he alone
was responsible for Bender's death."[27]

At the time of the release of the DeCavalcante and DeCarlo tapes in the
summer of 1969, the Boiardo gang and friends were on the ropes. DeCavalcante was indicted for conspiracy to operate an interstate numbers game
and was awaiting trial in federal court on an extortion indictment. Tony
Boy was awaiting trial on federal charges relating to a corruption scandal
that ensnared the mayor of Newark, Hugh Addonizio, and the city council.
The Boot, eighty years old, was appealing a conviction on gambling and
conspiracy charges and was facing a three-year prison term. Gyp DeCarlo,
who was suffering from cancer, began serving a twelve-year prison sentence for extortion.

Little Pussy, meanwhile, was in Trenton prison, ironically, for refusing
to talk; he would not answer questions at a state grand jury hearing about
corruption and racketeering in Monmouth County. He also was found
guilty of perjury for lying to the state commission investigating corruption
in Long Branch. After filing an unsuccessful appeal, he began serving his
three-to-five-year sentence the following March.

It was fortunate for Little Pussy that he was already safely behind bars
when the DeCarlo and DeCavalcante tapes were released to the public. The
recordings exposed Sam, Gyp, and Little Pussy. Gyp seemed to have had a
premonition that trouble was in the air; he didn't know he was being taped,
but perhaps he had a sixth sense that for some reason he might be summoned to a barbecue at the farm. He wasn't afraid, of course, or so he said:

DeCarlo: If he [Boiardo] told me to meet him up there, I'd walk right
in. I don't take nobody with me.
Russo: Oh, don't do that!
DeCarlo: The hell with him!
Russo: Where, at the farm?

DeCarlo: Yeah, if he ever takes me, him and his son is dead the same day.

Russo: What good is that? No use going like a moron.

DeCarlo: They don't kill people when they know they ain't gonna get away with it. If I don't come back—don't Si [an associate] and them know where I went?

Russo: So, what's the difference? You're dead. Take somebody up with you.[28]

Realistically, Gyp had nothing to worry about; he was a capo. Little Pussy, however, was vulnerable; he was simply a lieutenant. The only thing more damning for a soldier than to be caught trash-talking his capo was turning into a rat, informing on his boss and the family. Little Pussy was many bad things, but he was not a snitch, and that may have saved him too, for a little while.

CHAPTER 9

THAT OLD GANG OF MINE

*I don't hold any grudges. Every person has a job to do. Just using a hypo-
thetical case, just hypothetical, if you were a crook you should be good at it.
If you were a policeman it would be your job to catch the crook. . . . I'm as
honest as anyone in the world, or maybe, in half the world.*
                                                    —Richie "the Boot" Boiardo[1]

The Boot was a habitual early riser, even at an age when most men would
prefer to sleep in. Every morning as the first rays of the sun touched the
highest spires and gargoyles of the big house on his Livingston estate, the
seventy-seven-year-old don slid behind the wheel of a shiny black Plym-
outh, drove down a private five-hundred-foot roadway past two sets of
gates, the last adorned with armored knights bearing the family crest, and
cruised fifteen miles through the suburbs to Newark. Members of his crew
met with him, engaged in casual conversation, and carried grocery bags
and boxes to his car.

On February 3, 1967, three IRS agents who had been tailing the Boot
cornered the old man as he pulled out of the parking lot of a luncheonette
on Roseville Avenue. They searched him and found in his pocket a wad of
$2,500 in small denominations wrapped in brown paper and tied tightly
with string—apparently the Boot's share of a day's take from one small
pit stop in a far-reaching illegal lottery, horse-bookmaking, and sports-
gambling network that grossed $20 million annually and was at the time
the largest gambling operation in New Jersey. The lottery and bookmaking operation also was transmitted through a wire service to Florida, which
made it a federal case. Over the next few days, more incriminating evidence

was picked up in a coordinated sweep by thirty-six IRS intelligence agents who raided storefronts, social clubs, and apartments in Newark, Bloomfield, East Orange, Belleville, and North Arlington; they netted large quantities of "cut cards," horse and lottery bet slips, adding machines with tapes, recap sheets used to compute the day's action, along with suitcases full of brown manila envelopes, petty cash, and vials of aspirin. The aspirin, deemed immaterial by prosecutors, was not submitted as evidence.[2]

"I was shopping on the street and they picked me up for nothing," the Boot said to reporters, explaining that he was buying meat and vegetables. "I never gambled in my life. How can they make that kind of charge? No cards, no dice, nothing. I don't know how they can make a charge without catching you gambling."[3] At his arraignment, the Boot described his occupation as a security guard: "Speaking in a low voice with a slight accent, Boiardo said he served as a watchman a couple of hours a day at private garages in Verona and Newark. Asked the addresses of the garages, Boiardo said he could not remember."[4]

Much of the intelligence behind the raids came from IRS agent Dominic M. Germano, who infiltrated the gang by masquerading as a restaurant waiter. He gained the Boiardo crew's confidence by socializing at the small Roseville Avenue luncheonette, the gambling ring's headquarters, and making regular small bets. The unassuming waiter became fast friends with Joseph Cipriano, one of the Boot's crewmembers. In passing conversation, Cipriano confided that "Boiardo was the big boy, the boss" in charge of the lottery, and was considered the "boss of the Eastern seaboard."[5] "Boiardo could have a guy knocked off," Cipriano bragged to the agent.[6]

The Boot and eighteen of his underlings were indicted for operating an illegal gambling ring that "had more than four hundred runners whose average action was thirty thousand dollars per year."[7] Also arrested was Andy Gerardo, who would later become the Boot's key lieutenant after the death of Big Pussy in 1978, and an associate named Angelo Sica. At its height, the operation averaged about $32,000 a day in gambling transactions from the First Ward alone. "Gambling in Newark is said to provide the mob with fifty million to one hundred million dollars a year according to Essex County officials," the *New York Times* reported in 1964. "But . . . the big action . . . involving loan sharking, numbers rackets, union racketeering, sports and horse race betting, narcotics . . . funnels close to one billion" to the northern New Jersey organized-crime groups.[8] Numbers banks relied on the Boot to bail them out when their gambling operations took a heavy hit from payouts to winners. In one instance, the Boot bankrolled a $100,000 cash deficit on a football pool.[9] The raid concluded an IRS surveillance of about six months. Prosecuting U.S. Attorney David M. Satz Jr. crowed that it was "among the most significant raids ever made in the United States."[10]

At the same time, Tony Boy, who was very ill with stomach ulcers, was being heavily monitored by law enforcement. Also, several informants who were very close to the Boiardos began leaking information to the FBI; the most damaging source was Angelo Chieppa, who had been an associate of the Boot for over thirty years. The gambling indictments, betrayals, and ongoing pressure from law enforcement chipped away at the Boiardo family's ability to control an extensive network of criminal enterprises and created an opening for other crews, crime families, and unaffiliated minority gangs to make inroads.

In a few neighborhoods, the Boot faced a new and different kind of turf battle. In the summer of 1968, one year after the Newark race riots, the Boot "discussed the Negro question in Newark" with an unnamed associate who was supplying information to the FBI. The informant met the Boot on his estate and described the patriarch as being in poor health; he lost his balance several times and dragged his feet when he walked. "His hair has grown to unusual proportions and he had a few days' growth of beard," the informant observed.[11]

The Boot was in a cranky mood. He "was critical of the politicians who were allowing the Negroes to loot the various cities while instructing the police not to interfere." The Boot was concerned that the unrest was affecting his business. Black-run gambling operations were spreading throughout the black neighborhoods. Black numbers runners working for him were beaten up and shot. "The negroes want these Negro runners to give the work to them rather than give it to the whites," the Boot said, complaining that no one was doing anything "because everyone is afraid to do anything about the colored."[12] He suspected that "this Negro group must have been reading books about the Mafia because they have organized themselves like the Mafia."[13]

Harold McLeod, a gambler who "was tied up with the colored gambling element,"[14] was involved in a string of holdups of Tony Boy's black-run numbers operations. McLeod and two stickup men associated with Charlie Graves, an independent, "well-known Negro hoodlum in Newark," robbed a Boiardo numbers bank of $18,000 and a numbers runner of $3,500 dollars. McLeod was shot-gunned to death, according to an FBI informant, by "someone from Tony Boy's mob."[15]

When some of the Boot's white numbers people in downtown Newark "were having a problem with the Negroes in that area," they came to him for assistance in solving their problem. The Boot advised his men that unless they were ready to "go in there and shoot," they "should go ahead and give them the numbers."[16] According to another FBI informant, the Boot and some of his fellow capos were gradually learning to adjust to the times. They understood that unless they accommodated this new wave of activity in the black neighborhoods, "the people now involved in these operations will be forced into other areas in order to make a living." They believed that bookmakers in the black neighborhoods were largely uneducated and unskilled and that running gambling operations was their sole means of earning a decent living. Since they knew "nothing else," if they were pushed out they would "probably turn to more violent crimes, such as kidnappings, bank robberies, and the like, in order to make a living."[17] The Boot, a practical leader, clearly saw the writing on the wall; he instructed his men that black operators "should be allowed to take over the numbers in the Negro community provided that they only take action from the Negro numbers players and not the whites."[18]

The Boot and his fellow gang lords faced many challenges as the complexion of Newark and other Jersey cities dramatically changed. An article that appeared a few years later in the *New York Times* discussed these challenges, reporting that numbers runners working for the Boot in the black lower Vailsburg and North Newark sections of Newark—once white strongholds—were increasingly being robbed and kidnapped by street gangs. After four black men working for the Mafia were shot and killed, law-enforcement officials believed an arrangement was made that allowed a local black gang to assume control of gambling in those neighborhoods and to use the Boiardo organization for laying off bets and paying protection money for its police and political connections. Meanwhile, in Newark's South and Central wards a black gambling ring led by a woman, D'Alama Sutton, forty-nine years old, was allowed to operate freely, while a small black narcotics operation in Asbury Park was loaned money by a white loan shark connected to Little Pussy. Investigators believed this development at the Jersey Shore was especially significant, as years ago it was unheard-of for Mafia loan sharks to lend money to blacks engaged in legal or illegal activities. The *New York Times* article concluded that the Mafia had come to the realization that it was more practical for blacks rather than white men to be on the streets, running operations locally. These rackets were just too lucrative for the mob to jeopardize over a matter of principle—and race; the white racketeers decided to stay one step ahead of the competition and became equal-opportunity employers well before the federal government enacted the Equal Opportunity Employment Act of 1972.[19]

Mob tolerance and coexistence with these emerging gambling rackets marked the beginnings of black organized crime in Newark. A few years later, in 1975, black drug dealers like Frank Lucas of Harlem and his brothers would establish the Country Boys crew in Newark to distribute heroin, paving the way for greater organization and self-sufficiency among black gangsters.[20]

The Boiardo gang, meanwhile, had other pressing and immediate issues to contend with. The Hughes Commission, launched by

Governor Richard J. Hughes to investigate the causes of Newark's race riots of 1967, blamed the unrest on Newark residents' "pervasive feeling of corruption."[21] FBI and newspaper revelations regarding illicit mob gambling and influence in Newark brought tremendous pressure on government officials who were suspected of aiding and abetting organized crime. The hammer came down hard on Newark Police Director Dominic Spina, who had been placed in his position through the influence of the Boot, DeCarlo, and Catena. When a county grand jury that was investigating corruption issued subpoenas in 1965 to government officials, Tony Boy and Eugene Catena, in a discussion taped by the FBI, expressed misgivings about Spina: "they felt that he may turn on those who were paying him."[22] In February 1968, under pressure from the Hughes Commission, Mayor Hugh Addonizio set up a special gambling squad that was disbanded within two months by Spina because of an alleged manpower shortage.

In May 1968, another special grand jury was convened to investigate Newark corruption. Spina was indicted two months later, accused of not enforcing the state's gambling law and "of having deliberately overlooked a 'vast network of crime at his feet.'"[23] Witnesses testified to the grand jury that Newark police were observed delivering gambling slips to mob banks. Spina submitted his resignation, but Addonizio turned it down.

Spina, who started his career as a street cop walking a Newark beat in 1933, turned out to be a rogue operator who worked with his Mafia overlords but also acted independently, setting up his own gambling network with the collusion of officers in the police department.[24] His operations competed directly with those of the mob, which did not appreciate the rivalry. On November 23, 1962, an urgent radiogram from the Newark FBI office to the home office in Washington quoted Eugene Catena grumbling that the "Newark police director is well on his way to becoming 'the worst hood' in this area. Gene complained that [name redacted] is shaking down every gambler in Newark . . . and meeting personally with the most prominent hoods in the area to arrange working agreements."[25] In a taped conversation, a mob-connected bar owner complained about the increase in shakedowns of tavern owners for alleged liquor-license violations by city police captains who routinely sent personal drivers to pick up collections, which ranged from $800 to $1,000 a pop. Cops were selling tavern "routes" for as much as $10,000.[26]

Three days before Spina was indicted a shotgun blast "ripped through his living room window, missing him only because he leaned forward at that instant to pet his dog."[27] Although Spina attributed this drive-by to the "enmity and hatred of the lawless element," suggesting that the attempt on his life was a result of his tough stance on street crime, outside agitators, and black militants, the FBI believed it was actually a poorly executed mob hit.[28] An informant reported to law enforcement that before the attack an emergency mob meeting had been held in the back room of DaVinci's Restaurant in Newark; it was attended by Tony Boy, Andrew Gerardo, Vincent "Jimo" Calabrese, Angelo Sica, Toby Boyd, and a man named Al or Allen who was described as an associate of Walter Van Riper, a former New Jersey deputy attorney who was Spina's lawyer. The Boot apparently wasn't able to attend because it was held too late at night.

> The informant advised that the hoodlum element was very upset about the impending indictment of Spina because of the effect it may have on their illegal activities, as well as the fact that he understands that Spina had been on their payroll for several years. The informant also advised that concern had been expressed since some of the group attending the meeting had also been indicted by the Essex Grand Jury for gambling violations. The informant advised that it is his understanding that the purpose of the meeting had been to discuss what course of action should be taken with regard to Spina's indictment and the effect the indictment would have on the hoodlum element's illegal activities. He also advised that Spina was looking for a big bundle between now and the time of his trial.[29]

After the attempt on his life, Spina telephoned Gerardo and requested that $100,000 in cash be delivered to him by the afternoon of August 1, 1968. The payment appeared to be hush money. According to the FBI informant, the cash was delivered.[30] It turned out not to be necessary; a week later Spina was acquitted by the trial judge because of lack of evidence. He was never forced to testify against his mob friends. "There is no proof that the defendant ever requested or suggested that any subordinate desist from enforcement of the gambling laws, and there is no proof that he with knowledge of gambling at a specific location withheld appropriate police action."[31]

Richie the Boot and his cohorts also narrowly escaped federal charges in the gambling case because of a legal technicality. A federal conviction hinged on the mobsters' failure to register as gamblers and to purchase a fifty-dollar tax stamp. The registration and stamp law had been ruled unconstitutional by the U.S Supreme Court because it violated the federal self- incrimination statute. However, Essex County and the State of New Jersey were permitted to proceed and prosecute using federal evidence and witnesses. The state trial, presided over by Superior Court Judge Ralph L. Fusco, lasted two months, with the jury spending some sixty hours deliberating over a six-day period.

On April 28, 1968, all the defendants were found guilty. When issuing the sentences Judge Fusco stated that "this case cost [the IRS] more money than the entire budget for the year to break up this mob. Even after they were caught they wouldn't tell what was going on."[32] The defendants received one- to three-year sentences with fines and later appealed the decision.

On February 17, 1970, the state police raided another Essex County numbers ring, a $15 million-a-year business that was also alleged to be one of the Boot's operations, though he was never charged.[33] Joseph Sarrecchia, a Boot underling who was out on appeal for a 1969 gambling conviction, was rearrested in this new case, and his bail was revoked.[34] At the time, the FBI also began pursuing leads into the Boot's loan-shark business, which was taking in over a million dollars a year. Apparently, Essex County organized-crime factions pooled their monies to create a fund of half a million dollars for their sixty or so representatives to lend out at exorbitant rates.[35]

All legal appeals by the Boot and his associates in the 1969 state conviction were eventually tossed out; the aging crime lord attributed this failure to bad press. According to an FBI source, "Boiardo felt that the recent disclosure of the taped conversations of Angelo 'Gyp' De Carlo and his associates indicate that 'some guys talk too much.'"[36]

Although the Boot's federal criminal case was dismissed on the tax-stamp technicality, his conviction on state charges allowed the IRS to place a lien on his extravagant Livingston estate in the amount of $527,863.59. Anticipating the IRS lien, the Boot had squirreled away his expensive antiques, paintings, and home furnishings in the house of his aide Angelo Chieppa.[37] A "bespectacled" IRS agent accompanied by two armed Livingston police officers showed up at the farm and demanded payment of the lien. "Five thousand dollars?" the Boot cagily asked, feigning deafness. When the IRS agent corrected him, announcing the six-figure total, the Boot said he didn't have that much. The IRS subsequently seized more than half the acreage of his property and put it up for auction.[38]

At the time rumors circulated that law-enforcement authorities might conduct a "dig" at the estate. An FBI informant stated that Livingston police officials had asked the Boot to allow them to inspect the incinerator on his property. "Boiardo told them they could if they so wanted but he would like about three days' notice so that he could 'clear the bones and skulls' from the incinerator."[39] The New York Daily News reported that a U.S. attorney general "refused to comment on whether his office would dig into a suspected crematorium at the baronial estate. . . . Federal sources indicated that it was unlikely because it now is five years since the incinerator was publicized as the disposal instrument for gangland rubout victims, and any possible evidence would have been removed."[40] A follow-up New York Daily News story appeared to contradict the previous story: "The feds are planning to do a little excavating of their own, just in case some kinds of bones are buried there."[41] The stories and innuendos amounted to nothing. A forensic examination of the property was never conducted by federal, state, or local officials.

After being convicted on criminal charges for the first time in almost forty years, the Boot was shipped off to Leesburg State Prison on October 9, 1970, to serve a 2½- to 3-year sentence. The front page of the *Star-Ledger* carried a picture of the Boot sitting in a paddy wagon while his crew members were being loaded up; the caption read, "That old gang of mine." He insisted, as he was being led off, that he was not a criminal, that he was simply "an avid gardener and proud grandfather." When a reporter asked how he felt about going to prison, the Boot glibly replied, "I've been all over the country," and he sneered at his handcuffs, dismissing them as mere "Indian bracelets."[42]

The Boot was incarcerated in a familiar place, Leesburg, and there he resumed his old habits. "His new assignment at the prison is that of gardener," an FBI report noted. "[He] has planted many of the flowers in and around the newly built prison."[43] The Boot was released on parole one year later. He was eighty-one years old.

CHAPTER 10

CAUSE FOR INDICTMENT

Thunder and lightning, bolts and forks,
tempest and storm clouds, rain, and wind
filled up the sky and plains and hills.
The fury grew; it never stopped.
The poison serpent and its brood,
all creatures that inhabit forests—
foxes and doves—were struck by hail,
defenseless all against the gale.

—*Matteo Maria Boiardo,* Orlando Innamorato, *320*

Tony Boy Boiardo lived in a comfortable split-level home in Essex Fells, a leafy suburb. He was a family man, father of two daughters and a son, and a prosperous executive at Valentine Electric, one of the state's largest building contractors. Tony Boy's declared income in 1966 was $264,053, and his firm raked in $11 million from work for the municipal housing authority, the city, the county (a courthouse complex), and the federal government, as well as for the thirty-story Gateway office building next to Penn Central Station in Newark.[1] Tony Boy was an apparent model citizen who was described by Fells Police Chief Fred Rohnstock as "ordinary." "The Boiardos," said a neighbor, "have never said 'boo' to anybody."[2]

But at the end of the sixties, right before Christmas 1969, as the troubled decade of love began to turn a hard corner, Tony Boy and Newark's bull-necked mayor Hugh Addonizio emerged as the principal players in a soap opera of racketeering, extortion, and murder that played out on the front pages of big-city papers across the country. The *New York Times* was giddy about the Addonizio case, "the most graphic study in American criminal annals of the complete subversion of a city . . . and, indeed, of much of a state . . . by the money and muscle of the underworld," reported the paper in a Sunday magazine cover story in February 1970.[3] A Justice Department official commented to the *New York Times*, "We found a city of impacted rackets. At some point, the rackets grew from public nuisance to an alligator devouring the city."[4]

William Brennan 3rd, a young assistant state attorney general at the time and the son of Associate Justice of the U.S. Supreme Court William J. Brennan Jr., told the press that the Mafia had infiltrated "every facet of public life in the state except the church." He was famous at the time for a public outburst that was widely quoted: "Yes! Virginia, there is a Mafia in New Jersey," he said. "And it is more dangerous than any other calamity facing the United States."[5]

Addonizio, Tony Boy, and thirteen accomplices, including Newark city council members, were indicted for raking in millions in kickbacks for municipal construction projects, many of which employed Tony Boy's "legit" company Valentine Electric and other mob-infested businesses. Although Addonizio was called "the Pope" by his mob cohorts, it was Tony Boy who, according to a star witness at the trials, was "the real boss of Newark" and who, according to court testimony, personally threatened to break the legs of a recalcitrant contractor.[6] Tony Boy, the Boot, and their cronies were at the center of a deeply embedded ring of mobsters, gamblers, contractors, government officials, and hit men whose decades-long plunder of the city of Newark was said to have had an underlying effect on the bloody race riots of 1967 and the near total financial and social collapse of the city, which to this day has yet to fully recover.

Very much like Tony Soprano of the fictional HBO program *The Sopranos*, Tony Boy Boiardo had issues. He struggled to cope with the pressures of raising a conventional middle-class family in a profession that was totally unconventional, and deadly. And so he got help. Although it was never reported or confirmed then, rumor had it he was seeing a shrink. The only other Cosa Nostra capo known for taking to the couch was dapper Frank Costello, who admitted seeing a socially connected Park Avenue shrink named Robert Hoffman.[7]

The rumors about Tony, it turns out, were not rumors. Tony Boy was the patient of a prominent West Orange psychiatrist. William Furst was a war hero, a combat doctor, a major with the Seventy-fifth Infantry Division in World War II; he saw action in the Battle of the Bulge. "The soldiers coming off the battlefield had shell-shock, what we now call post-traumatic stress syndrome," Henry Furst, son of the late William Furst, explained. "He was the battalion psychiatrist, with about twenty-five thousand patients."[8]

Furst's experience with traumatized soldiers on the bloody battlefields of Europe inspired him to pioneer the practice of group, or self-help, therapy in psychiatry once he returned to the States. His expertise also made him eminently qualified to handle the traumas of the new kind of soldier of the suburbs that was Tony Boy. "[My father] was very interested in drug therapy," said Henry Furst, who explained that his father's battlefield residency with combat troops led to experimentation in pharmacology. "You couldn't wait three and half years until an analyst came up with a breakthrough and dug up their repressed memory. You had to turn them around and get him back out into the battlefield."[9]

An informant who was close to Tony Boy told the FBI that the heir apparent was a workaholic: "He worked hard in his business, was an early riser and traveled frequently on business trips and unlike his father, the Boot, he was a worrier."[10] Tony Boy had much to fret about; unbeknownst to his neighbors and family members, his life was about to be turned upside down.

On December 10, 1969, Newark Mayor Hugh Addonizio appeared before a federal grand jury investigating corruption in the Essex County municipal government and was asked in open court if he knew Tony Boy Boiardo. Addonizio, who was described by a federal prosecutor as "a man of easy conscience and flabby pride,"[11] had until then refused to answer questions, invoking the Fifth Amendment, but he shocked the court when under pressure he finally replied, in a statement that was intended to be exculpating but instead became famously damaging: "I do know him, and my answer may tend to incriminate me." The judge sarcastically replied, "Well, I guess that disposes of that one."[12]

One week later, in Washington D.C., U.S. Attorney General John N. Mitchell, a Richard Nixon appointee, announced the federal indictments of Addonizio, Tony Boy, two other gangsters, one contractor, a judge, a lawyer, and eight other Newark politicians for extortion and income-tax evasion.[13] It was the culmination of a nineteen-month federal investigation that also netted fifty-five hoodlums who were charged with running a gambling ring in Jersey associated with Sam the Plumber.

Tony Boy was on the lam again, refusing to answer subpoenas to testify at the grand jury hearings that led to the indictments. U.S. deputy marshals and Treasury agents scoured the state and searched in Boca Raton, Florida, for the truant Mafioso. Although he was not in the courthouse during the grand jury hearings, his presence was felt as one witness after another testified about the "boss" and his influence in city hall.

The Boot meanwhile was preoccupied with his own troubles; he was appealing his conviction by an Essex County court for running a $20 million lottery ring. The Addonizio deal was Tony's show, and, like a true star, he showed up late to his party, building suspense until his arrival on the day of his arraignment at the Federal Court House in Newark a few days before Christmas, December 19, 1969. Tony Boy's appearance created a stir among spectators and press at the courthouse. The *Newark Evening News* and the *New York Times* both said he was "tanned and smiling," with the *News* describing his wardrobe as "a light blue, glen-plaid suit, white shirt, blue tie and polished black shoes." The *Times* described the same attire as "a gray suit with a light blue basket weave pattern." As for the tan, according to the *Newark Evening News*, Tony Boy told the press that he "had been under a sun lamp. However, it was reported he had been in Antigua in the West Indies in the past two weeks."[14]

Tony Boy and the other fourteen defendants, including the mayor, pleaded not guilty to the charges. They were all released on bail in the range of $10,000 to $25,000, with Tony Boy's the steepest at $50,000.

The trial started on June 2, 1970. Prosecuting attorneys Frederick Lacy and Herbert Stern filed a sealed motion several weeks later, requesting revocation of Tony Boy's bail, which was granted. Three witnesses had received death threats over the telephone—they were told they would be "killed by nine pm tonight" on June 25[15]—and the court received an anonymous tip that a government witness, Paul Anderson, who had been killed in a car accident on the way to the trial, had been forced off the road intentionally by another car.[16]

Paul Rigo, who was described by the *New York Times* as "a dapper slender man who uses a long cigarette holder and wears pancake makeup in the winter to look tanned," was the star witness in the Addonizio case.[17] Rigo owned a helicopter, an Oldwick estate with a helipad, and a chauffeur-driven limo, all paid for through lucrative contracts with the city of Newark, including, appropriately, a municipal sewer job. Rigo testified that Tony Boy demanded a 10 percent kickback on all his government construction jobs.[18]

"There are a lot of mouths to feed at City Hall," Boiardo had told Rigo. "I take care of the mayor, the council. I take care of anybody else that has to be taken care of down there."[19] When Rigo balked at the demand, Tony Boy barked: "You'll pay 10 percent and pay it in cash."[20] Rigo eventually cooperated, paying kickbacks for the privilege of working these jobs to Tony Boy, who funneled allotments to the mayor and the city council; on one occasion Rigo handed $14,000 in cash directly to Addonizio.[21]

Tony Boy decided to raise the cost of doing business with Newark, and when Rigo refused the payoff increases, Tony Boy threatened to break his legs. Rigo fled to Mexico and eventually wound up in Washington, singing to the Justice Department. Rigo testified that he was forced to pay $253,000 in kickbacks and was coerced into becoming a bagman delivering payoffs to Addonizio, Tony Boy, and others.[22] After agreeing to testify, Rigo was constantly threatened by Tony Boy's associates. "Keep your mouth shut and remember you have a pretty daughter in Suffolk," a hoodlum warned the contractor. One day Rigo found a note on the seat of his car: "This could have been a bomb. Keep your mouth shut."[23]

After testifying, Rigo lost his estate in Oldwick, his yacht, helicopter, and limo, and he took his family into seclusion, guarded by federal agents. He told a reporter who tracked him down that he had no regrets about testifying: "If we had not gotten free, they not only would have controlled our pocketbooks, they would have controlled my soul and the soul of my family," he told the reporter. "The only thing to do is what we did and hope for the best. If you die, you die." If he had to do it all over again, Rigo said, "I'd kick Boiardo in the teeth and run like hell."[24]

There were other canaries in the Addonizio case, including Irving Kantor, a mob accountant with a phony plumbing-supply company and a dummy bank account that was used for laundering kickbacks for the Boiardo gang. He had been stricken with Lou Gehrig's disease, losing the use of his arms and legs, and was barely able to speak. In a bizarre turn the trial was moved to an auditorium in a hospital where he was being treated. A crush of onlookers created pandemonium in the hospital, with patients pushing and shoving to get a glimpse of the star defendant, Tony Boy. "'Is that Tony?' asked a little man, tugging at the wrinkled sleeve of a fellow patient. 'I'll bet that's him I can tell. Hi'ya Tony Boy!' . . . The locked-in smile on [Tony Boy's] tanned face took in anyone and anything, drifting with random radiance on patients, doctors, nurses, attorneys, newsmen, fire extinguishers and exit signs."[25]

Kantor's voice was so weak the dying man had to mumble responses to questions to his wife, who sat beside his rolling hospital bed holding his hand, occasionally wiping his mouth with a tissue and interpreting his answers for the court. "His voice sound[ed] very much like a phonograph recording being played below volume, and two speeds lower than its intended revolution," the *Newark Evening News* reported.[26]

The judge and jury strained to hear Kantor's words, some of it so garbled it was impossible to believe that his wife understood. At one point the judge questioned Mrs. Kantor on her ability to act as interpreter and repeat his answers "without correction, omissions or embellishing."[27] She replied that she had no reason to misrepresent or falsify her husband's answers. She added that she knew her husband best and was the most qualified to interpret his responses accurately. When the judge asked Kantor, whose facial expressions were distorted and awkward, the identity of his boss, no interpreter was needed. He barked out loudly: "Tony Boy Boiardo!"[28]

Mario Gallo, an asphalt and concrete contractor and defendant in the case, also was scheduled to testify against "the Pope" and the "real boss" of Newark, but he never got that far. He was killed in a car crash after suffering a heart attack at the wheel. A mob killer known as Joey Black, who wrote the autobiography *Joey the Hitman: The Autobiography of a Killer* in 1973 with David Fisher, speculated that Gallo was whacked with "a new weapon. It's a certain type of gas that you spray in someone's face. Not only does it kill him immediately, it leaves the same aftereffects as a heart attack."[29] The FBI investigated Gallo's death and confirmed that it was an accident.

With his bail revoked, Tony Boy was sent to Somerset County jail. He told one of his co-defendants that his jail cell was "a real sweatbox."[30] Tony Boy was fifty-six years old, he had a history of ulcers and gall-bladder trouble, and his doctor informed the court that he had suffered a minor heart attack around the time of his indictment. On July 6, Tony Boy complained of shortness of breath and chest pains. It was another attack. He was hospitalized while federal prosecutors scrambled.

They were faced with a possible suspension of the five-week-old trial until the "Boss of Newark" recovered, or they could sever his case, continue with the case against the Pope and the others, and eventually retry Tony Boy. The court sent its own physician to report on Tony Boy's condition; the doctor confirmed a coronary occlusion, and the court granted a severance. After several weeks in a hospital, where he was held as a prisoner without bail and received visits only from his family, Tony Boy was freed on bail and sent home to recuperate in Essex Fells. By October his condition had worsened, and he checked into Montclair Community Hospital where he remained for almost a month.

Addonizio and four other defendants, including three council members, were meanwhile convicted of sixty-four counts of extortion and conspiracy. Addonizio had served two terms as mayor of Newark; he was a popular figure who attended baptisms, bar mitzvahs, and social events and supported black politicians, including his successor, Kenneth Gibson. He was a graduate of Saint Benedict's Prep School in Newark, where he was an all-state quarterback, and Fordham University, and he had served with the Sixtieth Infantry in North Africa, Sicily, and Normandy. After the war he was elected to Congress and served six terms before running for mayor of Newark.

A bulky man, balding, with dark eyes and bushy eyebrows, Addonizio was described as a "tough talking Democratic politician of the old school."[31] Even while on trial, Addonizio was in a run-off election for his third term against Gibson and Anthony Imperiale, a white-supremacist leader of the First Ward. Gibson won the election, and Addonizio was sentenced to ten years in prison and fined $25,000. Prosecutors cited his municipal administration as the first one in the United States to have been taken over by organized crime. He served sixty-two months and was released on parole. In the last few years of his life, Addonizio took up raising homing pigeons at his home in Rumson. He died on February 2, 1981, at the age of sixty-seven.[32]

Tony Boy lingered in ill health for years. The federal prosecutor, Fred Lacey, repeatedly attempted to get him back into court, but doctors determined he was too ill to stand trial. Tony Boy was frequently spotted playing golf, but for the most part he struggled with poor health for eight long years after the Addonizio trial. He receded into the shadows, no longer "the little man who talked big."[33]

Tony Boy finally passed away in Montclair Community Hospital at the age of sixty-three in 1978. The cause was listed as heart illness. His final resting spot is the Gate of Heaven Catholic Cemetery in East Hanover, New Jersey. He has a clean granite headstone, like all the others in this relatively new burial ground, and he is in familiar company: John "Big Pussy" Russo is buried close by, having died of cancer in 1978. Another First Warder, Peter Rodino, is in the Gate of Heaven, as is Hugh Addonizio.

Although devastated by the death of his son, the Boot soldiered on. His old cronies had passed away, mostly violently, but he continued to run rackets with a new generation of gangsters with names like Thomas "Pee Wee" DePhillips, Vincent "Skippy" Squatrito, and Anthony DeVingo.

CHAPTER 11

THE ITALIAN WAY

He grit his teeth. He shouted, "Traitor!
There is no way you can escape!
Four hours from now, or less, these walls
will fall before my sword, and I
will swiftly seize this citadel
and scatter it across the plain,
and I will massacre these men,
and I say you will die with them!"
                    —*Matteo Maria Boiardo,* Orlando Innamorato, *138*

Kenneth A. Gibson decisively beat Hugh Addonizio in a hard-fought runoff election and became the first black mayor of a major American city on June 16, 1970. Addonizio was under indictment along with Tony Boy Boiardo for corruption, and not surprisingly he lost the election. It was a long, racially explosive contest with Italians from Newark's North Ward, formerly the First Ward, led by Anthony Imperiale, a white militant councilman who ran in the race on a "law and order" platform, trading insults with black activists led by LeRoi Jones (Amiri Baraka), the poet and playwright who fantasized that the Gibson administration would "nationalize the city's institutions, as if it were liberated territory in *Zimbabwe* or *Angola.*"[1]

After the votes were counted, Gibson vowed to replace Newark Police Director Dominic Spina, who was implicated in the Addonizio case and was a friend of the Boot's mob. Gibson and his followers declared that the Mafia's services in Newark were no longer needed, and then the thirty-eight-year-old former City Housing Authority civil engineer did what any seasoned politician would do: he went on vacation, flying to the British West Indies, where the Boot and other mobsters held silent interests in most of the casinos, and the slots were rigged to favor the house with ninety-to-one odds.

According to an FBI informant who had furnished reliable information in the past, while Gibson was on his junket, the Boiardo crew hatched a strategy to reverse the outcome of the election in Newark. In an FBI memorandum dated June 19, 1970, the FBI Newark office described information received from an informant who "earlier today had been in the company of Boiardo mobsters Andy Gerardo and Nunzio Sica [Angelo's brother] who were discussing to bring one [name omitted] from California to murder the newly elected mayor of Newark, New Jersey, Kenneth A. Gibson." According to the memorandum, "a plot is being considered by a New Jersey racket element to murder Gibson and . . . should we receive any further information in this regard he will be so advised. This will enable mayor-elect Gibson to take necessary precautionary measures which would provide whatever protection he deems appropriate."[2]

On the same day, an FBI teletype reported that the informant overheard Gerardo and Sica talking about a gunman originally from Newark who lived in Beverly Hills and had been hired to "hit" the newly elected mayor of Newark: "The informant has been unable to obtain additional information concerning this matter but will remain alert to this situation and immediately report any new information or details. . . . Newark proposes to personally contact mayor elect Kenneth Gibson and advise him that the FBI has received information from one of its sources that the new mayor was 'to be hit.'"[3]

A Newark government official released a statement revealing the plot to the *Newark Star-Ledger*, which reported it at the time, but neither the government nor the Gibson campaign apparently was told who was behind the conspiracy. There was some speculation that the threat might have come from disgruntled supporters of Addonizio or Anthony Imperiale.[4] During the riots in 1967, Imperiale had led a band of armed white vigilantes through the streets of his neighborhood ranting "when the Black Panther comes the white hunter will be waiting."[5]

The FBI was never able to identify the alleged contract killer from Beverly Hills, and no one was arrested in connection with the plot. In the end, the Gibson episode may have been bluster, or perhaps the Boiardo crew, feeling the heat, simply called it off. Considering the Boiardo mob's predilection for murder and disappearing witnesses, it seems likely that the threat was real and that the FBI actually foiled an assassination attempt that would have had lasting repercussions.

The FBI had asked the Gibson camp not to reveal the agency as the source of the tip: "Gibson will be further advised that the FBI is continuing to check this information and therefore requests that Gibson must not identify the FBI to any one as the source of this information for fear of compromising the source."[6] They knew the Boot suspected one of his key lieutenants was talking to them. The Boot himself realized that someone close to him was spilling his guts to the feds, and his suspicions focused on Angelo "Chip" Chieppa, an overweight, balding, otherwise ordinary citizen of Essex County, who was one of the Boot's key bagmen.

According to an FBI report, "For some twenty years Richie Boiardo had suspected that Chieppa was an informant despite contrary opinions by some of Boiardo's close associates."[7] Chip was a long-time protégé of the Boot; they went all the way back to the old neighborhood. He was born September 23, 1919, the year that the Volstead Act was ratified, ushering in the age of Prohibition. His father, Antonio Chieppa, was a factory worker, and his mother, Giovannia Pucillo, was only eighteen when she gave birth to Chip.

Chip's father was a contemporary of the Boot and may have worked for the old man in some capacity, but it was his son who fell squarely into the patriarch's orbit at an early age. Chip was the same generation as Tony Boy Boiardo. The Boot kept his son off the street when he was growing up, and the two boys evidently did not spend time together. That would change.

Over the years, Chip held various legitimate jobs as a truck driver, gas-station manager, coal salesman, oil-company representative, and contractor, but these positions were a diversion. He thrived and prospered in the illegal booze trade and would boast that it was his "specialty." He bragged even to police that he was friends with every major bootlegger from Massachusetts to Philadelphia, New York, and New Jersey. He was so good at what he did that he kept plugging away at bootlegging long after the repeal of Prohibition.[8]

Chip knew how to put together an alky-cooker from scratch, planning and overseeing the construction of the still and managing production. He and a crew of twelve once assembled and operated a distillery on a five-hundred-acre estate known as Indian Hill Farms near Southfields in Orange County, New York. The massive operation pumped out one thousand gallons of 180-proof booze a day. The still was made of a copper column thirty inches in diameter with a seventy-five-horsepower high-pressure boiler and mash capacity of thirty-six thousand gallons. When the feds busted the joint in 1955, they claimed it had cheated the government of an estimated $18,000 a day in taxes. At the time the District Attorney's office said it was one of the largest post-Prohibition stills in existence.[9]

Prohibition was repealed in 1933, but this did not signal the end of bootlegging, especially for the Boot and his crew. Federal excise taxes on alcohol as high as ten dollars per gallon in 1952, coupled with high state and city taxes, kept legal liquor out of the reach of average consumers and made it difficult for bars and restaurants to make a decent profit, so many continued to buy raw, untaxed liquor in five-gallon cans from bootleggers; it was a brisk business in Jersey as late as the 1960s. The government lost considerable liquor revenue to these post-Prohibition stills and responded by stepping up raids.

The Boot's operations were aggressively targeted by federal agents and the state police; they hammered away at his empire, and luckless Chip always seemed to be there when the G-men came crashing through the door. His criminal rap sheet was long, beginning with his first clip at the age of twenty-one on November 11, 1940; he was charged with violating

Internal Revenue liquor-tax laws, fined $700, and placed on probation for five years. Almost every year thereafter for almost two decades Chip got nailed or served time or both. He was indicted for conspiring to run a still, possession of an unregistered still, operation of a still, engaging in the business of a distiller—the list goes on.

Chip had as many aliases as he had arrests: Angie, Ash, Martini, Little Angie Londos, Angie Cantapulo, James Cantapulo, James Cantelup, A. Marino, Angelo Marione, John Marione, A. Martini, A Martino, John Politano, Joseph Rotundo. He served time in the county jail in Flemington, New Jersey; the U.S. Penitentiary in Lewisburg, Pennsylvania; Federal Detention Headquarters in New York City; the District of Columbia jail in Washington, D.C.; and the U.S. Penitentiary in Atlanta, Georgia.

Chip was the Boot's fall guy, and the patriarch was indebted to his soldier. When he was released on parole from Georgia in 1959 after serving two years, the Boiardos were there to help ease him back into society. The Boot deeded him five acres of land next to his own sprawling forty-acre compound in Livingston; Chip built a large ranch home on the property for $75,000—a lot of money back then. FBI surveillance often spotted Tony Boy and Chip together at a driving range on Eagle Rock Mountain Reservation, and they were frequently seen coming and going from the offices of Valentine Electric.

Chip told the feds he was employed in the purchasing and dispatching department at Valentine; however, informants told the cops he actually didn't work for the company.[10] Instead, Chip was doing what he did best—he ran a bootleg operation for Tony Boy, specifically a still and liquor-bottling plant in a rented bungalow at White Meadow Lake in Rockaway Township. The feds closed the plant down on January 6, 1964, arresting two underlings. Chip narrowly escaped capture.

Around this time Chip made a big career move, perhaps as a reaction to the bust at White Meadow Lake or perhaps he—and the Boot—realized he was a walking bull's-eye for the feds, who kept a close eye on him. There was too much risk in bootlegging—stills were not easy to hide—and there was not enough upside. The federal government eventually had relaxed liquor taxes; bootleggers could not compete with legal booze. Times were changing, Chip was ready to jump, and the Boot came through, setting up his loyal soldier in a glamorous new profession as a travel agent.

The Boot held silent interests in several legitimate casinos in the West Indies, and these needed a constant diet of tourists. The Boot hung up a legitimate shingle in Montclair—Caribbean Ventures—an agency that packaged travel junkets to the islands and fed the gaming tables with high rollers who were given credit to play. Chip ran the office and took a percentage collected after the Boot claimed his share. If the high rollers couldn't pay up, they were extended high-interest rate loans that had to be repaid, or else.

After the fall of Fulgencio Batista in Cuba in 1959, Fidel Castro shut down the multimillion-dollar gambling industry that had made Havana the Las Vegas of the Caribbean. Racketeers who owned a stake in such celebrated gaming establishments as the Capri Hotel and Casino, the Riviera, the Nacional, the Seville Biltmore, the Sans Souci, the Deauville, the Havana Hilton, and the Tropicana were forced out and lost fortunes. The Boot was a major silent partner in the Capri with Lucky Luciano, Fat Tony Salerno, and a number other smaller mob investors. The Boot as well as other Havana casino stakeholders like Meyer Lansky, Jerry Catena, and Santo Trafficante Jr. counted their losses after the revolution and quickly sought out more fertile fields in the nearby archipelago of Caribbean islands. The racketeers found these exotic resorts to be as accommodating as Cuba once had been, and even though Sam "Mooney" Giancana of Chicago had been given this territory by the syndicate, the spoils were eventually divided, with members of the Jersey mob including the Boot and the Blade hoisting their flags in Antigua, Curacao, and the Bahamas.

Chip acquired a stake—through the Boot—of a Holiday Inn in Antigua and the Flamboyant Beach Hotel (named after a local variety of tree not a lifestyle) in Curaçao, both of which operated casinos. As an owner, he managed their gambling operations, which meant skimming money from the house's winnings. Later, the feds learned from informants that Chip had interests in houses of prostitution on the islands and had been skimming money from the Reef Casino in Antigua.[11]

Chip was the Boot's bagman; he was skimming at the Boot's bidding. It was a sweet deal, a cushy job with lots of perks, but he still could not completely abandon his roots. With the Boot's backing he also acquired an interest in Leeway Liquors Limited, which was in the business of "manufacturing, distilling and distributing whisky in Curacao," according to FBI reports.[12]

Chip was finally being rewarded for years of taking the rap for his boss. The bagman from Newark, now a newly minted island baron, was so infatuated with the Caribbean lifestyle he applied for residence in Antigua. He was living the good life and was so proud of it and so confident in himself and his good fortune, he took to boasting about it back in Jersey—to all the wrong people.

On April 4, 1967, FBI agents caught up with Chip in the parking lot of a Howard Johnson's restaurant off the Garden State Parkway in Union. He was in a chatty mood, even after the officers identified themselves. According to the FBI report of the conversation, Chip was "factual on information furnished and appeared completely cooperative." The former bootlegger rambled on about his past triumphs in the illegal liquor trade, admitting his affiliation with the Boiardo mob, though he "pointed out that he has never been asked to participate in a 'hit' nor would he do so if asked."[13] Chip did not give up family secrets in this particular conversation; however, his casual blabbing about the Boiardo crew was a violation of the mob's fundamental unwritten code to never admit to anyone, let alone law enforcement, that the Mafia existed.

The Boot's people suspected Chip was chummy with a few agents, and they were growing wary of him. The signs were all there. When the Boot was busted on the gambling charge in 1967, even though Chip was very close to the boss, he was never named or brought to trial. And when Tony

Boy and his crew were indicted in the Addonizio corruption scandal, Chip was never fingered, even though he was closer to Tony Boy than most of the other accused conspirators. According to FBI reports, while the Boot was serving time at Leesburg, more rumors circulated among mobsters that Chip "had become a little too friendly with a government alcohol agent."[14]

In January 1973, an FBI informant reported that the Boiardo gang was planning to bribe "a high Justice Department official."[15] On May 23, 1973, an FBI communiqué stated, "Our Newark Office reports that Chieppa was the source of the information . . . which was received from Bureau of Alcohol, Tobacco, Firearms Assistant Director Jack Caulfield concerning the allegations of a bribery attempt of a high Justice Department official."[16]

Not only was Chip an informant, but he was suspected of being a federal deputy agent working for "alcohol tax authorities." An FBI document reported that "someone saw Chieppa drop a badge, which he hastily retrieved, as he was getting out of his automobile."[17] Clearly, the informant assumed it was some sort of law-enforcement badge.

In April 1973, the New York office of the FBI requested that a body recording device be installed on one of their key Boiardo informants. The home office of the FBI rescinded the request, saying it was premature. Although much of the information in this request was redacted by the FBI, it appears that the informant, if it wasn't Chip himself, was someone close to him. The home office recommended instead that "it would appear direct confrontation and an interview of [blank] would be the desirable step to take at this time prior to utilization of a body recording device."[18]

The case was related to an investigation of the Conforti and Eisele Construction Company, based in New York. According to the FBI the company was controlled by Tony Boy Boiardo and Chip, and it was the corporate entity behind the purchase of the Flamboyant Beach Hotel in Curacao. The investigation was connected to a "possible violation of [the] ITAR [Interstate Travel in Aid of Racketeering] extortion statute."[19] The feds were obviously digging up more evidence about the Boiardos and their offshore gambling activities, and Chip was at the center of the inquiry.

An FBI report claimed that Chip had begun informing on the mob as far back as 1959, when he was released from prison.[20] Why did one of the Boot's closest confidantes turn on him? By 1972 Chip was in poor health; he was diabetic, suffered from high blood pressure, was missing a kidney, and had had heart bypass surgery in Texas a few years before.[21] The criminal life was strenuous, and there was the constant threat of arrest and spending time in prison. Lots of mobsters flipped for less.

Another theory? A State Commission of Investigation source speculated that "Chieppa might have been caught in the middle of a power struggle . . . as the mob sought to determine a successor to the aging crime boss."[22] Popular sentiment in the mob was against Tony Boy's succeeding his father, and Chip was close to Tony Boy. Perhaps he realized this would put him in danger after the Boot passed away.

The Boot's long-held suspicions about Chieppa finally seem to have been acted on in May 1973. At the nondescript offices of Branch Brook Building Supply in Newark, Bruce Scrivo, the company president, Joseph Paterno, James Palmieri, and Big Pussy Russo presided over a hastily called meeting about the execution of a "contract" on an "unknown individual." The Intelligence Unit of the New Jersey State Police had gotten wind of the meeting and notified the FBI, but the word came too late.[23]

The Cadillac sedan of Chieppa's wife, Eleanor, was found in the parking lot of a Two Guys department store in Kearny on May 20, 1973. It had been missing, along with Chip, who had driven off in the car from their Livingston home and hadn't returned. Eleanor was concerned that he might have suffered a diabetic seizure, fainted somewhere, and needed his medication— this is what she told police when she called them on the morning after the first day of his disappearance. By the fourth day Eleanor suspected something worse than a fainting spell. Before he left Chip had told her he was going to meet John "Big Pussy" Russo. There was nothing unusual about this—Big Pussy was one of Chip's old friends and business partners—but he also was an enforcer, a right-hand gun for the Boot. Not returning from a visit with Big Pussy was not a good sign.[24] Coincidentally, on the day Chip disappeared the FBI was running surveillance on his sprawling ranch house as well as the Boot's mansion next door, and they saw Chip just outside his garage talking to the Boot before driving away in the Caddy.

When the cops pried open the trunk of Eleanor's car they found the body of a fifty-three-year-old, 250-pound male, wearing a gold and gray sports jacket and red trousers, with one thirty-eight-caliber bullet hole behind the left jaw and another behind the left ear. There could be no doubt; it was Chip. According to the police he was shot at close range with a Smith and Wesson revolver, and it was likely the killer was in the back seat. They had taken him for a ride.

Chip's body was stripped of his watch, wallet, and jewelry. In mobster idiom this meant that the dead man was killed for stealing—his personal effects were not really his and were taken back. Several FBI informants said they believed Chip was killed on the Boot's orders for taking money from the skimming operations at the Caribbean casinos he was managing for the Boiardo gang.[25]

The press described Chip as the Boot's bodyguard, and the *New York Times* speculated that his killing was linked to "the emergence of a struggle for control of the narcotics and numbers rackets between daring and ambitious black operators and the entrenched Mafia."[26] The Boot appeared to corroborate this hypothesis when he confided to an FBI informant "that Chieppa's recent death resulted from having been money hungry and implied that he . . . was also involved in narcotics."[27] The *New York Times* story was a convenient distraction for the Boot, shifting suspicion away from him and his gang; however, the authorities were not buying the story. The *Star-Ledger* reported: "State and Hudson and Essex officials denied a published story linking Chieppa to an alleged struggle between black and white drug pushers for control of illicit drug traffic in North Jersey. 'There is no evidence to substantiate the story,' a SCI [State Commission of Investigation] source said."[28]

From the start, Big Pussy was a key suspect in the Chieppa case. A man of few words but many deeds, most of them illicit, Big Pussy was interviewed by the FBI one week after the murder at his younger brother's offices in Long Branch. Little Pussy was in the room, and the brothers were in an unusually lighthearted mood considering a friend and associate had just been brutally slain. Big Pussy claimed dismissively that he had had little contact with Chip and had no idea the victim was connected to Tony Boy and Valentine Electric. When agents asked Big Pussy how he made a living, he said he helped his younger brother manage his business interests. "Tony has all the money," said Big Pussy about his brother "in a jocular vein" according to the report.[29] Little Pussy laughed at the comment. The FBI agents confronted Big Pussy with Eleanor Chieppa's statement that her husband said he was on his way to meet with him the day of the murder. Big Pussy denied it, explaining to the feds that Chip often used this type of excuse when he was going to see his girlfriend. "If he was [coming to see me] he knew it, but I didn't," said Big Pussy, coldly.[30]

The Boot did not attend Chip's funeral. A picture of a feeble old man identified as the Boot ran in the newspapers. According to an informant, "Boiardo was very pleased that television news media and newspaper photographs mistakenly identified an individual known as [left blank]" as him. This individual appeared to be in extremely poor health and Boiardo felt that it would gain sympathy for him in any future publicity.[31]

Although he told friends he was upset about the death of his friend, the Boot did not waste time mourning. He slipped into overalls and returned to his spring gardening, vigorously turning the earth and planting his tomatoes. Summer was coming soon, and he had a lot of work left to do. After all, in this thing of theirs, it was a business routine, an expected outcome. The Boot lived up to this basic principle all his life and explained as much to an associate who ironically also was an FBI informer:

These Italian associations live by the rules and the struggle[s] between the associations are basically similar to disputes which would arise among competing clubs or political parties, however, the settlement is handled the "Italian way." The informant states that Boiardo feels that the killings should be of no concern to others so long as outsiders are not hurt, since the participants understand the rules by which they live and conduct themselves.[32]

A few months later, Newark police received an anonymous call warning detectives to expect a hit. In a parked car in the North Ward they found the body of John Malanga with a bullet wound behind the right ear. The authorities believed he was killed over a gambling debt.[33] Malanga, sixty-eight, was another close and long-time associate of the Boot; they had worked together running stills and gambling operations. Malanga was convicted in 1968 along with the Boot on state gambling charges.[34] The Boot came under suspicion in this murder as well. According to an FBI source, the Boiardo "group is more prone to kill its own than any other group he [an informant] knows of."[35]

CHAPTER 12

ON THE JOLLY TROLLEY

*The thief said, "Better pardoned is
the sinner who can blame himself,
and I confess that I take all
I can from those less powerful."*
—*Matteo Maria Boiardo*, Orlando Innamorato, *406*

The Jolly Trolley Casino was a Las Vegas grind joint located in a dreary shopping mall on the northwest corner of the Strip and Sahara. The casino was built in a former butcher shop, and it incorporated an old meat cooler that greeted patrons when they walked in the front door with steak loins hanging behind glass doors. In a city that specialized in selling gimmicks, the Trolley's bait was to offer guests cheap steak dinners sold by the ounce and cut to their own specifications, as well as ninety-nine-cent burgers. Another selling point for carnivores: the Trolley featured the only strip club in Las Vegas, starring a conga line of naked go-go dancers on a stage at the edge of the gambling pit. Well-known strippers and porn stars appeared at the Jolly Trolley, including Marilyn Chambers, who performed a one-woman show, "The Sex Surrogate," on the casino stage.[1]

The Trolley was not the Capri. It was a dive and an easy mark for an old-school hoodlum who desperately wanted to continue living the life as the mob's glory days waned. Little Pussy was just such a thug; he infiltrated this sawdust joint on behalf of the Boot and himself and made everyone some money, but he also made quite a few more enemies in the process, and as usual he couldn't keep his mouth shut.

In 1970, Pussy was one of nine high-profile mobsters serving time for contempt, including Jerry Catena and Angelo Bruno. In 1971 he was paroled but found himself facing charges from the IRS for failure to file income taxes on two companies he owned. He pleaded guilty and was back in Trenton State Prison, sentenced to eighteen months and fined $50,000. During this stint, Little Pussy got caught in a melee in the prison mess hall and was stabbed twice in the lower back by black inmates. Newspapers reported that the prison stabbings were related to "racial conflict," but insiders attributed the violence to a turf war instigated by black militants over the control of drugs within the prison.[2] Five of the assailants were black, while six of the seven victims were white.

Little Pussy was released briefly from prison a year later to undergo surgery for a cancerous kidney condition and was again released a year later for surgery to correct poor circulation in a leg; he was treated at Golden Isles Hospital, Hallandale, Florida. While he was still serving time, the FBI suggested to the State Commission of Investigation that they ask him questions about La Cosa Nostra that would appeal to his ego. "Questions so directed to him should result in fairly positive answers."[3]

He testified in a closed session before the commission, answering all their questions despite his attorney's attempts to stop him. He admitted breaking bread with organized-crime members, but "he never set up rackets in the New Jersey Shore area," and, despite the DeCarlo tapes, he denied to the best of his recollection ever having conversations with Gyp. He also claimed to have never injured or killed anyone and denied he killed "Harold the Jew," as recorded in the tapes.[4]

Little Pussy eventually paid off his IRS debt by selling his New Jersey properties, and in November 1974 he was released from prison. His nemesis, Tony Boy, was out of the picture; at that time the heir apparent was still convalescing after his heart attack, taking it easy at home and on golf courses around the state. DeCarlo died from cancer in 1973, and Jerry Catena was getting ready to retire, so Little Pussy fell under the direct oversight of the Boot. Little Pussy appeared to be the last man standing in the Boiardo crew, along with his older brother Big Pussy, who was not in good health. The Boot also was dealing with health and age issues and, according to the newspapers, was losing the respect of "young turks" in the underworld.[5] It was to the Boot's advantage to overlook Little Pussy's past indiscretions, including the trash talk in the DeCarlo tapes, which had been released to the public years earlier. The Boot needed an earner on his team; he needed Little Pussy.

This leadership vacuum gave Little Pussy more leverage in the Boiardo gang. He seized the opening by establishing a foothold in legitimate enterprises, including a meat-and-fish distribution business for restaurants, and he invested in an Arthur Treacher's franchise and the Cedarbrook Inn in Lakewood, New Jersey. He continued to run operations for the Boot at the Jersey Shore and in Florida and helped open up new opportunities for the gang in Las Vegas and Denver.

He also tried to arrange a deal to build a multitower Ramada Inn hotel and casino in Atlantic City with 350 rooms and elevated walkways, and he secured a $3.6 million loan commitment from the New Jersey Economic Development Authority to build another Ramada Inn in Highlands, Vito Genovese's town.[6] His activities were closely monitored by the FBI. The agency planted listening devices in his Long Branch office: one inside telephone on his desk and the other in a bathroom ceiling, which captured the sound of the flushing toilet.[7] Little Pussy sensed that he was being monitored; he grew paranoid and took to driving erratically and at high speeds to lose agents he was convinced were tailing him.

Drug dealing was providing big easy money for many gangs in the seventies, especially in New York, and in spite of the Boot's strict ban prohibiting his crew from dealing in narcotics—like Vito Corleone the Boot believed drug trafficking was a dirty business that would destroy his political connections—Little Pussy began nibbling at the fringes, lending money to dealers and shaking them down at the Jersey Shore and in Florida. He kept this activity under the radar and out of the Boot's sight until a series of murders befell mobster emissaries who attempted to collect on loans made to drug traffickers.

Patrick "Patsy" Truglia, thirty-six, a known drug dealer living in Fort Lauderdale, Florida, with roots in Long Branch, New Jersey, reneged on a $50,000 loan and failed to pay up even after being beaten. On April 2, 1976, a trio of enforcers was dispatched to Truglia's home: James "Big Jim" Capotoria, who was six foot four and weighed three hundred pounds, and his associates Wayne Neeld and Bobby Dee. Capotoria demanded that Truglia and his wife, Mary Lou, turn over their Lincoln Continental along with some jewelry. Mary Lou refused. Big Jim punched her, knocking out a tooth. They slapped Patsy around and Neeld aimed a gun at him. Capotoria gave the signal to shoot. Patsy reached under a dining room table, pulled out a concealed Browning automatic pistol and fired thirteen shots, killing all three men. When the police arrived, Patsy denied he was involved in drug dealing but admitted he owed money to a man named Nick Russo. He was charged with homicide. His case went to trial, but he was found innocent by reason of self-defense.[8]

The following year, one of Little Pussy's associates, Joseph Agnellino, was murdered, apparently by drug dealers. In order to exact revenge, and also perhaps to make amends for his own drug-related transgressions, Little Pussy requested and received permission from the Boot and the Genovese family bosses in New York "to rid Monmouth County of drug dealers by taking their money and throwing away their drugs"[9] and to kill the men responsible for the Agnellino murder, including Truglia, who he believed was involved. In taped conversations between Pussy and another associate, he declared that "he would not bury the person responsible" but "would leave them out in the open so everyone will know that if any[one] gets out of line that's what's gonna happen with them."[10] Little Pussy put so much pressure on local drug dealers that they requested police protection. Vincent DeMarzo, an addict, who had been arrested at Agnellino's murder scene, pled guilty to the killing and was found hanged in his cell at Trenton State Prison in December 1978. Prison officials called his death a suicide.

Little Pussy's crackdown came to an end when police arrested two of his henchmen, including his personal driver Patrick Pizuto, who later turned informant. Truglia escaped Little Pussy's wrath and continued his life of petty crime; in 1984 he was sentenced to fourteen years in prison for attempted murder; in 1995 he was arrested in Florida along with his brother for participating in a telemarketing scheme that defrauded elderly people of $500,000.[11]

From 1976 to 1978, Little Pussy focused his attention on the Jolly Trolley Casino. According to the FBI, Pussy's assignment in Vegas on behalf of the Boot was to control a major casino or two and to pay off local politicians to ensure that there would be no interference with organized-crime members in the Las Vegas area—in particular, the Chicago gang headed by Anthony "the Ant" Spilotro, who dominated organized-crime operations in the city. The initial scheme was to establish a joint Boiardo-Spilotro skim in the Jackpot Casino.[12] Little Pussy ended up managing to pay off Philip Leone, a lone, corrupt Vegas police sergeant in the department's anticrime unit (Leone also was on Spilotro's payroll); and although Little Pussy boasted "of his influence in several major Las Vegas Casinos and of hidden interest held by other La Cosa Nostra figures in other casinos in Las Vegas,"[13] his actual sphere of influence was limited to the strip-mall casino with a meat locker in the entranceway.

Little Pussy insinuated himself into the Jolly Trolley by strong-arming its owners. He dispatched a pair of a goons to a New Jersey restaurant owned by Peter DeLamos, the Jolly Trolley's vice president, and threatened to start labor problems at the casino unless the owners paid tribute.[14] Labor unrest was not as persuasive an argument to DeLamos, Paul Bendetti, the casino's president, and Dennis Mastro, its food and beverage director, as the fact that they were already in debt to Spilotro for $150,000. A partnership with the Boiardo-Genovese crew could provide financial support, political influence, and protection both from the law and from the volatile Chicago hoodlum. While visiting Las Vegas to finalize the deal, Little Pussy took a room at the Jockey Club; the FBI occupied an adjacent room and electronically eavesdropped on his conversations with various cohorts, including Leone. Russo boasted about ownership of the El Mirador Motel and about involvement in mob ventures at the Money Tree, the Jackpot, and Honest John's casinos, and in an adult bookstore. There was also mention of cash payments to Leone and Sheriff Ralph Lamb of Clark County, Nevada.[15]

Not only did Little Pussy collect tribute from the Jolly Trolley owners, but he took charge of the casino: orchestrating the skim, arranging loans for the casino, even hiring and firing employees. "He was a totally vicious man," DeLamos later testified before a federal jury. "He came from another era but sometimes managed to continue his extortionate practices, but was running out of victims."[16] According to a joint investigation launched by the New Jersey State Police and the Nevada Gaming Control Authority, the Boot's organization skimmed approximately $13,600 per month from the Jolly Trolley from 1975 to 1979. The scheme was revealed by FBI surveillance in Las Vegas and New Jersey. A Monmouth Beach paving contractor and loan-shark victim named Richard Bohnert agreed to wear an eavesdropping device while dealing with Little Pussy, and so did Little Pussy's driver and confidante, Patrick Pizuto.[17] The undercover work, including the bugs in Little Pussy's office, netted hundreds of hours of incriminating conversations, with Little Pussy once again on tape bragging about his prowess and cunning, discussing his relationship with his Boss and Tony Boy, and basically digging himself an even deeper hole than the one he barely managed to crawl out of after the DeCarlo and DeCavalcante tapes were made public.

The FBI now had the Boot, Big Pussy, and Little Pussy, along with their Jolly Trolley partners, in its crosshairs for a Racketeer Influenced and Corrupt Organizations (RICO) Act conspiracy indictment. The bureau decided to approach Little Pussy to see whether he would cooperate. On August 22, 1978, they arranged an interview and informed him "in some detail" of the evidence they had amassed in cooperation with the New Jersey State Police and the Las Vegas Gaming Control Authority. Their efforts to turn Little Pussy into an informant failed. "Russo made no admissions," an FBI report read. "He was attentive throughout the interview, but remained uncooperative."[18]

Little Pussy was already deep in hot water; two months earlier the Boot had called him to a meeting with Big Pussy in the Long Branch office and chastised the younger brother for making decisions on his own and for late delivery of the family's share of the casino skim and loan-shark operations. "I'm the boss!" the Boot angrily declared. When Little Pussy attempted to explain that he was being squeezed by other mobsters, the Boot replied, "You're no help yourself. You have to lead. If you no lead, you shoot. Leave 'em with ten cents."[19] According to sources, it was only out of respect for Big Pussy that the Boot refrained from punishing the Jersey Shore hoodlum.[20] Ordinarily, holding out or not collecting vigorish payments in the mob was a capital offense. "Wiseguys," the Boot said to Little Pussy. "I've taken wiseguys out [killed them] because I distrusted them." Little Pussy said to the Boot: "I lived on [Newark] Street when I was a kid. You raised me. What have I got to worry about?"[21]

According to the FBI, Little Pussy had a lot to worry about, and he and his brother knew it. Big Pussy had once told an associate that "it would never be good for them [the Russo brothers] to be together in the event one was hit, for then the other would go also."[22]

At the end of that fateful year, in December 1978, the errant hood clearly saw the writing on the wall when his big brother died of cancer. The loss was a devastating blow. Little Pussy's legendary braggadocio and his voracious appetite suddenly vanished; he didn't eat for days. At the wake, he cried, and he was overheard to mutter, as he gazed down at his dead sibling, "There goes my insurance policy."[23]

Little Pussy's insurance coverage finally lapsed on the evening of April 26, 1979, when he returned to his apartment in Harbor Island Spa residence in Long Branch after a trip to Florida. Two men dropped by to visit him that night, according to neighbors who later heard a loud sound that resembled a "truck backfire."[24] The next morning, John A. Russell, a Jersey City attorney, stopped by Little Pussy's office in West Long Branch, and, surprised that his client wasn't in yet—Pussy usually showed up in his office no later than seven o'clock in the morning—he decided to drop in the Harbor Island Spa. Little Pussy didn't answer his apartment buzzer, and management let the attorney inside. The luxurious fourth-floor ocean-front suite was filled with stuffed cats and pictures of cats—momentos of Little Pussy's cat-burglar past—and in the bedroom Russell found Little Pussy's body lying lifeless in his bed, which was soaked in blood. "It took me a few seconds but I knew he was ice cold," Russell said. "I always found him to be a nice guy. I am sure he's done his share of bad things."[25]

Almost two decades later, an informant named Little Pussy's execution-ers: Thomas "Pee Wee" DePhillips, a key lieutenant of the Boot; Anthony DeVingo, who was Big Pussy's direct report; and Joe "Joe Z" Zarro, a Boiardo associate based in Passaic County. The men had waited for Little Pussy to return from his Florida trip; Pee Wee and DeVingo went up to the apartment sometime after dark while Zarro remained in a getaway car outside. Little Pussy offered his visitors a drink, and when he turned they fired. The killers locked the door as they left.[26]

The police never found a weapon, and there wasn't enough evidence to indict anyone, but there was much speculation in the press about the motives of the killers. The murder did take place just one month before indictments were to be announced in the Great Mob Trial, in which Little Pussy and the Boiardo gang were targeted for racketeering,[27] and it was said that Little Pussy's associates were worried that the Jersey Shore hood-lum had been living in such luxury that he might try to avoid jail at all costs even if it meant betraying his boss and his crew in court.[28]

The day after Russo's murder, the Boot confided to a close associate: "Perhaps it was for the best. He talked too much."[29]

THE MAFIA EXISTS!

The robber answered, "What I do
is done by all great lords on earth.
They massacre their enemies
in war just to enrich their states.
I hold up seven, maybe ten;
they madly kill ten thousand men,
and they do so much worse than me,
taking what they don't even need!"

—*Matteo Maria Boiardo,* Orlando Innamorato, *406*

It was as if the ghost of Little Pussy had come back to haunt his killers. On May 25, 1979, one month after Little Pussy's body was found in a heap among his collection of stuffed cats, State Attorney General John J. Degnan announced the arrest of eight reputed New Jersey mobsters on a twenty-four-count indictment alleging they had created a nationwide criminal conspiracy. The charges were the result of a two-year investigation triggered by the electronic surveillance of Little Pussy. The defendants in the case included several people who would later be implicated in his murder.

Although, since the days of Prohibition, the existence of the Mafia had generally been accepted as a given, no one had ever attempted to prove its existence in a court of law until the death of Little Pussy and the appearance of Degnan, an ambitious Harvard Law School graduate who, at the age of thirty-three, became the youngest man ever to serve as state attorney general; he later ran unsuccessfully for governor. "There have always been lingering doubts in the minds of some public officials, our citizens and even a few law-enforcement officials that there was such a national conspiracy, simply because no one ever had to prove it," Degnan told the press. "We are prepared to do just that—to demonstrate, in the course of proving other charges contained in this indictment, the existence of organized crime in the United States."[1]

Degnan's plan sounded noble and historic, finally an attempt to crush the horrible power and reach of the mob. Unfortunately the imagery just wasn't working. The prime suspect in this heroic effort was a frail, stooped old man who prided himself on being a grandfather, a great-grandfather, and a gardener; at age eighty-nine he was one of the oldest defendants ever to be tried on organized-crime charges. The Boot did not fit the picture of an arch villain and neither did his craggy crew of middle-aged, balding lieutenants—Thomas "Pee Wee" DePhillips, Anthony DeVingo, Andy Gerardo, Angelo Sica, James Vito Montemarano, Louis Ferrari, and Anthony Lardiere. Two other defendants in the case, Little Pussy and his older brother John, were already dead. The Boot and the Russos were considered the ringleaders; the fact that the Russos were out of the picture reduced the impact the case might have had, according to observers at the time.[2]

The defendants were charged "with murder, extortion, robbery, loan-sharking, gambling, and conspiracy to organize and operate Cosa Nostra for illicit financial gain."[3] Altogether the charges listed seventy-nine criminal acts including killing a numbers runner named Paul Campanile and plotting to kill Patsy Truglia and two other hoodlums. The Boot was accused of serving as capo and answering to the Genovese family bosses in New York. The bulk of the evidence consisted of clandestinely recorded conversations that took place in the West Long Branch office of Little Pussy and at two Newark locations—Kelly Ann's luncheonette and Lectrician's, an electrical-supply company said to be owned by Andrew Gerardo. Additional evidence was the eyewitness testimony of Little Pussy's chauffeur, Patrick Pizuto, who had murdered a Passaic grocer and received a reduced sentence and a place in the federal witness-protection program in exchange for his cooperation.[4] Evidence also came from Monmouth Beach paving contractor Richard Bohnert, a loan-shark victim who agreed to wear a wire to record meetings with Montemarano. Bohnert was forced to pay over $400,000 in interest over three years on a $75,000 loan made by Little Pussy.[5]

Politicians and journalists dubbed it the "Great Mob Trial," which quickly became a misnomer; far from great, the proceedings became mired in minutiae and triviality. There was early infighting over the admissibility of evidence that allegedly had not been packaged correctly. Pizuto vacillated, refusing to testify one day and then agreeing the next. One of the defendants, Louis "the Killer" Ferrari, was severed from the trial because of heart trouble and emphysema. At one point, a lawyer for one of the defendants grew so frustrated with the process he burst out, "This is a circus!"[6] But the biggest blow to the relevance of the proceedings was the absence of its star defendant, the Boot, who was severed from the case after pleading in court that he was too ill to stand trial: "I'm in agony and pain," he cried out. "Come tell Saint Peter to bring me to heaven."[7]

After a lengthy preparation and discovery process, the three-month-long trial was held in Freehold; it offered rare moments of absurdity and pathos. The indictment charged the defendants with being part of a "nationwide criminal cartel," and yet the presiding judge told jurors that this grandiose wording was "descriptive" and advised them that they could convict for conspiracy even though all the crimes occurred in New Jersey.[8] In one of the tape recordings submitted as evidence, Little Pussy was overheard talking to Pizuto about a contract to kill Campanile, who had been implicated in an unsanctioned shooting of a mob family member in a Pennsylvania restaurant. Pizuto was ordered by mob bosses to "hit" Campanile, who was taken for a ride that ended in a service area on the Garden State Parkway, where his body was found. In court, Pizuto claimed he was merely the driver of the car in which Campanile was murdered and blamed DeVingo for doing the actual dirty work.[9] In another taped conversation, Little Pussy discussed, in his characteristic Jersey style, managing a Shylock operation with Pizuto: "Youse got the . . . whole territory. It took me . . . 30 years. So you get some nice kids that you can trust. Don't bring me a . . . kid you say he's good, because if the kid's no good, you're gonna go with the kid. Youse can make all the money youse want, youse got bookmakers, everybody here, guys that are shying."[10]

On June 20, 1980, a state grand jury convicted four of the defendants of running a criminal syndicate in New Jersey: Sica; Montemarano; Gerardo, who was described by the prosecution as the acting head of the New Jersey branch of the Genovese crime family; and DeVingo, who was convicted of conspiracy but acquitted of the Campanile murder. The prosecuting assistant attorney declared the convictions proved that a national crime conspiracy called the Mafia existed and therefore it was not "a figment of Hollywood's imagination."[11] DeVingo ridiculed the results, claiming the convictions would not affect organized crime: "Ford closed its Mahwah plant today," he said, making an analogy. "But Ford didn't go out of business."[12]

Outside the courtroom, the defendants encountered a *New York Times* reporter who wrote that Sica could "pass for a bank president," that Montemarano was a former altar boy who said "he was needed at home to look after his sick father and take care of his pets and plants," and that Gerardo praised "the virtues of color-coordinated goatskin loafers."[13] DeVingo, who was brought up a strict Catholic in a household of nineteen children, "seemed the most complex" according to the *Times* journalist, who reported the alleged hit man's contempt of undercover detectives: "The state police, he said, rented an empty house across from his sandwich shop in Newark and put a plywood shield on a window to hide themselves. However they apparently could not see the shop from the house because of trees, and so they cut a tunnel through the leafy branches while Mr. DeVingo and his friends watched with interest."[14]

DeVingo was sentenced to two and a half to three years in prison. Gerardo received nine and a half to fourteen years and a $6,000 fine. Montemarano got slapped with a sentence of twenty-two and a half to thirty years and a $1,000 fine. Sica got six and a half to nine years and a $3,000 fine. Pee Wee DePhillips pled guilty but was already in prison for an unrelated offense; he received four and a half to six years.

Four months after the state had issued indictments in the Great Mob Trial, a federal grand jury had handed out indictments for the skimming operation at the Jolly Trolley Casino. The feds fingered the Boot, Montemarano, Las Vegas Detective Phillip Leone, and the three Jolly Trolley executives—Peter DeLamos of Rumson, Paul Bendetti, and Dennis Mastro, both formerly of Long Branch. The men were arraigned before a familiar face, Frederick Lacey, now a judge at the U.S. District Court in Newark, and all but the Boot and Leone pled not guilty to thirteen counts of RICO charges. Just as in the state trial, the Boot was severed from the federal trial for failing health, and Leone also was separated for medical reasons.

The federal trial finally began on October 1, 1981, more than a year after the Great Mob Trial convictions, but it lasted only three weeks. In court, Little Pussy's attorney, Jack Russell, admitted that he was in the mob leader's West Long Branch office when Jolly Trolley executives were coerced into signing an ownership agreement making Little Pussy a 28 percent partner in the casino. "He testified the defendants appeared 'upset, hesitant and frightened' at the meeting, while Russo was 'aggressive, loud, menacing' . . . [saying] 'just sign it and let's get out of here.' . . . Russo was 'crazy.' . . . Russo 'had a gun on his desk.'"[15] Russell claimed that he was at the meeting simply to witness the signing and that he had no knowledge of the purpose or content of the contract.[16]

The prosecution did not have enough evidence to convict Montemarano, and he was acquitted.[17] DeLamos, Bendetti, and Mastro were found guilty of all thirteen counts of conspiracy. They were sentenced on November 25, 1981, receiving three-year jail sentences plus fines of $60,000 each. The jury returned a special verdict finding that Little Pussy, Big Pussy, and the Boot were part of the RICO conspiracy. Lacey called the Boot and Little Pussy "societal scum."[18]

The FBI's investigation into the Jolly Trolley conspiracy eventually segued into a full-scale probe into the infiltration of Las Vegas casinos by Anthony Spilotro and his Chicago bosses. On June 23, 1986, the partially nude and mutilated bodies of Spilotro and his brother Michael were found in a shallow grave in an Indiana cornfield. According to authorities "recent convictions of five crime syndicate chieftains on charges of skimming profits from Las Vegas casinos 'had to be the coup de grace for Spilotro.'"[19]

These last trials took their toll on the Boot, who repaired to his farm, tending to his garden and passing the mantle of leadership to Gerardo and cohort Pee Wee DePhillips, who presided over the last gasp of the long-lived Boiardo mob. The empire had deteriorated dramatically, reduced to petty loan-shark schemes, swag, gambling, and bookmaking ventures operating out of rinky-dink luncheonettes, barren storefronts, electrical supply shops, garages, seedy pizza parlors, and stucco-covered social clubs in North Newark—places that required little overhead as real estate prices dropped and white residents continued to vacate the city in the drawn-out aftermath of the riots and a lingering recession.

Gerardo, like the Boot, commuted from Livingston, basically making the same rounds that the patriarch had already established in Bloomfield, Belleville, and the Roseville section of Newark, West Orange, and North Arlington. Gerardo, fifty-eight, was handsome, lean, and square-jawed with dark eyebrows, a head full of white hair, and a lacquered tan. He was called the White Haired Guy and the Silver Fox. Unlike many of the Boiardo crew's colorful alumni from the past, he was soft-spoken and cordial. Pee Wee, fifty-seven, was short, thus his name, with a rubbery face and a comb-over; he too was quiet, his voice a whisper. He suffered from a blood disease that required transfusions, and he came down with the shakes if he missed an injection.[20] He once told a judge that he never used violence, that it was just a bluff when he threatened people for not paying back usurious loans, but this little man was allegedly a cold-blooded killer responsible for murdering his friend, Little Pussy. His fellow assassins Anthony DeVingo and Joseph Zarro were also in the crew. It was an over-the-hill gang, made up of mostly fifty-somethings who lived in suburban enclaves like West Caldwell, North Caldwell, and Roseland and never worked a day in their lives, as the cop Mike Russell wryly observed after he helped bust the entire gang in an elaborate sting operation that was captured on film in the HBO documentary *Confessions of an Undercover Cop*.[21]

The story of this bust could have been an episode of *The Sopranos*; in fact the fictional mob series was inspired in part by the documentary and the banal assortment of low-life Jersey thugs who were exposed in it. In 1984, Mike Russell, a retired East Orange cop, came to the aid of an older white man who was involved in a traffic-accident "altercation" with two black men. "I went to help the white guy, it was two against one," said Russell in the film. "I evened up the odds. I smacked one guy, knocked him on his ass and then was invited into the luncheonette for breakfast by the white guy."[22]

The white guy was Andy Gerardo, and the luncheonette was the modest headquarters of a highly lucrative gambling, numbers-running, loan-shark, and bookmaking empire, an operation that had been grandfathered into this North Newark neighborhood by the Boot. Gerardo introduced Russell to the gang, and he was treated like a hero. Russell vaguely realized what he had stumbled onto. He contacted his friends in the police department, and they rehired him to spearhead a dangerous covert investigation. Russell became an associate of the mob, and, without the knowledge of the hoodlums or the cops, he filmed the entire affair with hidden cameras.

The investigation became known as Operation Intrepid, and it resulted in the indictment of sixteen individuals on arson, gambling, loan-sharking, racketeering, and theft charges by a state grand jury in May 1987. Charges included operating a $20 million-a-year gambling ring, robbing $3 million from a union dental-health plan, and laundering the cash through a Morris County contractor.[23] Gerardo's lawyers fought the case, arguing that because he was being similarly charged at another trial, he was facing double jeopardy. In the *Confessions of an Undercover Cop* film, the Silver Fox and his crew are marched into an arraignment hearing; Gerardo is dressed in a white shirt and blazer and, with handcuffs on, clutches a small white shopping sack. "Here comes the big guy," Russell says in the film, derisively. "Look at him with his little handbag!"[24]

Gerardo was said to have retired from the underworld completely after Operation Intrepid. His Livingston house was raided by the FBI in 1993, but Gerardo was not home. He was living comfortably in his second home in Aventura, Florida, by then, apparently nursing health ailments. A business, a social club on Bloomfield Avenue, and another private home were raided too; an FBI spokesperson would say only that the raids were part of an ongoing investigation into the Genovese crime family.[25]

Pee Wee took over command of the gang in 1992, after he was released on state charges, but he was busted again three years later for gambling and loan-sharking; he was nailed with five other men, including Vincent "Skippy" Squatrito, a former Newark cop who left the force in the 1970s, and Ronald Castellano, an enforcer who lured a loan-shark victim to Branch Brook Park in Newark and stabbed him in the stomach. Pee Wee and the others ultimately pleaded guilty to the charges. When asked by the judge whether he was a member of the Gerardo faction of the Genovese crime family, Pee Wee simply said "Yes."[26] The diminutive hoodlum and last acting capo of the fabled Boiardo clan died after a long bout of illness at the age of seventy while serving a six-and-a-half-year sentence in his Belleville home, an arrangement that was allowed by a federal judge. His death appeared to mark the bitter end of "a flamboyant era in organized crime, one that began in the waning days of Prohibition and extended into the latter half of the century."[27]

But it really wasn't until January 29, 2012, that this epitaph could be written. "He was dearly beloved by a special group of men who were the most loyal of friends," read a line from Andy Gerardo's obituary.[28] The retired capo died at his Florida home, age eighty-one, and his body was shipped back to Jersey. His wake was held at Lamonica Funeral Home in Livingston, not far from the house where he had lived for many years, a homely split-level at 224 Laurel Avenue with a driveway guarded by small mortar lions on brick pedestals and a full-size tennis court in the backyard.

His wake was attended by family and his "most loyal of friends." Their Mercedeses, BMWs, and Cadillacs choked the parking lot; Livingston police directed traffic; and inside the main room containing the open casket, with floral arrangements lining the walls, that old gang of his paid their last respects. The gathering was festive, not mournful. Gerardo was laid out like a "Silver Fox" in a silver-gray metallic casket, wearing a silver-gray double-breasted suit, his long white hair plastered down neatly, his folded hands clutching a black rosary.

Gerardo's funeral was held on Friday, February 3, 2012, at Saint Lucy's church in the old First Ward. It was a modest event; one car for the casket, a flower car, and one limousine for the immediate family. The church filled quickly—about two hundred people—and everyone watched as eight sturdy pallbearers carried the casket up the steps, into the church, and down the center aisle with priests leading the procession. They stopped midway, said a prayer, and then continued to the altar. Mourners seemed to come from all walks of life; most dressed in their Sunday best with a few in black leather and wearing gold chains. A full choir and a baritone soloist provided the music. In his eulogy, the pastor said Gerardo had simply gone off to "sleep" and in a whispery voice spoke about how the Gerardo clan had always been generous to the church. The family name was engraved in stone in the church's outdoor plaza. They had donated significant funds to help rebuild the church. Finally he mentioned that the Gerardos were especially helpful and skilled at managing Saint Lucy's bingo nights.[29]

CHAPTER 14

THIS THING OF THEIRS

My garden has variety.
I've planted it with love and war.
The fierce souls prefer the fights,
while fine and gentle hearts like love.
                    —*Matteo Maria Boiardo*, Orlando Innamorato, *537*

"That's where the barbecue used to be, way up in the back there," says Roger Hanos, pointing at a development of sprawling suburban homes on land that was once part of the Boot's thirty-acre estate in Livingston.[1] The barbecue he refers to was a large outdoor grill about eight feet square with six-to-ten-foot walls made of the same stone that the Boot's mansion was constructed of—stone that was salvaged from the old Newark Post Office. The fire pit was covered by a huge metal grate and another cooking grate on top of that. This former picnic area was once remote and wooded, the perfect location for doing things in secret.

The fireplace is long gone. The land was confiscated from the Boot by the IRS in the 1960s and was auctioned off; it is now home to families who probably have no idea what once was there. Legend has it the Boot burned the bodies of his enemies and other victims on a grate in a furnace on his property. Roger was raised on the estate, along with his family, his cousins, and their families, and during the many years he lived here none of them ever saw a furnace on the property. Could it have been the old barbecue?

The specter of brutal murders and the allegations of human cremation have haunted the Boiardo clan for years, and as far Roger is concerned they are untrue. He doesn't believe that his kindly, generous grandfather,

Richie the Boot, was capable of such atrocities. However, would Little Pussy Russo, a La Cosa Nostra lieutenant, make statements incriminating himself and his capo in multiple murders and disposal of the evidence by burning the bodies if they weren't true?

Roger walks the old property line, conjuring ghosts as he stares at estate buildings that still stand and have fallen into disrepair and decay, including the Boot's twenty-nine-room mansion. He hasn't been back in years; he seems nostalgic and sad. Everything has changed. The rambling woods are gone, the animals too, long replaced by a maze of cul-de-sacs and small winding roads that twist and turn and lead nowhere; their purpose is to feed into the broad driveways of the new mansions.

The estate also is weathered and desolate, hidden behind a tangle trees from the surrounding suburbs. The main house is visible beyond a padlocked rear gate on a dead-end street aptly named Twilight Court. In the statuary garden only the Boot and his charger, Chief, still stand, chipped and weathered with white paint flaking; the other busts disappeared years ago.

When *Life* magazine published the article about the farm, the story of a crematorium upset the Boot, but he was more disturbed by the photos of the busts of his grandchildren. He didn't want them to be exposed and persecuted, but they were. Roger Hanos remembers that, for him, the exposure was devastating and lasting:

> It wasn't until seventh or eighth grade that I had some knowledge of my grandfather's gangster past. During a lunch recess a classmate brought in a newspaper article about my grandfather being a reputed organized-crime leader. The kid was teasing me in front of some others sitting at our table. I was offended and started arguing with him when a teacher-monitor came over and questioned what was going on. The teacher read the article and said, "Reputed gang leader doesn't mean that he is; it means that it's possible that he is." However, that was short lived. After the *Life* magazine came out along with the infamous tape recordings regarding mob hits and bodies being incinerated on the estate where

we lived, it's been a never ending nightmare for many of us. It's difficult to escape the thought that friends and acquaintances form opinions or judge you by who you are related to or the fact that you resided "up on the farm." In college, a public-speaking-course professor, during class, recognized my name and statue likeness in the *Life* magazine spread and asked if I would like to stand up and talk to the class about it. Of course I declined and said that it wasn't me it was someone else who had the same name and quietly sat down. I was humiliated.

As the Boot aged and became less involved in La Cosa Nostra, he spent most of his days on the estate working in the garden. The Boot's friends and associates would stop by, including Roger's uncle Tony Boy, and they would walk away and talk. Roger was often within earshot of their conversations, but they talked in Italian or in terms that were vague and hard to decipher. The Boot was always careful not to discuss any of his other business in front of his grandchildren.

Some of these associates, it turned out, had become FBI informants. The bureau built a large file of documents that paraphrased, summarized, and recorded verbatim conversations with the Boot as he busied himself among his roses and tomatoes and rambled on amiably about the past, revealing much about the man, but very little about "this thing of ours," much to the disappointment of law enforcement. Many of these reports, memos, teletypes, and radiograms are likely based on recordings of Angelo "Chip" Chieppa, who lived next door to the Boot and frequently dropped in. The Boot was surrounded by spies; whether he knew exactly whom he could trust is uncertain. Most of the names are redacted in the documents.

It's clear, however, that the Boot seldom let his guard down. He confided to one turncoat that he worked the garden to stay strong and mentally alert. "If his associates ever feel that he is becoming senile or illogical in his thinking, they will immediately cast him aside."[2] In another report, the FBI learned that the Boot "takes pride in being almost 81 years of age and in being in good health. He likes to brag a little that he still enjoys sex twice a week—every Monday and Friday. He attributes this ability, at his age, to a clear mind and strong will power and not to any physical prowess."[3] He typically discussed his health or complained about reporters and the "Muslims" whom he felt were running roughshod in Newark following the riots and were "never punished for their crimes."[4] He also liked to talk about politics: he supported George Wallace for president because "he is a hell of a guy" and has "the right ideas about law and order."[5] And he admired Richard Nixon: "Boiardo's contention is that he feels President Nixon is the best president this country has ever had if the [Watergate] allegations against him are true. Boiardo said that Nixon showed a lot of guts in shaking down millionaire businessmen and government contractors who are robbing the country blind."[6] He also had great respect for J. Edgar Hoover, "an honest man who is only concerned with doing a good job."[7]

The Boot could be cordial to a fault, but often this masked his wicked cunning. When FBI agents showed up at the house, they were looking for tips and hoping that the Boot, in his old age, might slip and turn into a stool pigeon himself, or what the agency called a "high-echelon informant." At first the Boot was evasive with bureau agents who dropped by, refusing to admit his identity, claiming that he was the brother of the Boot, who was in the hospital.[8] He eventually warmed to them, reminiscing about his past as a Prohibition bootlegger but never giving up anything new or important and obviously playing them, fishing around for information that he wanted.

Agents and informants routinely probed the Boot for tidbits about missing and murdered people, often other mobsters like Tony Boy when he skipped town after the Fremont Tavern incident; Michele Miranda, who periodically fled New York when the police were looking for him; Thomas Eboli, the errant Genovese boss who was killed in Brooklyn by underlings; Chieppa after he was found dead; and Eugene "Gino" Farina, a button-man and frequent guest at the farm who suddenly vanished.

Farina was one of the Boot's trusted associates; he managed the Newark Police Department payoffs and the accounting and distribution of the take from gambling activities. He eventually earned enough money to buy a comfortable home in a wealthy neighborhood in Madison, New Jersey. Farina's appearance was striking—olive-skinned, with a bushy black moustache and always impeccably dressed. Farina was a frequent invited guest at the Boiardo estate until 1968, when he disappeared.

Roger recalled visits to the compound by Farina, the well-groomed man with the dark glasses who explained, at least to Roger, that he injured his eye while playing with firecrackers. Once, when Farina came over to the house to attend a party, the Boot spit on Farina's pants. The Boot always spit while chomping on a cigar. Roger's mother often reprimanded him for spitting on the floor. Farina was upset; he said, "Hey, Boot, stop," and the patriarch and his other guests laughed. Farina sullenly observed to the others that the Boot also spit on his dog.

The Boot revealed very little about Farina after he disappeared. He told an informant that "'Farina used to be with me,' but stated that he ran off . . . and they too [his gang] were looking for Farina. He then added that Farina's big problem was that he wanted to be a boss."[9] On another occasion, the Boot played down the issue, claiming that Farina simply ran off with a Sicilian girl.[10]

Finally, in 1973, an informant stepped up; he told the bureau that Tony Boy had caught Farina absconding with gambling funds. Farina was murdered in the back room of a restaurant owned by Jimo Calabrese, a Boiardo lieutenant and enforcer. Calabrese did the killing. In planning this murder, Tony Boy had done the right thing, which he did not always do: he got the appropriate approvals, adhered to the organization's chain of command, and delivered the okay to Andy Gerardo.[11]

After months of playing cat and mouse with prying FBI agents, one day the Boot very casually dropped a bombshell: he admitted to agents that "he took the oath in blood many years ago and swore to God that he would be faithful to the organization."[12] The agency received this news enthusiastically, calling it "an encouraging development" and a "breakthrough," and the Washington bureau sent out a "recommendation for commendation" and "incentive awards" to the agents involved.[13]

Unfortunately for the bureau, the breakthrough was short-lived. In subsequent drop-ins, eager federal agents faced a sphinx-like patriarch; the Boot turned cold, was evasive, denied he knew anything about La Cosa Nostra. He told the determined G-men they were welcome to drop by again anytime, but he gave up nothing in follow-up meetings. Bureau agents grew frustrated, though they remained persistent, returning time and time again to listen as the Boot reminisced about the glory days and engaged in small talk.

Federal agents also were determined to get to the bottom of a persistent rumor, one that still lingers to this day, that the Boot buried a vast treasure of money and jewelry on the grounds, specifically in his Godfather Garden, deep in the thorny, protective jungle of his massive rose bushes. In one conversation with a visitor who was later interviewed by the FBI, the Boot claimed that the apocryphal stash had already been "dug up" and then several minutes later confided that the cache was still buried on the grounds: "He stated that if [anyone] wanted it after he died, they would have to find it and added that there was no 'map' as to its location. All the information was in his 'head.'"[14]

According to Roger Hanos, the Boot did indeed squirrel away a secret fortune on the farm, but it was not buried in the rose garden. It was hidden in the boiler room in the basement of the main house, in a hollow compartment beneath a trick window ledge that opened like a treasure chest and contained cigar boxes filled with silver coins and plastic garbage bags stuffed with bundles of cash in large denominations. The Boot disclosed the secret to Roger near the end of his life, a couple years before he passed away. Roger had a sense that his grandfather was worried that he would die and no one would know about it or that that government would search his house and confiscate it. Roger does not know what happened to this treasure; it remains a mystery to this day.

Meanwhile, the outside world continued to stumble into the Boot's sacred Godfather Garden; and so he created an ad hoc line of defense. He asked Roger, whom he called "Rogee," and his brother, Darrel, to walk the thirty-acre estate with shotguns to hunt down varmints that were preying on his vegetables and the birds in his aviary. "In retrospect, we unwittingly played a role of providing security on the estate," said Roger. "My grandfather's visitors and friends couldn't help noticing our presence."

For most of his adolescence, Roger was unaware of the full scope of his grandfather's criminal background. Roger was close to the Boot yet also disconnected. "It's amazing how little we knew. I am eternally grateful that my mother did the best she could for her children in a difficult environment and that my grandfather shielded us from his first family."

One thing Rose shielded her sons from was knowledge of a possible murder that took place on the farm. It appears she accidentally stumbled into the middle of a crime in progress. She held onto this story for years, revealing it to Roger just before she passed away.

> I was in the downstairs kitchen with Papa and John Russo [Big Pussy], and an associate of theirs stopped by. Papa offered him a cup of espresso, and he refused. Maybe he thought he was going to be poisoned. Then Papa told me to take you upstairs. You were small and still in a highchair. After climbing up to the third floor, where the bedrooms are located, I heard a loud bang. I was curious; however, I waited a little while, then went down to see what happened. As I walked into the kitchen I saw blood on the floor and Papa cleaning it up. The associate was not there. There also was the distinct smell of smoke in the kitchen. I started to help Papa clean up the blood when Tony Boy came in and was a bit upset and told me to go back upstairs. Later a news story came out that said Papa's associate had disappeared.[15]

It was hard to be completely insulated from the mob. The Boot's most trusted hit man, Big Pussy, was Roger's confirmation sponsor. Tall and elegant, Big Pussy stood up at the altar at Saint Philomena's Church in Livingston and later handed Roger a diamond ring and a solid gold Omega watch as a confirmation gift. When Roger graduated from high school, the Boot instructed him to visit Big Pussy at Toppeta Motor Sales in Newark.

Big Pussy handed Roger the keys to a brand-new car. In 1960, when Big Pussy was shot in the Fremont Tavern incident and almost died, Roger and his father visited him at his home in Wayne, where he recuperated.

> All of our lives we were surrounded by Grandpa's associates, many of whom were friends and either socialized or grew up with the family in the First Ward neighborhood: Abe Zwillman, Jerry and Gene Catena, Andy Gerardo, Michele Miranda, Carmine Battaglia, John Russo, Anthony Russo, Gino Farina, Charlie "the Blade" [Tourine], Johnny Coke, Louie Coke, Angelo Chieppa, Pee Wee [DePhillips], Billy Jinks, Jimo Calabrese, Toby Boyd. In addition, there were many famous celebrities who visited the Livingston estate.

Joe DiMaggio's visit to the farm was the occasion of an awkward incident. "Joe DiMaggio was having dinner at the house and my cousin Mario, who was about ten at the time, said, 'Hey Joe, catch,' and he threw a baseball at Joe, who wasn't expecting it while he was sitting there. Grandpa gave Mario a quick smack across the face." It was the only time Roger saw the Boot hit any of the grandchildren.

When Roger's sister, Lillian, got married in 1966, the Boot hired the Four Seasons to perform at the wedding. The reception was held at Thomm's, a grand eating house in Newark formerly owned by the Boot and called the Sorrento. The Boot picked up the tab and gave away one silver dollar to each of the five hundred guests; waitresses distributed the coins from cigar boxes. When Frankie Valli and the boys started up, word got out to the community and locals tried to crash the party.

After he was severed from the Great Mob Trial and the Jolly Trolley case, the Boot became almost a recluse at the farm. The death of his son, Tony Boy, and Big Pussy's sudden passing in 1978 left the Boot managing the New Jersey Genovese faction's family interests largely from home. Andy Gerardo was made acting capo, and after he was sent to prison following the Operation Intrepid convictions, Pee Wee was placed in charge. With the disarray in his organization's leadership and his income decimated, the Boot sold most of his belongings—antique furniture, fixtures, and art work—to pay legal expenses and doctors' bills. The estate and property had already been deeded to Tony Boy's wife in the early 1950s. He held on to a few weapons. "Until the day he passed away, he kept a loaded gun hidden under a hat on top of his bedside night stand," said his grandson Roger.

The Boot's health spiraled down quickly; he suffered from cardiac problems, arthritis, a double hernia, and a lengthy bout with the shingles. He lived alone at the Livingston estate with intermittent hospitalizations; close family and friends visited on a regular basis to help out. Somehow he soldiered on, defying the odds, taking care of business.

When the Boot could no longer take care of himself or feed himself or go to the bathroom, friends and family began showing up more frequently, acting as nursemaids. Once Roger left him in the bathtub for five minutes. When he returned he found the water had drained from the tub and the Boot lay there naked, freezing cold. Another time, Peter Penna found the Boot lying on the garage floor; he had been there for twenty-four hours. During one hospital stay, the Boot asked Roger, as a favor, to obtain some poison from a local funeral home so that he could kill himself. Roger ignored the request.

As his condition deteriorated, the Boot was admitted to University Hospital in Newark. He was on a pacemaker; his blood pressure and heart rate were perilously low. Fluid was building up in his lungs; when they took x-rays, the doctors saw the shotgun pellets still in his chest from the 1930 assassination attempt. "He was ninety-three; you'd think they'd let him fade away," said Roger, "but they really worked on him." He was so sick and tortured with a feeding tube in his stomach, he instructed Roger to go home and retrieve his pistol so that he could shoot himself. His grandson leaned over, kissed him, said he loved him and would never do such a thing. "I honestly believe that he would have killed himself if he had the means to do it," said Roger.

Just before his last hospitalization, the Boot gave his grandson specific instructions regarding his funeral arrangements. He actually picked out the suit, shirt, and shoes he wanted put on. He said to Roger, "When I die, plant some flowers on my grave."

On November 17, 1984, the Boot passed away in his hospital bed. Roger received the call from Newark's University Hospital at 4 A.M. and notified his family and Pee Wee, who requested that Roger not publicize the wake or funeral arrangements because he would like "friends of his grandfather's" to be allowed to attend the wake without any publicity. Roger agreed, but only for the first day of the wake; the second day would be for family. On the first night of the wake, Pee Wee and about eight of his lieutenants arrived; they stood at attention, like a military unit, and marched to the coffin to pay their respects, one by one. "Pee Wee was crying uncontrollably," said Roger. "What impressed me the most was how sincere and loyal these guys were to my grandfather. I sensed that he was like a father figure to them since he knew them all of their lives and knew their parents also."

The Boot's funeral mass was held in Saint Lucy's Church in the North Ward, beneath the magnificent stained-glass window that the Boot had donated to the church many years before. It was a modest service attended by one hundred mourners, mostly close family friends and forty relatives including almost all of his thirteen grandchildren and nine great-grandchildren. There was no eulogy. Reverend Michael Fuino read from Saint Paul's Letter to the Romans: "But why do you judge your brother? Or why do you show contempt for your brother? For we shall all stand before the judgment of the seat of Christ."[16]

A cortege of seventeen cars including a hearse, two flower cars, and four limousines transported the Boot a few miles out of the city to the Holy Cross Catholic Cemetery in Arlington. After a simple graveside ceremony, the Boot's body was laid to rest alongside his wife, Jennie, his infant daughter, Carmenella, his mother, Maria Carmine Favarulo, and—unknown to all the mourners—the tiny body of Sara Carmela Serpico, aged one year, seven months, and twenty-two days. She was the daughter of John Serpico, one of the Boot's close friends from the old days in the North Ward and perhaps even further back to Italy.

Serpico emigrated from Marigliano, where the Boot was raised as a small child, and he arrived in the United States in August 1901, four months before young Ruggiero Boiardo. Serpico was the barber who helped start the Boot in his notorious career, selling him hair-tonic alcohol during Prohibition. According to records kept in the Megaro Funeral Home in Belleville, Sara died in Newark Babies Hospital on August 19, 1929, of appendicitis. She had a proper funeral with a hearse (cost seventeen dollars), limousine (six dollars), flower car (eleven dollars), and church service (five dollars). Her pine box was shipped to the funeral home from Philadelphia. A barely legible handwritten notation on the invoice appears to read: "Paid per R."[17]

The Boot's exact arrangement with John Serpico for his daughter's burial remains a mystery. No one in the Boiardo family was aware of the circumstances. One can imagine that the funeral was paid for by the Boot, that his friend, struggling to make a living in the New World, did not have the money for a ceremony or a burial. The gangster offered his own family plot; the alternative was a pauper's grave, and the Boot would have none of that, not for an innocent child. His gesture was as an act of ultimate kindness and perhaps contrition. Sara Carmela Serpico was laid to rest beside the Boot's mother and his infant daughter Carmenella. Two weeks after the service, the Longy War began with the shooting of Ralph Russo.

Richie the Boot was a curious puzzle, a monster and a saint; he could be unselfish, generous and yet terrifyingly brutal. Life meant everything to him, and nothing. He lived by the gun and died in a bed. He came to the New World to pursue a dream and ended chasing a nightmare.

THE CURSE

"Body in Rug Believed to be Grandson of Mobster"

The headline in the *Star-Ledger* of November 22, 2006, was an anachronism, a throwback to the sixties, when the paper was called the *Newark Star-Ledger* and grisly Mafia hits in New Jersey and New York were commonplace. Michael Balestro, forty years old, was identified as the body in the rug. The mobster was Richie "the Boot" Boiardo. He hadn't appeared in the news in thirty years, though he had been a household name in the Garden State for decades. Balestro was the son of one of the Boot's daughters. He had grown up on the Boot's Livingston estate, which had gates and fences patrolled by snarling Belgian shepherds and, allegedly, was guarded by men in black suits with guns. He got whacked by the mob. That was the impression created by the press reports.

Missing-persons reports had been filed on Balestro months before, when a friend and relatives couldn't find him at home. He had moved out of the estate years ago and was living in a small wood-frame two-bedroom off Northfield Avenue, about one mile away from the old compound. Livingston Detective Ron Barbella and a handful of Livingston police officers and crime-scene detectives from the Essex County prosecutor's office went to the house and broke in through a side window. The place was empty. In the living room a large rectangular patch had been cut out of the carpet. The officers also found large bleached-out patches of carpeting in the dining room, as if someone had scrubbed away spots, and bloodstains on the floor and walls. "We checked out the basement," said Barbella. "Michael had a lot of junk stored down there. The stuff was piled up nice and neat, nothing seemed out of the ordinary. The place didn't smell, except for the smell of mildew, which was normal for Michael's house. Mildew, stale alcohol, old food; that's what it smelled like."[1] The Essex County crime-scene investigators also searched the house and took samples of the stains. And then they sealed off the house.

Barbella had known Balestro well. They had gone to school together and had been friends; but Michael drifted away in high school, became a loner and recluse. He had been collecting disability checks for chronic depression. His skin was pale and sickly; he had a thick bushy mustache, wore thick prescription glasses, and always wore a New York Yankees cap. He looked odd, to say the least. "Nicest guy in the world," said Barbella, "wouldn't hurt anyone."

The Livingston cops returned again the next day with State Police investigators and officers from the Essex County prosecutor's office with Voodoo and Nero, a pair of German shepherd cadaver dogs. The police searched the house, but didn't disturb anything; they were not looking for a body at first. "Finally they let the dogs go," Barbella recalled. "They bolted right into the house and right into the basement and they went crazy around this couch that was stacked with boxes." The officers moved some boxes and found a rolled-up carpet that was like the carpet in the living room. The dogs were agitated; they circled, whined, and scratched on the concrete floor in the direction of the carpet. One of the officers poked a knife deep into the rolled up carpet and liquid poured out, spilling to the floor. "The smell, God it was horrible. It was the smell of death," said Barbella.

Balestro's body was found inside, wrapped in a sheet and fully covered with a heavy layer of spray-foam insulation. Over that was a heavy layer of duct tape head to toe; another sheet was wrapped around the tape and then the piece of carpet. "Basically he was mummified," said Barbella. "You couldn't smell him until the carpet was punctured."

It was later determined by the county coroner that Michael was shot point blank in the back with a forty-five-caliber pistol. The bullet exited through his lung and heart. His body had been in the basement, rolled up in the carpet, for over a month.

Detective Barbella had been at his desk when the first missing-persons call came in. It was mid-August. Barbella and his partner, Dave Fischgrund, ran the Livingston Police Department's juvenile division; typically in the summer and on holidays they collared shoplifters at the Livingston mall, but when they were not working juvenile cases, they took whatever came over the transom.

"John Kirby called," Barbella recalled. "He's a good friend of Michael Balestro. He said he had something weird to tell me. Every year he and Michael get together for Fourth of July. But Michael didn't call. So John called him, left messages, and got no reply." Kirby had stopped by the house a few times; no one was home, and Michael's car, a blue 1976 Dodge Dart, was missing from the driveway.

Another call came in from Mary DelMaestro, an aunt of Michael's. She told Detective Fischgrund that her birthday came and went—on July 2—and she didn't hear from her nephew. Michael always called on her birthday. She decided to call him. Michael's roommate, David Scioscia, answered. They spoke for a few seconds, and then he abruptly cut her off, said he had to go and would call her back; but he never did. She was worried.

A third call came into the department from Anthony Balestro, who lived at the Jersey Shore and was an uncle of Michael's. Uncle Tony also hadn't spoken to Michael for months, no return phone calls, nothing. He had driven up to Michael's house to check on him, but no one was home. Uncle Tony spoke to a clerk at Michael's bank, Valley National in Livingston. The clerk told him Michael had been in recently and had cashed a Social Security check.

Barbella also knew Scioscia, the roommate, and tracked down a cell-phone number for him. Scioscia told Barbella that he had seen Balestro four days earlier and said he might be playing in a band in a bar in

Whippany. Barbella checked. Balestro wasn't in Whippany. He hadn't been there for months.

From the start, when the suspicious disappearance of Michael Balestro was brought to the attention of the Livingston cops, they were under no illusions. They didn't believe that the Mafia was involved. They knew Michael too well. "He was a mess," said Tommy Paranzine, a Livingston patrol officer. "I used to go to his house a dozen times a month or more. Nuisance calls. He fought with his father constantly. They were both drunks. They'd hit each other. The neighbors called us. I remember he was lying in his bed, all bloody after a drunken bout with his old man. I said to him, 'Michael, come on get up, let's go.' He got up and there was a bag of marijuana on his bed, out in the open. I said, 'Michael, come on. How stupid is that?' And I'd have to arrest him. He'd spend the night in jail, and he was back out the next day. He was a disaster."[2]

His father died—of natural causes—and Michael got lonely. He'd call up the police station just to talk to someone. "He'd say to me, 'I know you. You're so and so.' He thought I was someone he went to school with," said Paranzine, "and that wasn't me. But he insisted. He was a sad case. We never thought that Michael's disappearance had anything to with anything other than him being a fuckup."[3]

Michael was a dysfunctional child from a dysfunctional family that had lived on the estate of a Mafia don. His father operated a small-scale Italian lottery out of his house to make a living. Michael and young Mario often found their father at the kitchen table, lottery slips spread out in front of him.[4] In the fall of 1966, two detectives from the prosecutor's office slipped into the compound by concealing themselves in the trunk of the car of adoption-agency representatives who had an appointment to see Michael and little Mario. When the car pulled up to their home on the estate, the officers jumped out, barged into the home, and seized $595 in horse race slips and $105 in lottery slips. They also confiscated betting account books, account sheets, a daily racing sheet, and three telephones, and they arrested Mario. At the time the Balestro boys did not know they were adopted, and at the request of the family local newspapers reported the incident discreetly, mentioning only that the officers "entered the property under a ruse." The secret was kept from the boys. More than twenty years later Michael found out he was adopted; his older brother never did.

On October 17, 1973, Phyllis Balestro was standing on a three-foot step-ladder cleaning a window in Michael's bedroom. She was a small woman and had to pull down the top portion of the storm window and lean out to clean the exterior glass. The police later said a "tension spring mechanism" locked after pushing the lower portion of the storm window up. Phyllis lost her footing on the ladder and was left dangling, her neck locked in the window, which acted as a vise.[5]

When Michael came home after school, he couldn't get into the house. He went to his aunt Rose's house next door. They tried to reach Phyllis by telephone. When no one answered, they went back to the house. Rose broke a window to get in, and Michael found his mother hanging by the neck in his bedroom window. He was only eight years old. Rose raced to the bedroom and tried to hold Phyllis's body up to keep her from chok-ing until help arrived. But it was too late; Phyllis was dead. The incident was reported in the *Newark Star-Ledger*, which didn't fail to mention that Phyllis was the daughter of "aging mob kingpin Ruggiero . . . Ritchie the Boot . . . Boiardo and the brother of Anthony . . . Tony Boy . . . Boiardo, the reputed heir to his father's underworld dealings."[6]

"When we got there we found the woman with her head wedged between a storm window that slammed shut and the upper window sill," a Livingston policeman told the *New York Times*, which published an unusually long article considering this was the accidental death of a sub-urban mom. "The estate has been shrouded in secrecy for years," the *Times* reported, "and is described by neighbors as a very private place, with a winding road leading up to the gargoyled homes, which are not visible from the public road."[7]

Phyllis was the daughter of a Mafia don, and rumors quickly spread. It was too bizarre; how could someone be killed by a storm window? Had one of the Boot's many enemies infiltrated the heavily guarded estate, some-how eluded the pack of Belgian shepherd attack dogs, and sent a message to the Boot by murdering his daughter on his own turf? The neighbors whispered these things.[8]

The kids at Livingston public school gossiped in the hallways, despite the fact that the coroner's office ruled the death an accident. Michael Balestro heard it all, and because he had seen his mother dead, he took it very hard. He became despondent, as did his father, who began drinking and taking sedatives. "They put themselves into a hole," said Aunt Mary. "We invited them to family dinners and parties, and they never came."

In 1977 Michael's older brother, Mario Jr., graduated from high school and went out celebrating with four other classmates in an International Scout with a canvas roof. At 1:30 in the morning the driver of the Scout tried to dash across Route 10 from a side street. A car driven by a young woman struck the Scout, and the boys were thrown through the canvas top. Mario was the unlucky one. The others were tossed into the trees; Mario hit the pavement, and his head slammed into the curb. He was the only one killed.

Mario Sr. and Michael became even more withdrawn. The house on the farm fell into disrepair. They argued with each other. A few years after young Mario's death they sold the house, moved out of the Boiardo compound, and bought the cottage just off Northfield Avenue. It was not a happy move. Away from the influence of the Boot and the rest of the family, the sanity and health of father and son declined rapidly. They tuned out the rest of the world, lived like hermits, and constantly fought with one another.

During one battle, in anger, Mario Sr. revealed that Michael was an orphan and not his real son. The news shocked Michael. "The boys were adopted through a doctor in Newark," said Aunt Mary. "Phyl couldn't have kids. She tried, but something was wrong. So the doctor told her about these two unmarried young girls, the doctor's patients, who were giving up their babies. Mario and Phyl took them." Michael began to search for his birth mother. "He wanted to find out about her, who she was," said Aunt Mary. "He tried and tried but couldn't find her. He dropped it eventually, but it never stopped bothering him, this idea that he didn't know who his real parents were. It was awful for him."

Michael's father died in 2000, age seventy-four. Michael was left alone in the house. He spent his days drinking and practicing the guitar—he was a self-taught musician—sometimes playing music in bar bands in the area. One day an old friend, David Scioscia, showed up on his doorstep. He had been kicked out of his house by his mother and needed a place to stay. Michael rented him a room for $300 a month. Scioscia was a loner and a misfit, like Michael. They had gone to Livingston High together, both graduating in 1983. Scioscia went from job to job and frequently drifted around the country, but he always returned to Livingston.

Vinnie and Anna Marie Falzo, who owned Cammarata's Pizzeria on South Livingston Avenue, told a local news reporter that Scioscia had worked for them on and off for five years a decade before. He was hard-working and well-liked by the customers, they said, but he appeared mentally unbalanced at times. He would talk to himself and was prone to sudden mood shifts. He would fail to show up for work one day and not reappear for months, and then without an explanation. "He was a little strange," Vinnie Falzo said. "He had kind of a split personality."[9] Public records show Scioscia had addresses in Wilmington, North Carolina, and Aurora, Colorado, in the late 1990s. But the Falzos said they never hesitated to rehire him because he never caused problems in the pizzeria and did his job well. "He really is a very nice person," Anna Marie Falzo said.[10]

The Falzos said that more recently he had worked as an auto mechanic at the Gulf station on South Livingston Avenue and at a Sears auto center and had also worked as a courier. In his high school yearbook Scioscia was pictured with neatly combed hair and was described as a nature enthusiast who loved camping trips and visits to the Shore. It said he planned to join the Coast Guard and learn to be an electrician. "Live life the way you want it to be for yourself," was the quote printed under his photograph.[11]

After Michael was reported missing and Scioscia's story about his possible whereabouts didn't check out, Barbella contacted Valley National Bank, Balestro's bank. The manager found that Michael's debit card had been used at ATMs at local bank branches in Caldwell and at the Willowbrook Mall in Wayne; his account was now empty. The bank's security director retrieved video footage and photos of the person using the ATMs and sent them to the police. "It was someone dressing up as Michael and doing a half-ass job of it," Barbella said. "Michael always wore a Yankee hat, glasses, always had a funny mustache, long hair, very pale. The impersonator wore the hat and glasses, but sometimes had a mustache and sometimes didn't, and his hair was an obvious wig."[12] Barbella requested more ATM videos from the bank and finally recognized the imposter—Scioscia. He had been using Michael's card as far back as June.

Essex County prosecutors issued an arrest warrant. They also requested permission from the phone company to track Scioscia's cell-phone usage. Scioscia was tracked through his phone from Jersey to Florida to Minnesota to Del Rio, Texas, and into Mexico. Mexican border police turned him around at the border because he didn't have proper registration for his car. As he backed up to return to the United States, his tires were punctured by security spikes. U.S. customs officers brought him in, ran a check on the vehicle, and he was caught. Officers from Livingston flew down to Texas and took custody of Scioscia. During a layover at an airport in Houston, he blurted out, "I shot him." He then gave the police a full confession, telling them where he had hid the gun. The officers recorded it all on tape.

It turned out that Scioscia had learned that his friend was deeding his house to a Catholic charity in his will. The donation had been orchestrated by his neighbors. When Michael signed the will, Scioscia was there and co-signed the document as a witness. "He learned that Michael was worth something, and things went to his head," said Uncle Tony. "So he shot him in the back to make some money."[13]

In court, despite overwhelming evidence of his guilt—including his own confession that he had shot Michael—Scioscia pleaded self-defense.

Instead of going through a lengthy trial, Essex county prosecutors allowed Scioscia to cop a plea. He was sentenced to fifteen years in prison, but he immediately got the sentence reduced to fourteen years because he didn't have a criminal record. "I started fighting the sentence," said Uncle Tony. "But the court didn't care. Michael was just an alcoholic. They said it didn't matter. So I dropped it. Why keep proceeding when nothing means nothing?"[14]

Although in the end, despite all the rumors, Michael was not murdered by the mob, family members are convinced his death was indirectly related to the Mafia. "He was a victim of the family curse. You know, the sins of the fathers are visited upon their sons. That's what happened to Michael," said his uncle Tony Balestro, sitting in his house in Tom's River.[15] His sister Mary—Michael's aunt Mary DelMaestro—sat on a couch beside him crying. "It's such a shame; he was such a good boy," said Mary. "Yes, it was the family curse. It was because of what the Boot did. Poor Michael paid the price."[16]

TIMELINE

December 8, 1890	Ruggiero Boiardo is born and placed in a Naples orphanage. He is adopted in 1896 by Maria Carmine Favarulo and Antonio Esposito of Marigliano, Italy, in the Province of Naples.
December 18, 1901	Ruggiero emigrates to the United States with his parents and eventually lands in Chicago.
1906	Ruggiero relocates to Newark with his mother.
January 8, 1912	Ruggiero marries Giovannina "Jennie" Manfro.
August 1, 1913	Daughter Agnes is born.
September 3, 1914	Ruggiero "Tony Boy" Boiardo Jr. is born.
July 26, 1919	Daughter Mary is born.
January 11, 1920	The Boot is charged with operating a gambling house and is fined $52.05.
January 17, 1920	Date set by the Volstead Act for Prohibition, which banned the sale of alcohol, to begin.
September 11, 1920	Daughter Carmenella is born.
November 4, 1920	The Boot becomes an American citizen at the age of twenty-nine.
August 8, 1921	Daughter Carmenella dies.
January 12, 1922	The Boot is convicted and sentenced to twelve months of hard labor for manslaughter in the accidental killing of Antonio Romeo.

August 7, 1922	Daughter Rosina is born.
1924	The Boot's mother dies.
December 23, 1925	The Boot, Frank Mazzocchi, and Sam Angelo are arrested on a concealed-weapons charge; they are convicted and serve six months in Essex County Penitentiary.
May 20, 1926	Daughter Phyllis is born.
1928–1931	Castellammarese War. This conflict for the control of organized crime involved the two major Italian American crime families of New York led by Salvatore Maranzano and Joe "the Boss" Masseria. The end of this war led to the creation of an organized syndicate of Italian and Jewish gang leaders.
February 14, 1929	The Saint Valentine's Day Massacre takes place in Chicago.
May 13, 1929	The Atlantic City conference of the nation's top gang leaders convenes for the purposes of determining territorial boundaries and establishing a commission to resolve issues peacefully.
December 4, 1929	Rival Mazzocchi gang member Joseph Rosso is killed by John "Big Pussy" Russo.
May–December 1930	Some time during this period, Al Capone meets with the Boot and Longy Zwillman in an attempt to settle matters between them.
May 6, 1930	Rival gang leader Frank Mazzocchi is shot and killed.
October 5–6, 1930	The Boot/Zwillman peace banquet is held.
November 26, 1930	The Boot is the victim of an assassination attempt.
March 9, 1931	The Boot, who was tried and convicted of weapons possession, begins a 2 1/2-year prison sentence.
October 23, 1935	Dutch Schultz and three associates are murdered in Newark.

1945	The Boot leaves Newark and moves his family to the Livingston estate.
1946	The Boot takes the oath of La Cosa Nostra and becomes a "made" member.
October 22, 1946	The Boot's wife, Jennie, dies at age fifty-three.
April 30, 1950	The Boot's son, Tony Boy, marries Catherine Porreca.
October 4, 1951	Willie Moretti, a mob leader in Passaic and Bergen counties and Boot rival, is murdered.
May 2, 1957	Frank Costello steps down from La Cosa Nostra and resigns as boss of the Luciano family. Vito Genovese takes over; the family becomes Genovese.
November 10, 1957	The second largest mob meeting in the nation is held at the Boot's Livingston estate.
November 14, 1957	The Apalachin national mob meeting is held in upstate New York.
1958	The Boot turns over day-to-day operations to Tony Boy.
April 4, 1959	Vito Genovese is convicted of drug conspiracy and sent to prison. Jerry Catena is named acting boss of the Genovese family.
September 23, 1960	The Club Fremont shooting incident. The Boot comes out of retirement and takes back control of his crew.
1961	The FBI begins electronic eavesdropping of Sam the Plumber and Gyp DeCarlo.
October 1963	Joseph Valachi testifies in a U.S. Senate committee hearing that the Mafia exists; names Jerry Catena a boss, the Boot a captain, and Tony Boy a soldier in the Genovese family.
October 18, 1963	The Boot is called to testify at an Essex County grand jury hearing in response to Valachi's revelations.
July 13, 1966	Two teenagers are shot while trespassing on the Boot's estate.

February 3, 1967	The Boot is arrested for running a $20 million gambling operation.
September 1, 1967	*Life* magazine publishes an article exposing the Boot's Livingston estate.
April 28, 1968	The Boot and eighteen underlings are found guilty of running illegal gambling operations in Essex and Bergen counties.
December 1969	Tony Boy, Newark Mayor Hugh Addonizio, and others are indicted in a corruption-conspiracy case.
March 14, 1970	Jerry Catena is jailed for refusing to testify before a state crime commission.
July 6, 1970	Tony Boy suffers a heart attack and is severed from the corruption-conspiracy case.
September 22, 1970	In the corruption-conspiracy trial Hugh Addonizio is convicted and sentenced to ten years in prison and a $25,000 fine for taking kickbacks.
October 9, 1970	The Boot starts serving his prison term.
November 16, 1971	The Boot is released from prison at the age of eighty-one.
May 20, 1973	Angelo Chieppa's body is found stuffed in a car trunk in Kearny, New Jersey.
April 20, 1978	Tony Boy dies of a heart attack.
December 19, 1978	Big Pussy dies of natural causes.
April 26, 1979	Little Pussy is murdered.
September 27, 1979	The Great Mob Trial begins.
November 17, 1984	The Boot dies at the age of ninety-three.
April 23, 2000	Jerry Catena dies at the age of ninety-eight.
August 21, 2006	The Boot's grandson Michael is murdered.

CAST OF CHARACTERS

Henry Abrams (Kid Henry) A former pugilist and partner of the Boot in the Vittorio Castle Restaurant and the Rex B, an Italian lottery.

Hugh Addonizio (the Pope) Mayor of Newark from 1962 to 1970; convicted in the 1969 corruption-conspiracy case and sentenced to ten years in federal prison.

Anthony Alfone (Money) An early Boot gang member, thief, and cohort of Ralph Russo.

Albert Anastasia (Mad Hatter, Lord High Executioner) Murder Inc. boss, Mangano crime-family boss, and New York labor racketeer; executed by the mob in 1957.

Phyllis Boiardo Balestro The Boot's youngest daughter; resided at the Livingston estate with her husband, Mario Sr., and children, Mario Jr. and Michael.

Tony Bananas See Antonio Caponigro.

Amiri Baraka (formerly LeRoi Jones) Newark poet and black activist during the 1967 riots and throughout the election campaign of the city's first black mayor, Kenneth Gibson.

Mary Boiardo Barile The Boot's second oldest daughter; lived in South Orange, New Jersey, with her husband, Joseph, and children.

Edith Bencivengo The Boot's long-term girlfriend and housekeeper.

Tony Bender See Anthony Strollo.

Big Pussy See John Russo.

Ruggiero Boiardo Sr. (Richie the Boot, Diamond Ritchie) Newark Prohibition bootlegger and gang leader who became a Genovese family caporegime (captain, capo) and one of the most powerful and enduring mob chieftains on the East Coast.

Ruggiero Anthony Boiardo Jr. (Tony Boy) The Boot's son, Genovese lieutenant, and businessman; managed gambling, loan-shark, and extortion operations and owned legitimate enterprises.

Vincent James Calabrese (Jimo) A lieutenant and enforcer in the Boiardo gang; supervised some gambling operations.

Paul Campanile A Trenton, New Jersey, gangster and numbers runner.

Alphonse Capone (Al, Scarface) A Brooklyn, New York, gangster who became the boss of Chicago's underworld during Prohibition; had a vested interest in uninterrupted booze shipments from New Jersey and New York, which the Boot and Longy Zwillman controlled.

Antonio Caponigro (Tony Bananas) Newark Fifth Ward crime leader and Boot associate known for his violent temper; he rose to become consigliere, or counselor, of the Bruno crime family.

Joe Casey See Joseph Juliano.

Francesco Castiglia (Frank Costello) Succeeded Lucky Luciano as boss of the Luciano crime family, which became the Genovese family; resigned after an assassination attempt on his life.

Eugene Catena (Gene) One of Jerry Catena's younger brothers; lieutenant who oversaw Port Newark waterfront gambling and union racketeering.

Frank Catena One of Jerry Catena's younger brothers; a powerbroker in the International Longshoreman's Association, Local 1235, which controlled the Port Newark waterfront.

Gerardo Vito Catena (Jerry) A Zwillman associate who rose to become acting boss of the Genovese family, a successful businessman, and a friend and partner of the Boot.

Angelo Chieppa (Chip) Long-term associate and informant of the Boot; managed multiple illegal stills, Caribbean gambling interests, and skim operations for the Boot and his son, Tony Boy.

Louie Coke See Louis DeBenedetto.

Frank Costello See Francesco Castiglia.

Agnes Boiardo Crescenzi The Boot's oldest daughter; lived at the Livingston estate with her husband, Louis, and son, Maurice.

Louis DeBenedetto (Louie Coke) A Boot lieutenant who oversaw gambling activities and skimmed profits in Las Vegas.

Angelo DeCarlo (Gyp, Ray) A Boot underling during Prohibition; became a Genovese capo overseeing parts of Union and Monmouth counties in New Jersey. His office was bugged by the FBI, exposing the operations of the Boiardo crew. He was pardoned by Richard Nixon.

Simone Rizzo DeCavalcante (Sam the Plumber) A crime-family boss whose Kenilworth (New Jersey) office was bugged by the FBI, yielding 2,300 pages of transcribed mob conversations.

Nicholas Delmore (Nick, Delly) A Union County (New Jersey) bootlegger and bookmaker, a close associate of Zwillman and Catena; took charge of organized crime in Elizabeth. His nephew, Sam DeCavalcante, assumed control of his crew, which became known as the DeCavalcante family.

Thomas DePhillips (Pee Wee) A Boot lieutenant; assumed control of the Boiardo crew after Andy Gerardo's retirement; implicated in the murder of Little Pussy.

Anthony DeVingo A Boot soldier and enforcer; implicated in the murder of Little Pussy.

Eugene Farina (Gino) A Boot lieutenant and enforcer; oversaw bookkeeping and police department payoffs for the Boiardo crew's gambling operations; disappeared in 1967.

Arthur Flegenheimer (Dutch Schultz, the Dutchman) A Harlem and Bronx bootleg and gambling boss who distributed beer in New Jersey through the Boot; murdered in Newark in 1935.

Mario Gallo A Newark contractor who was indicted with Tony Boy in the 1969 Newark corruption–conspiracy case; was about to turn stool pigeon when he was killed in a car accident.

Vito Genovese (Don Vito) Appointed acting boss of the Luciano crime family in 1936 but fled to Italy shortly afterward to escape a murder charge. In 1946 he returned, rejoined the family, and ousted Frank Costello in 1957, taking over what became known as the Genovese family. The Boot was a capo in this faction under Costello and later Don Vito.

Andrew Gerardo (Andy) A Boot lieutenant who became acting capo of the crew after the Boot died in 1984. He retired to Florida in 1991.

Sam "Mooney" Giancana Chicago crime boss and an associate of the Boot; implicated in the CIA plot to assassinate Fidel Castro.

Kenneth Gibson Mayor of Newark following the conviction of former mayor Hugh Addonizio.

Rosina Boiardo Hanos (Rose) The Boot's third oldest daughter; resided at the Livingston estate with her husband, Arger (Turk), and children, Roger, Darrel, and Lillian.

Anthony Imperiale A North Ward leader and New Jersey assemblyman who led a group of vigilantes during the Newark riots in 1967.

Joseph Juliano (Joe Casey, Joe Julian) An original member of the Boot's First Ward gang; was the Boot's chauffeur and bodyguard at the time of the attempted assassination.

Irving Kantor A government witness in the 1969 Newark corruption-conspiracy trial; operated a shell company that laundered illegal contract payments.

Meyer Lansky One of the original Jewish syndicate leaders; was a close associate of Bugsey Siegal, Lucky Luciano, and Abner "Longy" Zwillman.

John Lardiere (Johnnie Coke) A Genovese lieutenant, enforcer, and union racketeer; served under Gene Catena.

Little Pussy See Anthony Russo.

Charles Luciano (Lucky) Boss of the Luciano crime family; architect and leader of the Five Family commission; brokered the resolution of the Longy War; was a silent partner with the Boot and others in the Capri Hotel and Casino in Havana.

Frank Mazzocchi (the Rum King, Chichi) A Prohibition bootlegger in the First and Second wards; a partner of the Boot and then an enemy; murdered in 1930.

John Mazzocchi Frank's brother and lieutenant; murdered in 1932.

Dominic Mazzocchi Brother of Frank and John.

Harold McLeod A gambler who fingered banks and numbers runners in black neighborhoods under the jurisdiction of the Boot and his son, Tony Boy.

Michele Miranda (Big Mike) A Genovese capo and later consigliere based in Forest Hills, Long Island; close associate of the Boot and Tony Bananas.

James Vito Montemarano A lieutenant of Little Pussy.

Guarino Moretti (Willie) A rival of the Boot; based in Passaic and Bergen counties (New Jersey); partnered with Zwillman and New York crime leaders in the illegal-booze and gambling business.

Timmy Murphy See Thomas Pecora.

Frank Nappi A Boot gang member during Prohibition; shot in the leg and permanently crippled by Joseph Rosso.

Dominic Paselli (the Ape, Sully the Ape) A Zwillman gang member during Prohibition; murdered in 1930.

Edward Pecora A mob boss and Teamsters Local 575 organizer; reported to Gene Catena.

Joseph Pecora (Joe Peck) Secretary-treasurer of Teamsters Local 863 in Newark and mob lieutenant in the Genovese family under Catena.

Thomas Pecora (Timmy Murphy) A union organizer, racketeer, and alleged hit man; reported to Gene Catena.

Peter Penna A close friend of the Boot and caretaker of the Livingston estate; lived there with his family.

Patrick Pizuto Little Pussy's driver; turned state's evidence against his boss in the Great Mob Trial and was placed in a witness-protection program.

Anthony Provenzano (Tony Pro) A top Teamsters official; allegedly a member of the Genovese family reporting to Jerry Catena.

George Raft Hollywood movie star and friend of the Boot and other gangsters; worked at the mob-owned Capri Hotel and Casino in Havana as host and director of entertainment.

Nathan Reiner (David Zipper) A New York racketeer and an early associate of the Boot; dabbled in narcotics.

Paul G. Rigo A contractor who worked on jobs for the city of Newark; became the key government witness in the 1969 corruption-conspiracy trial.

Joe Rogers See Joe Stassi.

Doc Rosen See Joseph Stacher.

Phillip Rossi (Phillip Rosso, Phillip Ross, Young Dilly) Joseph Rosso's brother, Mazzocchi gang member, former pugilist, and drug addict; murdered in 1931.

Joseph Rosso (Joseph Rossi, Joseph Ross) A Mazzocchi gang member and enforcer; killed by Big Pussy in 1929.

Johnnie Russell See Ralph Russo.

Anthony Russo (Little Pussy) Younger brother of Ralph and John; was a Boot lieutenant, driver for Vito Genovese; became a Jersey Shore crime boss; murdered in 1979.

John Russo (Big Pussy) A key Boot lieutenant from Prohibition through the 1970s; died of natural causes in 1978.

Ralph Russo (Johnnie Russell) Older brother of John and Anthony; a Boot lieutenant who ran the gang while the boss was in prison; murdered in 1936.

Carmine San Giacomo (Big Yock) An enforcer for Zwillman and Willie Moretti during the Prohibition wars.

Sam the Plumber See Simone Rizzo DeCavalcante.

Dutch Schultz See Arthur Flegenheimer.

Angelo Sica A Genovese lieutenant who managed an illegal lottery for the Boot.

Dominic Spina Newark police director appointed by Mayor Addonizio, served from 1962 to 1970; provided protection for the mob's illegal gambling activities throughout the city.

Joseph Stacher (Doc Rosen) A Zwillman lieutenant during Prohibition and successful business partner; moved to Las Vegas to manage mob interests in casinos.

Joe Stassi (Joe Rogers) A Zwillman lieutenant, Boot ally, and professed hit man; seventy years later implicated the Boot and Zwillman in the Dutch Schultz murder.

Anthony Strollo (Tony Bender) A Genovese capo who oversaw the family's bar and nightclub operations in Manhattan; disappeared in 1962.

Charles Tourine (the Blade) A Boiardo gang member during Prohibition; managed the casino at the Capri Hotel in Cuba and other mob operations in the Caribbean and Europe.

Patrick Truglia (Patsy) A Florida petty criminal with roots in Long Branch, New Jersey; became a target of Little Pussy's for drug dealing and reneging on loans.

David Zipper See Nathan Reiner.

Abner Zwillman (Longy) One of the original Big Six syndicate bosses, Zwillman, as they say, put the "organize" in organized crime. Initially, the Boot's archenemy and fiercest competitor; in the end, one of his best partners and friends. During the Prohibition years and up until his suicide in 1959, his influence and organizational skills were sought after by mobsters and politicians alike. A great leader who fell victim to his own success.

NOTES

NOTES ON ORIGINAL SOURCE MATERIALS

Some of the original source materials used in this book and cited in the notes came from newspaper clippings found in scrapbooks put together over the years by Richie "the Boot" Boiardo. He was an avid though amateur historian-unfortunately he often snipped off the names of newspapers and the dates of articles. The same is true of newspaper and magazine clippings collected by his daughter, Rosina "Rose" Boiardo Hanos. In most cases, Roger Hanos and I were able to track down the origin of these clippings; a few articles eluded us, as did a few articles that came from the Newark Evening News morgue at the Newark Public Library, which contains a large scrapbook on the Boot and his son, Tony Boy, with clippings from the Newark Evening News and the Star-Ledger, many of them missing source identification and dates.

The *Newark Evening News* morgue was given to Newark Public Library at the behest of author and historian John T. Cunningham when the newspaper went out of business in 1972. Included were 380 handwritten annual index volumes, 800,000 photos, and two million clippings. A Microsoft Access index to the subject headings of the clippings folders has 162,000 entries. Funds for microfilming the clippings and creating the clippings-folders index were provided by the New Jersey Historical Commission, the New Jersey State Library, and the National Endowment for the Humanities. The morgue is an invaluable, although oftentimes frustrating, resource for writers and historians.

Most of the FBI files that served as source material for this book were accessed through the Freedom of Information/Privacy Act (FOIPA), Title 5, United States Code, Section 552/52a. Others were accessed on the FBI's website, www.fbi.gov. In the list below, source files from the FBI's website are marked with asterisks. Each listing includes the subject's name, the range of Bufiles (FBI Bureau files) researched, and the time frame of the documents reviewed.

Settimo "Big Sam" Accardo, Bufile: 115-102, 9/5/52–1/30/79

Hugh Addonizio, Bufiles: 92-HQ-6370–HQ-92-11658, 11/27/62–8/10/77

Albert Anastasia, Bufile: 62-98011, 9/26/52–7/4/58

Ruggiero "Richie the Boot" Boiardo Sr., Bufiles: NK92-375–92-HQ-2942, 10/23/52–11/30/81

Ruggiero "Tony Boy" Boiardo Jr. Bufiles: 166-HQ-915–HQ179-1525, 9/30/58–1/14/77

Toby Boyd, Bufiles: 92-1504–92-8374, 7/30/65–10/18/75

Alphonse Capone, Bufile: 69:180–62-20619, 3/21/29–2/16/36*

Antonio "Tony Bananas" Caponigro, Bufiles: 70-HQ-4294–92-HQ-2703, 7/25/38–1/27/75

Gerardo Catena, Bufiles: 62-23825–92-3172, 1/24/34–3/1/77

Angelo Chieppa, Bufiles: 92-HQ-6257–166-HQ-6178, 6/5/47–1/16/74

Frank Costello, Bufiles: 51-401–92-2869, 2/6/35–2/14/69

Angelo "the Gyp" DeCarlo, Bufile: 179-195, 11/27/68–7/10/73

Emilio "the Count" Delio, Bufiles: NK92-1265–92-6255, 9/19/62–10/25/91

Thomas "Pee Wee" DePhillips, Bufiles: NK166-1675–182-21, 11/1/65–6/30/80

Eugene "Gino" Farina, Bufiles: NK92-1062–92-5636, 10/31/61–10/2/74

Arthur "Dutch Schultz" Flegenheimer, Bufile: 23-2130,
7/22/35–10/20/38*

Vito Genovese, Bufiles: HQ-92-2938–NY-58-7146, 12/24/57–2/10/70

Andrew Gerardo, Bufiles: 92-1381–183-485, 4/23/63–6/30/80

Vincent "the Chin" Gigante, Bufile: 92-4238, 7/6/59–12/3/76

Meyer Lansky, Bufiles: 62-97928–166-3701, 9/5/52–8/17/78

John "Johnnie Coke" Lardiere, Bufiles: NK137-23882–
NY183B-3629, 7/11/72–11/2/89

Charles Lucania aka Charles "Lucky" Luciano, Bufile: 39-2141,
8/28/35–9/27/65

Michele "Big Mike" Miranda, Bufiles: NY39-291–92-2860-1,
2/5/47–2/27/74

Guarino "Willie" Moretti, Bufiles:
95-45571–HQ62-86305,12/24/47–2/8/84

George Raft, Bufiles: 62-99407–65-54233, 7/25/42–4/4/67

Anthony "Little Pussy" Russo, Bufiles:
NK92-747–92-5617,10/31/61–3/1/84

John "Big Pussy" Russo, Bufiles: NK92-739–92-7637, 6/26/64–10/26/78

Dominic Spina, Bufile: NK157-2842, 9/17/52–6/21/77

Charles "the Blade" Tourine, Bufiles: NY92-2989–179-HQ-452,
11/13/44–10/22/76

Abner "Longy" Zwillman, Bufiles: NK62-36085–NK58-4441,
11/4/35–3/3/59

ABBREVIATIONS FOR FREQUENTLY USED SOURCES

NN	*Newark Evening News*
NNM	*Newark Evening News morgue files, Newark Public Library*
NSE	*Newark Star-Eagle*
NSL	*Star-Ledger [Newark], formerly Newark Star-Ledger*
NYT	*New York Times*

PROLOGUE

1. Boiardo, Ruggiero, Sr., FBI Reports, 2/14/64, 9/3/64, 3.

2. "Ritchie Case Draws Colorful Crowd to Essex Court House," *NN*, 2/19/31.

3. *NNM*, 11/29/30.

4. Ibid.

5. Boiardo, Ruggiero. Sr., FBI Memorandum, 2/22/71.

6. Boiardo obituary, *NSL*, 11/17/84.

7. *NSL*, 7/14/86; Thomas Pannullo interview, 10/22/10; Agnes Manfro DellAc-qua interview, 11/3/10.

8. Boiardo, Anthony. FBI Report, 7/31/59, 8.

9. *NSE,* 11/26/30.

10. *NN,* 11/29/30.

11. Ibid.

12. Patrick Downey, *Legs Diamond: Gangster* (New York: CreateSpace, 2011), 30–32.

13. *NN,* 11/29/30. Although according to this Newark Evening News story, Frankie Yale was "taken for a ride"—in other words, was murdered by assassins who had kidnapped him in a car—most reliable versions have him killed in his car by a drive-by machine-gun attack on a Brooklyn street. According to one such account that appeared in the New York Daily News (5/1/98), Yale was wearing his belt buckle when he died, and his widow later sold it for $500 to help pay for the murdered gangster's funeral.

14. Ibid.

15. *NSE,* 11/26/30.

16. *Asbury Park [New Jersey] Press*, 11/26/30.

17. *NSE,* 11/26/30.

18. *NYT,* 11/27/30, 30.

19. *NN,* 11/26/30.

20. *NSE,* 11/26/30.

21. *NN,* 11/26/30, 1.

22. *NSE,* 11/26/30.

23. *NN,* 11/29/30.

24. *Asbury Park Press*, 11/26/30.

25. *NN,* 11/26/30.

26. Ibid.

27. *NSE,* 11/26/30.

28. *NN,* 11/26/30.

29. *NSE,* 11/26/30.

30. *Asbury Park Press*, 11/26/30.

31. *NN*, 11/29/30.

32. *NNM*, 2/19/30.

33. Ibid.

34. Sarah Ball, "An American Family," *Vanity Fair*, April 2012. http://www.vanityfair.com/hollywood/2012/04/sopranos-exclusive-slideshow, accessed 3/1/12.

35. Robert V. Baer, Plaintiff ,v. David Chase, DC Enterprises, United States District Court for the District of New Jersey, Civil Action No. 02-CV-2334 (JAP), Certification of David Chase, Clause #14, 4.

36. Boiardo, Ruggiero, Sr., FBI Memorandum, 5/3/72.

CHAPTER 1 — DIAMOND RITCHIE

1. Roger Hanos interviews. The author interviewed Roger Hanos, the grandson of Richie "the Boot" Boiardo, innumerable times from 2007 through 2012. Many intimate facts about the Boot and his immediate family and associates were disclosed during these conversations.

2. *NN*, 11/29/30.

3. Ibid.

4. *NN*, 6/11/69, 12.

5. Information about Newark in this paragraph and the next from Michael Immerso, *Newark's Little Italy: The Vanished First Ward* (New Brunswick, N.J.: Rutgers University Press, 1997), 7, 15, 16, 45.

6. *NN*, 7/28/21.

7. *NN*, 5/20/21.

8. *NN*, 1/26/27.

9. *Timelines of the Great Depression,* n.d., www.huppi.com/kangaroo/Timeline.htm, 1.

10. *Cumberland [Maryland] Sunday Times*, 7/2/34.

11. *Indianapolis Star*, 11/11/19, 14.

12. *NN*, 12/23/25.

13. Rich Walling, "Tales of the Unique and Stranger Side of a Rural Township." In *Weird East Brunswick* (East Brunswick, N.J.: East Brunswick Museum, 2003), 2–3. Also, in an FBI Memorandum (9/26/68, 5), the Boot claimed that in "the old days he operated stills and collected protection money from other still owners in the Mendham area."

14. Ibid.

15. *NYT*, 10/26/27, 50.

16. Rosina "Rose" Boiardo Hanos interview. Roger Hanos interviewed his mother for this book over the course of three years, from 2007 until her death on April 10, 2009.

17. *NN*, 7/9/29.

18. Boiardo, Ruggiero, Sr., FBI Memorandum, 5/12/54, 6–7.

19. Boiardo, Ruggiero, Sr., FBI Memorandum, 7/14/67.

20. *NN*, 11/29/30.

21. *NYT*, 1/13/30, 1.

22. *NYT*, 3/8/29, 14.

23. Laurence Bergreen, *Capone: The Man and the Era* (New York: Simon & Schuster, 1994), 286.

24. Robert Rudolph, "Solving a Two-Decade-Old-Mafia Hit," *NSL*, 2/9/98, 1.

25. "Man 65 Routs Robbers. Bandits Caught, but Some One Robs Jeweler during Excitement," *NYT*, 2/7/25, 5.

26. "Duffy Tells How First Ward Gang Reign Has Been Broken," *Newark Call*, 7/12/38,

27. *Asbury Park [New Jersey] Press*, 8/29/29, 1.

28. *NN*, 6/11/29, 1.

29. *NNM*, 12/4/29.

30. Ibid.

31. Ibid.

32. *NNM*, 12/5/29.

33. *NN*, 12/4/29.

34. Russo, John, FBI Report, 6/26/64, 6.

35. Fred D. Pasley, *Al Capone: The Biography of a Self-Made Man* (New York: Garden City Publishing, 1930), 114.

36. *NN*, 5/6/30, 1.

37. *NN*, 5/7/30, 1.

38. "Trial May End Ritchie's Power," *NN*, 11/28/30.

39. *NNM*, 3/20/31.

40. One of the Boot's men, Dominic Tetta, who had a police record going back to 1896—his first arrest was when he was eight years old—was found murdered in an apartment in downtown New York one month after the Boot was shot. "Two Slayings Mark Day's Crime Record," *NYT*, 14.

41. *NYT*, 3/21/31, 5.

42. *NYT*, 3/6/32, 25.

43. *Newark Call*, 6/12/38.

CHAPTER 2 —— THE LONGY WAR

1. "Ritchie May Lose Arm's Use," *NN*, 11/23/30, 2.

2. The legend that Longy was responsible for the hit on the Boot was cemented in gangland lore by the only biography written about the Jewish gang lord, *Gangster #2: The Man Who Invented Organized Crime*, published in 1985. The author, a Newark newspaperman named Mark Stuart, claimed his biography was based on exhaustive research and interviews, but his version of the assassination attempt, like much of the other material in the book, is pure invention. His account of the Boot shooting reads like a scene from a Jimmy Cagney movie or a Western showdown, with the Boot strolling down Broad Street in the middle of a spring day after a visit to his tailor, surrounded by "four of his best men, all well-armed." Longy's henchmen suddenly emerge from the opposite direction, and Boiardo's cohorts for some unexplained reason "[melt] swiftly away." One of Longy's henchmen is quoted in the book: "They disappeared like thin smoke rings from a lousy cigar." The Boot remains all alone on Broad Street and is unable to reach for his "holster" fast enough; Longy's men pull out their artillery and blast away. A simple check of newspaper archives, police records, and FBI files contradicts this fanciful account and many others in the book.

3. Warren Grover, *Nazis in Newark* (Piscataway, N.J.: Transaction, 2003), 42.

4. Brad R. Tuttle, *How Newark Became Newark: The Rise, Fall, and Rebirth of an American City* (New Brunswick, N.J.: Rutgers University Press, 2009), 98.

5. Stuart, *Gangster #2*, 23.

6. Grover, *Nazis in Newark*, 42–43.

7. Stephen Schneider, *Iced: The Story of Organized Crime in Canada* (Mississauga, Ontario: Wiley, 2009), 199–205. Stephen Fox, *Blood and Power: Organized Crime in Twentieth Century America* (New York: Morrow, 1989), 24–25, 28, 31, 32, 43, 53–54, 58. The information about the Bronfman family activities and the family's relationship to Reinfeld and Zwillman in this paragraph and the next six is contained in these two books.

8. "Plot Charged in Arrest," *NYT*, 2/5/27, 2.

9. Grover, *Nazis in Newark*, 44.

10. Stuart, *Gangster #2*, 53.

11. Thom L. Jones, "Gangsters Inc. Whack Out on Willie Moretti," *Gangsters Inc.*, 2010, gangstersinc.ning.com (accessed 2012), 1.

12. "Investigations: Willing Willie," *Time*, 12/25/50.

13. Carl Sifakis, *The Mafia Encyclopedia: From Accardo to Zwillman*, 2nd ed. (New York: Checkmark Books, 2005), 314.

14. Boiardo, Ruggiero, Sr., FBI Memorandum, 5/12/54, 7; Report, 7/23/57, 5.

15. Tuttle, *How Newark Became Newark*, 100.

16. Sifakis, *Mafia Encyclopedia*, 21.

17. Ibid., 398.

18. Tuttle, *How Newark Became Newark*, 98.

19. E. J. Fleming, *The Fixers: Eddie Mannix, Howard Strickling, and the MGM Publicity Machine* (Jefferson, N.C.: McFarland, 2005), 114.

20. John Austin, *More of Hollywood's Unsolved Mysteries* (New York: Shapolsky, 1991), 170; Tim Adler, *Hollywood and the Mob: Movies, Mafia, Sex and Death* (New York: Bloomsbury, 2008), 77.

21. "War Reported over Lotteries," *NNM*, 9/19/30.

22. "Gangster Slain," *NN* 11/5/30, 1–2; "Racketeer Slain on Hospital Cot as He Hides Out," *Asbury Park [New Jersey] Press*, 11/4/30, 1.

23. "Peace Sought in Racket War," *NNM*, 9/22/30.

24. Stuart, *Gangster #2*, 60–61; quote attributed to "Jake Rosenthal."

25. Ibid., 61; quote attributed to "Barney Goldfarb."

26. Boiardo, Ruggiero, Sr., FBI Report, 8/13/64.

27. Sifakis, *Mafia Encyclopedia*, 333.

28. "Dr. Gnassi Faces Three Charges in Gang Death," *NN*, 11/6/30, 1.

29. Catena, Jerry, FBI Report, 1/15/58, 5.

30. "War Reported over Lotteries," *NNM*, 9/19/30; "Peace Sought in Racket War," *NNM*, 9/22/30.

31. "War Reported over Lotteries," *NNM*, 9/19/30.

32. Catena, Jerry, FBI Report, 7/27/61, 15.

33. Ibid.

34. "Longy and Ritchie Merge," *NSE*, 10/7/30.

35. Ibid.

36. "Police 'Drop in' at Banquet to Newark Gang Leader," *NSE*, 10/6/30.

37. Ibid.

38. "Huge Bootleg Profits. Prosecutor Says Total in Nation Is Nearly Four Billions [sic] a Year," *NYT*, 4/8/26, 1.

39. Boiardo, Ruggiero, Sr., FBI Memorandum, 5/12/54, 4.

40. "Police 'Drop in' at Banquet to Newark Gang Leader," *NSE*, 10/6/30.

41. "Ritchie Marathon Dinner Peaceful, One Day Old and Going Strong," *NNM*, 10/6/30.

42. "Longy and Ritchie Merge," *NN*, 10/7/30.

43. "Ritchie Marathon Dinner Peaceful, One Day Old and Going Strong," *NNM*, 10/6/30.

44. Ibid.

45. "Things Pop as Ritchie and Longie Meet at Dinner—But Not Guns," *NNM*, 10/7/30.

46. "Ritchie Marathon Dinner Peaceful, One Day Old and Going Strong," *NNM*, 10/6/30.

47. Ibid.

48. "Things Pop as Ritchie and Longie Meet at Dinner—But Not Guns," *NNM*, 10/7/30.

49. Ibid.

50. Ibid.

51. Ibid.

52. "Ritchie Marathon Dinner Peaceful, One Day Old and Going Strong," *NNM*, 10/6/30.

53. "Hold 4 in Gang Slaying of Man in Hospital Bed," *Brooklyn Daily Eagle*, 11/4/30.

54. "Find Car of Slain Gangster," *NN*, 11/4/30, 2.

55. Ibid., 1.

56. "Gunmen Invade Hospital, Shoot Patient Dead; Victim Sought Refuge from Gang's Revenge," *NYT*, 11/4/30, 1.

57. Ibid.

58. Catena, Gerardo, FBI Report, 1/15/58, 1.

59. "Gnassi's Hospital Here Have [sic] Troublesome Sailing," *NN*, 12/4/30.

CHAPTER 3 — I'M NO CRYBABY

1. *NN*, 2/19/30.

2. *NN*, 4/30/69, 3.

3. *NN*, 11/29/30.

4. *NN*, 12/2/30.

5. *NYT*, 12/2/30, 23.

6. "US Jury Starts Ritchie Tax Quiz," *NNM*, 5/1/31.

7. *NN*, 1/5/30, 2.

8. Agnes DellAcqua interview, 11/3/10. DellAcqua is the niece of Richie "the Boot" Boiardo.

9. *NN*, 12/22/30.

10. *NN*, 1/6/31.

11. *NN*, 1/29/31.

12. *NN*, 1/28/31.

13. *NN*, 1/30/31.

14. *NN*, 2/18/31.

15. *NNM*, 2/19/31.

16. "Ritchie Case Draws Colorful Crowd," *NN*, 2/19/31.

17. Ibid.

18. Ibid.

19. *NNM*, 2/20/31.

20. *NNM*, 2/21/31.

21. "Ritchie's Substitute," *NN*, 8/5/31, 2.

22. "Giving Ritchie a Good Time at State Prison," *NN*, 8/7/31.

23. *NN*, 8/6/31, 8/3/31.

24. "Giving Ritchie a Good Time at State Prison," *NN*, 8/7/31.

25. *NN*, 11/14/32.

26. "Gangster's Pet Dog Fails to Balk Raid," *NYT*, 12/10/31, 2.

27. Martha H. Swain, Pat Harrison: The New Deal Years (Oxford: University of Mississippi Press, 2009), 41.

28. "Quiz Ritchie about Racket," *NN*, 7/5/39, 2.

29. "Boiardo, Aide Bailed as Zipper Witness," *NN*, 9/8/33, 10; "Russo Rubbed Out in Ride," *NN*, 2/18/36, 8.

30. "Gang Is Netted for Zipper Quiz," *NN*, 8/25/33, 1

31. *NYT*, 8/31/67, 26.

32. Boiardo, Ruggiero, Sr., FBI Report, 3/28/68, 3.

33. "Gangster in Jersey Found Slain by Road," *NYT*, 7/2/34, 20.

34. "Disagree on Murder Scene," *NN*, 7/3/34, 4.

35. "Schultz Dies of Wounds without Naming Slayers," *NYT*, 10/25/35, 16.

36. Richard Stratton, "The Oldest Mafioso Tells All," *GQ Magazine*, 4/16/74, 61–62.

37. Ibid.

38. Willis Clint, ed., *Wise Guys: Stories of Mobsters from Jersey to Vegas* (New York: Avalon Books, 2003), 158.

39. Caroline Crane, *Murder & Mayhem in the Catskills* (Charleston, S.C.: History Press, 2008), 75.

40. Clint, *Wise Guys*, 158.

41. "Schultz's Killer Freed in Trenton: Charles Workman Served 23 Years of Term," *NYT*, 3/11/64, 40.

42. "Richie to Appear Again before Grand Jury," *NN*, 8/28/39.

43. "Russo Rubbed Out on Ride," *NN*, 2/18/36, 8.

44. "Connect Slaying near Pittsburgh with Schultz Case," *New Castle [Pennsylvania] News*, 2/20/36, 1.

45. Boiardo, Ruggiero, Sr., FBI Report, 4/26/63, 2.

46. Boiardo, Ruggiero, Sr., FBI Report, 8/6/73, 2. "Source stated that the elder Boiardo and his 'Tony Boy' are trigger happy and that their group is more prone to kill its own than any other group he knows of."

CHAPTER 4 — FORTUNATE SON

1. "Addonizio Friend Lives Quiet Life," *NYT*, 12/12/69, 65.

2. Rosina "Rose" Boiardo Hanos interviews.

3. "Tape Shows Mobsters Don't Like or Trust Boiardos," *NN*, 1/12/70.

4. Boiardo, Anthony, FBI Report, 1/27/59.

5. "Boiardo Saga: Mob and Politicians," *NSL*, 12/14/69, 1.

6. Immerso, *Newark's Little Italy*, 119.

7. Richard Ben Cramer, *Joe DiMaggio: The Hero's Life* (New York: Simon & Schuster, 2000), 143.

8. "Ritchie Place Gets Warning," *NN*, 4/19/39.

9. "Boiardo Saga: Mob and Politicians," *NSL*, 12/14/69, 1.

10. "Ritchie in Wrecking Business," *NN*, 9/5/39.

11. "Relation of Ritchie to Lotteries Probed," *NN*, 4/17/39.

12. "Ritchie Indicted by U.S. Jury in Bootleg Plot," *NN*, 4/9/39; "Ritchie Freed in Still Plot," *NN*, 4/10/40.

13. Boiardo, Ruggiero, Jr., FBI Report, 1/27/59, 7–8.

14. Public Notice, *NN*, 6/7/44.

15. Boiardo, Ruggiero, Jr., FBI Report, 1/27/59, 22.

16. Ibid., 22–23.

17. Roger Hanos interviews,

18. Rosina "Rose" Boiardo Hanos interviews.

19. Roger Hanos interviews.

20. "Thirty-one Carloads in Cortege for Wife of Newark First Ward Figure," *NNM*, 10/25/48.

21. Ibid.

22. "Newark Killing, Police Payoff, Family Data Given in Transcript," *NN*, 6/11/69.

23. Sifakis, *Mafia Encyclopedia*, 188.

24. Nicholas Gage, *Mafia USA* (Chicago: Playboy Press, 1972), end chart.

25. Rosina "Rose" Boiardo Hanos interviews.

26. Roger Hanos interviews.

27. "Boiardo Wedding Glittering Festival, 'Son of Prohibition Era Figure Takes Bride,'" *NNM*, 5/1/50; "Thousands Attend Colorful Boiardo Wedding at S. Lucy's," *Italian Tribune*, 5/5/50.

CHAPTER 5 — JERRY

1. "The Gangster Next Door," *Sun Sentinel [Fort Lauderdale, Florida]*, 9/24/89.

2. Catena, Jerry, FBI Director Letter, 12/16/61.

3. "Catena, Riela Quizzed in Essex Crime Probe," *NSL*, 11/8/63, 1.

4. "2 Boiardos Chatty about Family Life," *NSL*, 11/1/63.

5. Ibid.

6. "Catena, Riela Quizzed in Essex Crime Probe," *NSL*, 11/8/63, 1.

7. "Catena's Neighbors Can't Believe He Has Mob Ties," *NSL*, 12/4/57, 10.

8. Ibid.

9. Catena, FBI Report, 9/26/57, 26. In this 1957 report, the FBI mentions that in 1939 Zwillman admitted knowing Catena twelve years earlier.

10. Catena, Gerardo, FBI Report, 7/27/61, 22–29.

11. "The Vito Genovese Family," FBI chart, circa 1963. The testimony of Joseph Valachi led the FBI to create a series of organizational charts that documented the command structure of some of the Mafia crime families. An original copy of the Genovese chart was found among the Boot's possessions by his family after his death and was passed on to Roger Hanos.

12. Boiardo, Ruggiero, Jr., FBI Teletype, 6/20/62.

13. Thomas Pannullo interview, 10/22/10.

14. "Meetings of Mafiosi in the U.S., 1928–1957," FBI map and report.

15. Roger Hanos and Rose Hanos interview, 8/12/07.

16. *NSL*, 12/4/57.

17. Catena, FBI Letter to FBI Director, 1/28/54, 5.

18. Moretti, Willie, FBI Teletype, 5/18/54.

19. "Suicide of Zwillman Gives Catena Clear Path to Take Over New Jersey Mobs," *New York Post*, 1/7/59, 3.

20. Catena, FBI Director Report, 1961.

21. Catena, FBI Intelligence Memorandum, 5/3/61.

22. Michele Miranda, FBI Informant Report, 1962.

23. Boiardo, Ruggiero, Jr., FBI Report, 7/26/62.

24. Rosina "Rose" Boiardo Hanos interviews.

25. Catena, FBI Memorandum, 4/23/63.

26. Catena, FBI decoded Radio Report, 2/6/64.

27. Miranda, FBI Memorandum, 5/16/63.

28. Catena, FBI Report, 7/27/61, 15.

29. Catena, FBI Report, 6/17/63.

30. "Inquiry on Crime Told of Bombings," *NYT*, 1/8/71, 15; "U.S. Jury Indicts Four Union Aides," *NYT*, 8/20/71, 13.

31. "Nation: 'Jail for the Pro,'" *Time*, 6/26/78.

32. Catena, FBI Report, 1/11/63.

33. "Tony Pro Says: 'I Love the Guy, but Jimmy Hoffa Became an Egotistical Maniac,'" *People*, 8/25/75.

34. Roger Hanos interviews.

35. Quoted in Peter J. Bridge and Joseph Volz, *The Mafia Talks* (Greenwich, Conn.: Fawcett Publications, 1969), 29.

36. Boiardo, Ruggiero, Jr., FBI Memorandum, 4/6/73, 2.

37. "The Gangster Next Door," 9/28/89, Sun Sentinel.com, accessed 7/28/12.

38. Catena, FBI decoded Teletype to Director, 12/19/61.

39. Estes Kefauver, *Senate Reports on Crime Investigations. Organized Crime in Interstate Commerce* (Washington, D.C.: U.S. Government Printing Office), 1951.

40. Catena, FBI Report, 7/27/61.

41. Catena, FBI decoded Teletype to Director, 12/20/61.

42. "Bally Manufacturing's Fortunes Are Still on the Rise," *NYT*, 8/17/77, 25.

43. Catena, Gerardo, FBI Reports, 12/27/57, 11; 2/18/58, 7–16. Also, Boiardo, Ruggiero, Jr., FBI Report, 1/27/59, 22.

44. Catena, FBI Report, 4/7/75, 5.

45. Catena, FBI decoded Radio Message, 4/26/62.

46. Alan A. Block, *Masters of Paradise* (New Brunswick, N.J.: Transaction, 1998), 47–48.

47. Catena, FBI Report, 7/27/61, 88.

48. Catena, FBI Teletype, 5/3/63.

49. Catena, FBI Director Memorandum, 4/18/62.

50. Catena, FBI Report, 6/27/61, 55.

51. "'Mafia Pressure' Charge Sworn to by Jersey Aide," *NYT*, 12/20/68, 1.

52. "Jersey Mafia Scandal Traced to New York Prohibition Gangs," *NYT*, 12/24/68, 9.

53. The City of Newark stopped using numbers to designate its districts sometime during the latter half of the 1950s, after urban renewal leveled much of the Italian neighborhood. When most former First Warders speak of the North Ward, they are thinking primarily of the area north of Bloomfield Avenue, where most lived during the 1960s and early 1970s. The phrase "Old First Ward" was used to distinguish the area around Saint Lucy's Church and Seventh Avenue, the remnant of the Italian colony. It was "old" because the city no longer had a First Ward but also because most of it had literally ceased to exist after urban renewal.

54. Wally Edge, "Entirely Too Comfortable with Organized Crime," *PolitickerNJ*, 5/25/07.

55. Catena, FBI decoded Radio Message, 4/20/62.

56. Catena, FBI Teletypes, 12/12/61, 12/13/61.

57. "Hughes Denies Mafia Link," *Daily Register* [Red Bank, N.J.], 1/8/70, 1.

58. Catena, FBI Report, 6/27/61, 51.

59. "Accused Mobsters Still Silent," *NYT*, 11/24/74, 91; *Jersey City Journal*, 12/9/74, 6.

60. "Jailed Crime Figure Files Suit on Fatal Poison in Wife's Soda," *NYT*, 6/17/74, 66.

61. Anthony Bruno, "What Are You Gonna Do Now Tough Guy," TruTV Crime Library, 2001, http://www.trutv.com/library/crime/gangsters_outlaws/mob_bosses/mike_coppolla/2.html, accessed 8/16/12.

62. "Mobster on Leave from Prison Is Shot and Killed in Bridgewater," *NYT*, 4/11/77, 40; "Trial for Accused Mafia Hit Man," *Philadelphia Inquirer*, 7/6/09.

63. "Alleged Mob Boss Wants Case Closed," *NSL*, 10/23/2008.

CHAPTER 6 — THE CLUB FREMONT INCIDENT

1. Boiardo, Ruggiero, Jr., FBI Memorandum, 9/30/60, 1.

2. "Mob Angles Eyed, All Detectives on Shooting Probe," *NNM*, 9/24/60.

3. Boiardo, Ruggiero, Jr., FBI, 3/30/1962, 10.

4. Ibid.

5. Photo from *Newark Evening News* picture morgue at Newark Public Library; reproduced in Richard Linnett, "The Real Sopranos," *Penthouse*, April 2007, 94.

6. Boiardo, Ruggiero, Jr., FBI Reports, 3/29/68, 1, 3–4; 6/5/63, 6.

7. Boiardo, Ruggiero, Sr., FBI Report, 2/2/62, 4.

8. Boiardo, Ruggiero, Jr., FBI Report, 9/6/66, 1.

9. "Dad Boosted 'Tony Boy,'" *NNM*, 12/10/69.

10. Boiardo, Ruggiero, Sr., FBI Report, 4/26/63, 3.

11. Boiardo, Ruggiero, Jr., FBI Report, 9/27/67, 1–2.

12. "Tape Shows Mobsters Don't Like or Trust Boiardos," *NN*, 1/12/70.

13. Ibid.

14. Boiardo, Ruggiero, Jr., FBI Report, 6/26/62, 4.

15. Russo, John, FBI Report, 6/26/64, 1–4.

16. Boiardo, Ruggiero, Jr., FBI Report, 2/14/61, 1.

17. Tony Boy's other meeting places were Marie's Luncheonette at 48 Stone St., in Newark's old First Ward; the Altruist Club, a social club at 654 4th St., in the Roseville section; and DaVinci's, a restaurant owned by Jimo Calabrese in North Newark. Boiardo, Ruggiero, Jr., FBI Memorandum, 1/6/62, and Teletype, 12/21/62.

18. Source for this paragraph and the next: Boiardo, Ruggiero, Jr., FBI Report, 12/2/60, 1–3.

19. "Mob Angles Eyed, All Detectives on Shooting Probe," *NNM*, 9/24/60.

20. Ibid.

21. "Wounded Ex-Con Had Police Badge" *NN*, 10/5/60, 2.

22. "Mob Angles Eyed, All Detectives on Shooting Probe," *NNM*, 9/24/60.

23. "Suspects Indicted," *NN*, 5/22/61, 1.

24. Ibid.

25. "Fourth Ex-Convict is Shot in Newark" *NYT*, 9/24/60.

26. Rosina "Rose" Boiardo Hanos interview.

27. Boiardo, Ruggiero, Jr., FBI Report, 9/23/60, 3.

28. Ibid., 4.

29. Boiardo, Ruggiero, Jr., FBI Report, 4/26/61.

30. "'Timid' Boiardo Refuses to Talk," *NNM*, 11/15/60.

31. Boiardo, Ruggiero, Jr., FBI Report, 1/27/59, 4. This report is based on a surprisingly candid voluntary interview Tony Boy gave to the FBI. Tony called an agent by phone "and stated that he understood the FBI had been making inquiries concerning him, and he would like to know if the FBI would be interested in interviewing him. He was invited to come to the Newark office on November 20, 1958." He was interviewed by three agents.

32. Boiardo, Ruggiero, Jr., FBI Report, 12/2/60, 2.

33. "Suspects Indicted," *NNM*, 5/22/61.

34. Boiardo, Ruggiero, Jr., FBI Report, 2/14/61, 2, 3.

35. Ibid., 3.

36. Ibid.

37. "Quiz of 'Tony Boy,' No New Light on Missing Man," *NNM*, 9/13/61.

38. Boiardo, Ruggiero, Jr., FBI Report, 4/26/61.

39. Ibid., 5.

40. Boiardo, Ruggiero, Jr., FBI Report, 8/18/61, 4.

41. Ibid., 1.

42. "Suspects Indicted," *NNM*, 5/22/61.

43. Ibid.

44. "Gang Shootings Witness Missing," *NNM*, 9/12/61.

45. Boiardo, Ruggiero, Jr., FBI Report, 5/29/62, 22.

46. Ibid.

47. "Charges Dropped in Club Shooting," *NN*, 1/6/66, 1.

CHAPTER 7 — CASTLE CRUEL

1. "Nike Missile Sites in New Jersey," http://alpha.fdu.edu/~bender/NYmsg.html, accessed 4/23/12.

2. Arlene Moretti Linnett interview, 3/18/09. A transplanted Newarker who moved to Roseland in the early 1950s, my mother, along with her neighbors, often saw the Boot on his horse trotting through town. Also, Boiardo family home movies, in Roger's possession, show the Boot riding horseback with his friends and associates in the suburbs that surrounded his house, including Roseland.

3. Roger Hanos interview, 8/12/07.

4. Rose Hanos interviews; and an interview with Lillian Hanos LaMonica, 10/20/10.

5. Rose Hanos interviews.

6. Rose Hanos interviews.

7. "Boiardo, Family Testify on Shootings at Estate," *NN*, 8/10/66, 30.

8. "No Action on Boiardo," *NN*, 8/23/66, 1.

9. "Boiardo, Family Testify on Shootings at Estate," *NN*, 8/10/66, 30.

10. Ibid.

11. "No Action on Boiardo," *NN*, 8/23/66, 1.

12. Roger Hanos interviews.

13. "Boiardo Home: A Feudal Baron's Castle," *New York Sunday News*, 2/1/70, New Jersey section.

14. Boiardo, Ruggiero, Sr., FBI file, 1/31/68.

15. C. B. DiCrollalanza, *History of the Genealogy of the House of Boiardo* (Florence, Italy: Istituto Araldico Coccia), 37, 64, 91, 93, 97.

16. Charles S. Ross, "Justifying Violence: Boiardo's Castle Cruel," *Philological Quarterly* (Winter 1994).

17. Sandy Smith, "The Crime Cartel—Brazen Empire of Organized Crime," *Life*, September 1, 1967: 16–17.

18. Fred J. Cook, "The People v. the Mob; or Who Rules New Jersey," *New York Times Magazine*, 2/1/70, 32.

19. Ibid.

20. "Tape Shows Mobsters Don't Like or Trust Boiardos," NN, 1/12/70, 5.

21. Ibid.

22. Ibid.

23. "Billy Jinks Has Them Guessing," *NN*, 2/25/51.

24. Boiardo, Ruggiero, Sr., FBI Memorandum, 7/26/68.

25. Boiardo, Ruggiero, Sr., FBI Report, 9/26/68.

26. "Boiardo Saves Woman's Body in Coffin," *NSE*, 1/3/33.

27. Boiardo, Ruggiero, Sr., FBI Report, 7/26/68.

28. Roger Hanos interviews.

CHAPTER 8 — LOOSE LIPS

1. "Secrets of Mafia Are Revealed in Transcript of FBI Bugging," *NYT*, 6/11/69, 1.

2. "Tape Shows Mobsters Don't Like or Trust Boiardos," *NN*, 1/12/70.

3. Henry A. Zeiger, *Sam the Plumber: One Year in the Life of a Cosa Nostra Boss* (New York: New American Library, 1970), 242.

4. Boiardo, Ruggiero, Sr., FBI file, "Portions of a conversation between Anthony Russo and Philip Leone," 6/9/78, 18.

5. Rose Hanos interviews.

6. "Tape Shows Mobsters Don't Like or Trust Boiardos," *NN*, 1/12/70.

7. Boiardo, Ruggiero, Sr., FBI file, "Portions of a conversation between Anthony Russo and Philip Leone," 6/9/78, 5.

8. Roger Hanos interviews.

9. Russo, Anthony, FBI Report, 10/31/61, 3.

10. Russo, John, FBI Report, 9/23/64, 2.

11. Russo, John, FBI Report, 3/29/68, 1–3.

12. Russo, John, FBI Report, 3/30/65.

13. "Bodies Linked to Organized Crime Families in Philadelphia," *The Progress* [Pennsylvania], 4/30/80, 11.

14. Robert Rudolph, "Solving a Two-Decade-Old Mafia Hit," *NSL*, 2/9/98.

15. Kevin Coughlin, "Organized Crime Seen in Loanshark Arrests," *NSL*, 9/22/84.

16. Russo, Anthony, FBI Report, 10/31/61, 5.

17. Russo, John, FBI Report, 9/23/64, 1.

18. Ibid.

19. "Tapes of F.B.I. Show Two Mafiosi Gave Conflicting Versions of an Execution," *NYT*, 1/1/70, 56.

20. Ibid.

21. Russo, Anthony, FBI Report, 5/11/62, 1–2.

22. Russo, Anthony, FBI Report, 5/14/69, 2.

23. Russo, Anthony, FBI Report, 2/20/62, 3.

24. Russo, Anthony, FBI Report, 6/28/62, 3.

25. "Tape Shows Mobsters Don't Like or Trust Boiardos," *NN*, 1/12/70.

26. "FBI Taped Conversation Sheds Light on 1962 Gangland Slaying of Strollo," *NYT*, 1/8/70; Sifakis, *The Mafia Encyclopedia*, 37–38.

27. "FBI Taped Conversation Sheds Light on 1962 Gangland Slaying of Strollo," *NYT*, 1/8/70.

28. "Prospect for Release of More Mafia Eavesdropping Data Called Doubtful," *NYT*, 1/11/70, 68.

CHAPTER 9 — THAT OLD GANG OF MINE

1. "Richie Must Stay in State," *NN*, 8/1/70, 1.

2. "U.S. Gaming Raiders Seize Boiardo," *NN*, 2/3/67, 1.

3. "Boiardo Named as Kingpin," *NN*, 2/4/67, 1.

4. *NN*, 2/3/67, 1.

5. Boiardo, Ruggiero, Sr., FBI Report, 7/3/69, 17; "Boiardo Characterized as Rackets 'Big Boy,'" *NN*, in cited FBI file; no date indicated.

6. Boiardo, Ruggiero, Sr., FBI Report, 7/3/69, 17.

7. Ibid., 17–18.

8. "Garden State Attorney Agrees with What He's Been Reading," *NYT*, 12/18/64, 4.

9. Boiardo, Ruggiero, Jr., FBI Memorandum, 10/18/68.

10. Boiardo, Ruggiero. Sr., FBI Report, 8/18/67, 6; "U.S. Gaming Raiders Seize Boiardo and 3; $20 Million Operation Alleged," *NN*, 2/3/67.

11. Boiardo, Ruggiero, Sr., FBI Memorandum, 8/9/68, 1.

12. Ibid.

13. Boiardo, Ruggiero. Sr., FBI Report, 9/26/68, 4.

14. Boiardo, Anthony, FBI Report, 5/2/63, 1.

15. Ibid.

16. Ibid., 2.

17. Boiardo, Ruggiero, Sr., FBI Memorandum, 11/6/69, 5.

18. Boiardo, Ruggiero, Sr., FBI Report, 9/26/68, 4.

19. "Black Racketeers Challenging the Mafia," *NYT*, 9/4/73, 1, 41.

20. "Three Thumbs Down: Ex-Newark Cops Feel Slighted by Portrayal in 'American Gangster,'" *NSL*, 11/10/07.

21. Governor's Select Commission on Civil Disorder, State of New Jersey, Robert D. Lilley, Chairman, *Report for Action* (Trenton: State of New Jersey, 1968), 20.

22. Boiardo, Ruggiero, Jr., FBI Report, 4/30/65.

23. "Newark Jury Told Spina Ignored Crime," *NYT*, 10/24/68.

24. "Newark's Police Chief Cleared of Charges," *St. Petersburg [Florida] Times*, 11/08/67, 12.

25. Addonizio, Hugh, FBI decoded Radiogram, 11/23/62.

26. Catena, Gerardo, FBI decoded Radiogram, 1/14/63, 1.

27. "Spina Indicted in Newark as Lax on Gambling Laws," *NYT*, 7/25/68.

28. Ibid.

29. Boiardo, Ruggiero, Jr., FBI Report, 8/26/68, C.

30. Ibid.

31. "Spina Acquitted on Judge's Order," *NYT*, 11/8/68.

32. "Boiardo, 18 Guilty; Blow to Mob Seen," *NN*, 4/28/69.

33. Boiardo, Ruggiero, Sr., FBI Report, 3/17/70, 4; "Cops Raid Huge 'Numbers Bank,'" *NN*, 4, in cited FBI file; no date indicated.

34. "Big Gambling Ring Raided in New Jersey," *NYT*, 1/17/70, 16.

35. Boiardo, Ruggiero, Sr., FBI Report, 7/3/69, B.

36. Boiardo, Ruggiero, Sr., FBI Report, 3/17/70, 5.

37. Roger Hanos interviews.

38. Boiardo, Ruggiero, Sr., FBI Report, 12/2/70, 3–4; "Seize Boiardo Land in U.S. Tax Claim," *NN*, in cited FBI file; no date indicated.

39. Boiardo, Ruggiero, Sr., FBI Report, 9/29/67.

40. "Doubt Mob Crematory Quiz," *New York Daily News*, 4/23/70. Quotes from Federal officials in this article are inaccurate; the alleged incinerator on the Boot's property was first publicized in *Life* magazine in September 1967, less than three years before.

41. "Only U.S. Digs the Boot's Estate," *New York Daily News*, 3/11/71.

42. "Boiardo Is Shipped Off to Prison," *NSL*, 10/9/70, 1.

43. Boiardo, Ruggiero, Sr., FBI Report, 5/28/71.

CHAPTER 10 ⸺ CAUSE FOR INDICTMENT

1. "Boiardo and Biancone Out of Valentine," *NN*, 4/19/70, 1; "Boiardo Said to End Ties with Company," *NYT*, 4/19/70, 87.

2. "Addonizio Friend Lives Quiet Life," *NYT*, 12/12/69, 65.

3. Fred J. Cook, "The People v. the Mob; or, Who Rules New Jersey?" *New York Times Magazine*, 2/1/70, 5.

4. "Newark Corruption Held a 'Textbook Case' for U.S.," *NYT*, 12/21/69, 1.

5. "Garden State Attorney Agrees with What He's Been Reading," *NYT*, 12/18/68, 43.

6. "Contractor Tells of Newark Graft," *NYT*, 6/24/70, 50.

7. Sifakis, *Mafia Encyclopedia*, 125.

8. Richard Linnett, "The Real Sopranos," *Penthouse*, April 1970, 4.

9. Henry Furst interview, April 2005.

10. Boiardo, Ruggiero, Sr., FBI Memorandum, 7/29/76.

11. "Hugh J. Addonizio, 67, Ex-Mayor of Newark Jailed 5 Years, Dead," *NYT*, 2/2/81, D9.

12. "Addonizio Ouster Weighed for His Silence in Inquiry," *NYT*, 12/11/69, 2.

13. Boiardo, Ruggiero, Jr., FBI Teletype, 12/8/69.

14. "Mayor, Tony Boy and 12 Deny Guilt," *NN*, 12/19/69, 1; "Addonizio, Boiardo and 12 Enter Pleas of Not Guilty," *NYT*, 12/20/69, 1.

15. Boiardo, Ruggiero, Jr., FBI Airtel, 6/26/70.

16. Boiardo, Anthony, FBI Teletype, 6/25/70.

17. "Break Laid to Informer," *NYT*, 12/13/69, 1.

18. "Contractor Tells of Newark Graft," *NYT*, 6/24/70, 50.

19. Ibid.

20. "Witness Quotes Addonizio as Wanting Pipe Kickback," *NN*, 6/23/70, 1.

21. Boiardo, Ruggiero, Jr., FBI Teletype, 7/9/70.

22. "Illness of Tony Boy Delays Newark Trial," *NN*, 7/6/70, 1.

23. "Guilty Plea Filed in Trenton Trial," *NYT*, 6/27/70, 1.

24. "No Regrets about Extortion Trial Testimony, Says Rigo," *NN*, 1/8/71, 3.

25. "Onlookers Focus on Tony Boy," *NN*, 6/9/70.

26. "Kantor Says Contractors Had to Pay Off 'Tony Boy,'" *NN*, 6/9/70, 1.

27. Ibid.

28. Ibid.

29. Joey with David Fisher, *Joey the Hitman: The Autobiography of a Mafia Killer* (Philadelphia: Da Capo Press, 2002), 59.

30. "Illness of 'Tony Boy' Delays Newark Trial," *NN*, 7/6/70.

31. "Hugh J. Addonizio, 67, Ex-Mayor of Newark Jailed 5 Years, Dead," 2/2/81, *NYT*, D9.

32. Ibid.

33. "Anthony Boiardo Is Dead at 60; Called Key Jersey Crime Figure," *NYT*, 4/23/78, 36.

CHAPTER 11 — THE ITALIAN WAY

1. Jerry Gafio Watts, *Amiri Baraka: The Politics and Art of a Black Intellectual* (New York: New York University Press, 2001), 363.

2. Boiardo, Ruggiero, Jr., FBI Memorandum, 6/19/70, 1–2.

3. Boiardo, Ruggiero, Jr., FBI Teletype, 6/19/70.

4. "Addonizio Aides Seek Softer Line," *NYT*, 6/12/70, 42.

5. Tuttle, *How Newark Became Newark*, 179.

6. Boiardo, Ruggiero, Jr., FBI Teletype, 6/19/70.

7. Boiardo, Ruggiero, Sr., FBI Report, 8/6/73, 2.

8. Chieppa, Angelo, FBI Report, 4/25/67, 3.

9. "13 Indicted Here in Running Still," *NYT*, 11/8/55, 23.

10. Chieppa, FBI Report, 4/25/67, 4.

11. Chieppa, FBI Airtel Memorandum, 6/7/73, 2.

12. Chieppa, FBI Air Mail Letter, 5/6/63, 1.

13. Chieppa, FBI Report, 4/25/67, 4.

14. Boiardo, Ruggiero, Sr., FBI Report, 8/6/73, 2.

15. Boiardo, Ruggiero, Jr., FBI Letter, 5/23/73.

16. Ibid.

17. Ibid., 2.

18. Chieppa, FBI Teletype, 5/2/73, 1.

19. Ibid., 3.

20. Boiardo, Ruggiero, Sr., FBI Report, 8/6/73, 2.

21. Chieppa, FBI Letter, 12/15/72, 2.

22. Bruce Bailey, "Cops to Probe Casino Ties of Slain Boiardo Bodyguard," *NSL*, date unknown (found in Rose Hanos's news-clip collection).

23. Russo, John, FBI Report, 6/26/73, 6–7.

24. Ibid., 6.

25. Boiardo, Ruggiero, Sr., FBI Report, 8/6/73, 2.

26. "Blacks Believed Defying the Mafia," *NYT*, 5/21/73.

27. Boiardo, Ruggiero, Sr., FBI "Contacts" Report, 5/31/73, 2.

28. Bailey, "Cops to Probe Casino Ties of Slain Boiardo Bodyguard."

29. Chieppa, FBI Report, 1/16/74, 11.

30. Ibid., 12.

31. Boiardo, Ruggiero, Sr., FBI "Contacts" Report, 8/6/73, 2.

32. Boiardo, Ruggiero, Sr., FBI Report, 9/29/72.

33. "Inquiry Planned on Gangland Killings," *NYT*, 12/18/73, 87.

34. "Boiardo Associate Found Slain in Gangland Style in Newark," *NYT*, 11/25/73, 62.

35. Boiardo, Ruggiero, Sr., FBI Report, 8/6/73, 2.

CHAPTER 12 —— ON THE JOLLY TROLLEY

1. "Artist, Former Casino Owner Petit Dies at 62," *Las Vegas Sun*, 9/14/98.

2. "Prison Stabbings in Jersey 'Racial,'" *NYT*, 2/15/72, 19.

3. Russo, Anthony, FBI Report, 5/8/74, 2.

4. Russo, Anthony, FBI Report, 8/23/74, 2.

5. "Inquiry Planned on Gangland Killings," *NYT*, 12/18/73, 87.

6. Ovid Demaris, *The Boardwalk Jungle* (New York: Bantam Books, 1986), 125.

7. Ibid., 126.

8. "Loan Shark's Envoys Slain," *Cumberland [Maryland] Sunday Times*, 1/4/76, 1; "Russo Anti-Drug Push Called Ploy to Find Agnellino Killers," *Daily Register [Shrewsbury, N.J.]*, 5/29/79, 1, 3; "Identity of 3rd Shootout Victim Sought," *Sarasota [Florida] Herald Tribune*, 4/5/76, 15.

9. "Russo Anti-Drug Push Called Ploy to Find Agnellino Killers," *Daily Register [Shrewsbury, N.J.]*, 5/29/79, 1, 3.

10. Ibid.

11. "Alphabet Companies Spell Trouble for Brothers," *Sun Sentinel [Fort Lauderdale, Florida]*, 6/3/95; New Jersey Supreme Court State v. Truglia (defendant), 9/11/84, 517, www.findacase.com.

12. Boiardo, Ruggiero, Sr., FBI Teletype, 6/14/78, 1–6.

13. Boiardo, Ruggiero, Sr., FBI Teletype, 4/19/78, 2.

14. "Casino Execs Testify They 'Humored' Reputed Mobster," *Kingman [Arizona] Daily Miner*, 10/15/81, 5.

15. Boiardo, Ruggiero, Sr., FBI Teletype, 6/8/78.

16. "Casino Execs Testify They 'Humored' Reputed Mobster," *Kingman [Arizona] Daily Miner*, 10/15/81, 5.

17. "4 Are Convicted of Running Criminal Syndicate in Jersey," *NYT*, 6/21/80, 25.

18. Boiardo, Ruggiero, Sr., FBI Teletype, 8/23/78, 1–2.

19. "An Aging Mob Boss," *NSL*, 1/4/80, 1, 16.

20. Demaris, *Boardwalk*, 131.

21. Ibid., 127, 130.

22. Russo, John, FBI Report, 6/26/64, 3.

23. Francis McKee, *Mobsters I Have Known and Loved* (Shelyville, Ky.: Wasteland Press, 2009), 243.

24. Demaris, *Boardwalk*, 132.

25. "Mobsters Slaying Is Probed," *Daily Intelligencer [Doylestown, Pennsylvania]*, 4/29/79, 4A.

26. "Solving a Two-Decade-Old Mafia Hit," *NSL*, 2/9/98, 1.

27. "8 Indicted as Members of National Mob," *NYT*, 5/24/79, B2.

28. "Solving a Two-Decade-Old Mafia Hit," *NSL*, 2/9/98, 1.

29. Ibid.

CHAPTER 13 — THE MAFIA EXISTS!

1. "State Sets Out to Prove There Is a Mafia," *NYT*, 3/16/80, NJ1.

2. Ibid.

3. Ibid.

4. "Jersey Wins Right to Play Tapes as Trial of Reputed Mafia Figure Starts," *NYT*, 3/11/80, B3.

5. "What the Jury Is Likely to Hear," *NYT*, 3/16/80, NJ25.

6. "State Seeks to Prove the 'Mafia' Exists," *NYT*, 3/16/80, 2.

7. "Boiardo Severed from Trial," *NSL*, 2/30/80, 1, 20.

8. "A Hit Man Derides Quality of Testimony," *NYT*, 6/29/80, NJ8.

9. "What the Jury Is Likely to Hear," *NYT*, 3/16/80, NJ25.

10. Ibid.

11. "4 Are Convicted of Running Criminal Syndicate in Jersey," *NYT*, 6/21/80, 25.

12. Ibid.

13. "A 'Hit Man' Derides Quality of Testimony,'" *NYT*, 6/29/80, NJ8.

14. *NYT*, 5/29/80, NJ8.

15. "Coercion Claimed in Casino Deal," *Syracuse [New York] Post Standard*, 10/13/81, A4.

16. Ibid.

17. "Reputed Crime Figure Is Cleared of Charges," *NYT*, 10/10/81, 28.

18. "3 Are Sentenced for Fronting for Gang Figures in a Casino," *NYT*, 11/25/81, B20.

19. "Mobster's Death Was Punishment for Errors," *Daily Intelligencer [Doylestown, Pennsylvania]*, 6/25/86, 8.

20. "Lawmen Gird for Release of Mobster," *NSL*, 8/22/93.

21. *Confessions of an Undercover Cop*, HBO, 1988.

22. Ibid.

23. "Major, Costly Organized Crime Cases Slow to Reach Jersey Courtrooms," *NSL*, 1/14/90.

24. *Confessions of an Undercover Cop*.

25. Guy Sterling, "FBI Raids Hit 4 Sites Tied to Genovese Mob," *NSL*, 11/24/93.

26. "Genovese Boss Admits Gambling, Loansharking," *NSL*, 1/22/95.

27. "Mob Boss' Death Signals End to Colorful Jersey Era," *NSL*, 11/05/97, 27.

28. "Andrew Gerardo Obituary," *NSL*, 1/30/12.

29. The descriptions of the wake and funeral of Andy Gerardo are based on my eyewitness account.

CHAPTER 14 — THIS THING OF THEIRS

1. Roger Hanos interviews. Much of the detailed, intimate information in this chapter comes from these interviews, which occurred from 2007 through 2012.

2. Boiardo, Ruggiero, Sr., FBI Memorandum, 7/14/67.

3. Boiardo, Ruggiero, Sr., FBI Memorandum, 6/11/70.

4. Boiardo, Ruggiero, Sr., FBI Memorandum, 5/31/68.

5. Boiardo, Ruggiero, Sr., FBI Report, 9/26/68.

6. Boiardo, Ruggiero, Sr., FBI Memorandum, 3/10/72.

7. Boiardo, Ruggiero, Sr., FBI Memorandum, 5/31/68.

8. Boiardo, Ruggiero, Sr., FBI Report, 9/3/64.

9. Boiardo, Ruggiero, Sr., FBI Memorandum, 5/31/68.

10. Boiardo, Ruggiero, Sr., FBI Report, 9/26/68.

11. Boiardo, Anthony, FBI Report, 5/18/73.

12. Boiardo, Ruggiero, Sr., FBI Memorandum, 8/3/66.

13. Boiardo, Ruggiero, Sr., FBI Memorandum, 8/18/66.

14. Boiardo, Ruggiero Sr., FBI Report, 5/31/68, 2–5.

15. Rose Hanos interviews.

16. "Jersey 'Godfather' Buried in Simple Ceremony," *NSL*, 11/23/84.

17. Megaro Funeral Home, Sara Serpico burial invoice, 8/19/29.

EPILOGUE

1. Ronald Barbella interview, 12/29/07. All information about the police work in the beginning of this chapter is from this interview.

2. Thomas Paranzine interview, 12/30/07.

3. Ibid.

4. Roger Hanos and Rose Hanos interviews.

5. "Boiardo's Daughter Strangled in Mishap," *NSL*, 10/18/73, 1, 26; "Boiardo's Daughter Killed while Cleaning a Window," *NYT*, 10/18/73.

6. "Boiardo's Daughter Strangled in Mishap," *NSL*, 10/18/73, 1, 26.

7. "Boiardo's Daughter Killed while Cleaning a Window," *NYT*, 10/18/73.

8. Information in this paragraph and the next four paragraphs from Mary Del-Maestro interview, 1/17/08.

9. "Livingston Drifter Charged in Roommate's Slaying," *NSL*, 9/6/06.

10. Ibid.

11. Ibid.

12. Barbella interview, 12/29/07.

13. Anthony Balestro interview, 1/17/08.

14. Ibid.

15. Ibid.

16. DelMaestro interview, 1/17/08.

SELECTED BIBLIOGRAPHY

Adler, Tim. *Hollywood and the Mob: Movies, Mafia, Sex and Death*. New York: Bloomsbury, 2008.

Albrecht-Carrie, Rene. *Italy from Napoleon to Mussolini*. New York and London: Columbia University Press, 1966.

Austin, John. *More of Hollywood's Unsolved Mysteries*. New York: Shapolsky, 1991.

Baraka, Amiri. *The LeRoi Jones/Amiri Baraka Reader*. Edited by William Harris. New York: Thunder Mouth Press, 1991.

Barnes, Ed, and Alison McFarlane. "The Mafia Road Map & House Tour." *New Jersey Monthly*, April 1, 1980: 57-63.

Bergreen, Laurence. *Capone: The Man and the Era*. New York: Simon & Schuster, 1994.

Blackwell, Jon. *Notorious New Jersey*. New Brunswick, N.J.: Rutgers University Press, 2008.

Block, Alan A. *Masters of Paradise*. New Brunswick, N.J.: Transaction, 1998.

Boiardo, Matteo Maria. *Orlando Innamorato*. Translated by Charles Stanley Ross. West Lafayette, Ind.: Parlor Press, 2004.

Bridge, Peter J., and Joseph Volz. *The Mafia Talks*. Greenwich, Conn.: Fawcett Publications, 1969.

Brill, Steven. *The Teamsters*. New York: Simon & Schuster, 1978.

Calderone, Carmen. *The Genealogy of American Organized Crime*. GreatUnpublished, 2004; available from Amazon.com.

Cohen, Rich. *Tough Jews*. New York: Vintage Books, 1999.

Confessions of an Undercover Cop. HBO. Directed by Christopher Jeans. Performed by Michael Russell. 1988.

Cook, Fred J. "The People v. the Mob, or, Who Rules New Jersey?" *New York Times Magazine*, February 1, 1970: 1, 9-11, 32-36.

Cramer, Richard Ben. *Joe DiMaggio: The Hero's Life*. New York: Simon & Schuster, 2000.

Crane, Caroline. *Murder & Mayhem in the Catskills*. Charleston, S.C.: History Press, 2008.

Cunningham, John T. *Newark*. Newark: New Jersey Historical Society, 1966.

Demaris, Ovid. *The Boardwalk Jungle*. New York: Bantam Books, 1986.

———. *The Last Mafioso: "Jimmy the Weasel Fratianno."* Toronto, New York, London: Bantam Books/published by arrangement with Times Books, 1981.

DiCrollalanza, C. B. *History of the Genealogy of the House of Boiardo*. Florence, Italy: Istituto Araldico Coccia.

Downey, Patrick. *Legs Diamond: Gangster*. New York: CreateSpace, 2011.

Duggan, Christopher. *A Concise History of Italy*. Cambridge: Cambridge University Press, 1994.

English, T. J. *Havana Nocturne: How The Mob Owned Cuba . . . And Then Lost It to the Revolution*. New York: HarperCollins, 2007, 2008.

Feder, Sid, and Joachim Joesten. *The Luciano Story*. New York: Universal-Award House, 1972.

Final Report of the Select Committee on Improper Activities in the Labor or Management Field. John L. McClellan, Chairman. S. Rep. No. 1139, 96th Cong., 2d Sess. 1960.

Fleming, E. J. *The Fixers: Eddie Mannix, Howard Strickling, and the MGM Publicity Machine*. Jefferson, N.C.: McFarland, 2005.

Fox, Stephen. *Blood and Power: Organized Crime in Twentieth-Century America*. New York: Morrow, 1989.

Gage, Nicholas. *Mafia USA*. Chicago: Playboy Press, 1972.

Governor's Select Commission on Civil Disorder, State of New Jersey. Robert D. Lilley, Chairman. Report for Action. Trenton: State of New Jersey, 1968.

Grover, Warren. *Nazis in Newark*. Piscataway, N.J.: Transaction, 2003.

Hayden, Tom. *Rebellion in Newark: Official Violence and Ghetto Response*. New York: Vintage Books, 1967.

Hoffman, Paul. *Tiger in the Court*. Chicago: Playboy Press, 1973.

Hoffman, Paul, and Ira Pecznick. *To Drop a Dime*. New York: Putnam, 1976.

Horan, James D. *The Mob's Man*. New York: Crown, 1959.

Immerso, Michael. "Crime Bosses of Newark." In *Crime Bosses of Newark*, 1-9. Newark: Newark Historical Society; New Jersey Historical Society, 2008.

———. *Newark's Little Italy: The Vanished First Ward*. New Brunswick, N.J.: Rutgers University Press, 1997.

Ingle, Bob, and Sandy McClure. *The Soprano State.* New York: St. Martin's Press, 2008.

Jeandron, Jack. *Keyport: From Plantation to Center of Commerce and Industry.* Charleston, S.C.: Arcadia, 2003.

Jones, Thom L. "Gangsters Inc. Whack Out on Willie Moretti." 2010. gangstersinc. ning.com (accessed 2012).

Justia Company. "Justia US Law.com." February 22, 1972. http://law.justia.com/ cases/federal/appellate-courts/F2/451/49/714 (accessed April 1, 2011).

Kefauver, Estes. *Senate Reports on Crime Investigations. Organized Crime in Interstate Commerce.* Washington, D.C.: U.S. Government Printing Office, 1951.

Lacey, Robert. *Little Man: Meyer Lansky and the Gangster Life.* New York: Little, Brown, 1991.

Lait, Jack, and Mortimer Lait. *U.S.A. Confidential.* New York: Crown, 1952.

Linnett, Richard. "The Real Sopranos." Penthouse, April 2007, 94-99.

Maas, Peter. *The Valachi Papers.* New York: Putnam, 1968.

Mangione, Jerre, and Ben Morreale. *La Storia.* New York: HarperPerennial, 1993.

McKee, Francis. *Mobsters I Have Known and Loved.* Shelyville, Ky.: Wasteland Press, 2009.

Moruzzi, Peter. *Havana.* Layton, Utah: Gibbs Smith, 2008.

Mumford, Kevin. *Newark: A History of Race, Rights, and Riots in America.* New York: New York University Press, 2007.

Pasley, Fred D. *Al Capone: The Biography of a Self-Made Man.* New York: Garden City Publishing, 1930.

Porambo, Ron. *No Cause for Indictment: An Autopsy of Newark.* New York, Chicago, San Francisco: Holt, Rinehart, and Winston, 1965.

Poundstone, William. *Fortune's Formula: The Untold Story of the Scientific Betting System That Beat the Casinos and Wall Street.* New York: Hill & Wang, 2005.

Raab, Selwyn. *Five Families.* New York: St. Martin's Press, 2005.

Reppetto, Thomas. *Bringing Down the Mob: The War against the American Mafia.* New York: Henry Holt, 2006.

Ross, Charles S. "Justifying Violence: Boiardo's Castle Cruel." *Philological Quarterly,* Winter 1994: 31-52.

Rudolph, Robert. *The Boys from New Jersey: The Fantastic True Story of How the Lucchese Crime Family Escaped Justice.* New Brunswick, N.J.: Rutgers University Press, 1995.

Schneider, Stephen. *Iced: The Story of Organized Crime in Canada.* Mississauga, Ontario: Wiley, 2009.

Sifakis, Carl. *The Mafia Encyclopedia: From Accardo to Zwillman.* 2nd ed. New York: Checkmark Books, 2005.

Smith, Greg B. *Made Men: The True Rise-and-Fall Story of a New Jersey Mob Family*. New York: Berkley, 2003.

Smith, Sandy. "The Crime Cartel-Brazen Empire of Organized Crime." *Life*, September 1, 1967: 15-22, 42B-45.

Stratton, Richard. "The Man Who Killed Dutch Schultz." *GQ*, September 1, 2001: 330-337, 373-374.

Stuart, Mark. *Gangster #2: The Man Who Invented Organized Crime*. Secaucus, N.J.: Stuart, 1985.

Swain, Martha H. *Pat Harrison: The New Deal Years*. Oxford: University of Mississippi Press, 2009.

Timelines of the Great Depression. n.d. http://www.huppi.com/kangaroo/Time line.htm (accessed January 31, 2011).

Turkus, Burton B., and Sid Feder. *Murder Inc.: The Story of the Syndicate*. New York: Farrar, Straus & Young, 1951.

Turner, Jean-Rae. *Newark: The Golden Age*. Charleston, S.C.: Arcadia, 2003.

Tuttle, Brad R. *How Newark Became Newark: The Rise, Fall, and Rebirth of an American City*. New Brunswick, N.J.: Rutgers University Press, 2009.

Urquhart, Frank J. *A History of the City of Newark-New Jersey Embracing Practically Two and a Half Centuries, 1666-1913. Vol. 2*. Charleston, S.C.: Nabu Press, 2010.

U.S. Treasury Department, Bureau of Narcotics. *Mafia*. New York: HarperCollins, 2007.

Volkman, Ernest. *Gangbusters: The Destruction of America's Last Great Mafia Dynasty*. New York: Avon, 1998.

Waldron, Lamar, with Thom Hartman. *Ultimate Sacrifice*. New York: Carroll & Graf, 2006.

Walling, Rich. "Tales of the Unique and Stranger Side of a Rural Township." In *Weird East Brunswick*, 2-3. East Brunswick, N.J.: East Brunswick Museum, 2003.

Watts, Jerry Gafio. *Amiri Baraka: The Politics and Art of a Black Intellectual*. New York: New York University Press, 2001.

Wikispaces. "The Death of Anthony Russo." n.d. http://darkpastoflongbranch .wikispaces.com/05.+The+Death+of+Anthony+Russo (accessed March 24, 2012).

Willis, Clint, ed. *Mob*. New York: Avalon Books, 2001.

———. *Wise Guys: Stories of Mobsters from Jersey to Vegas*. New York: Avalon Books, 2003.

Zeiger, Henry A. *Sam the Plumber: One Year in the Life of a Cosa Nostra Boss*. New York: New American Library, 1970.

INDEX

ABOUT THE AUTHOR

Richard Linnett was born in Newark, New Jersey, and was educated at George Washington University and Columbia University Graduate School of the Arts. He is the co-author, with Roberto Loiederman, of *The Eagle Mutiny*, the true story of a mutiny on an American ship during the Vietnam War and its tragic aftermath.